3 week

...ues &

...ltu...

Learning

A Collection of Papers
Reflecting Some
Contemporary Thinking

Commissioning Editor
Peter Barnes Ph.D. FRGS

D0552225

AfOL

Published by The Association for Outdoor Learning
(formerly the National Association for Outdoor Education)
Printed by Fingerprints, Barrow-in-Furness, Cumbria

ISBN 1 898555 04 4

Cover design/photograph and typesetting: Fiona Exon, AfOL

Values and Outdoor Learning

Foreword

Shirley M. Payne

The subject of values in relation to Outdoor Activities is of growing concern and debate both amongst those who work in the outdoors - either in a paid or a voluntary capacity - and those who have an interest in the development of our society.

I was pleased when Peter Barnes offered to commission and collate a series of articles, which the Association for Outdoor Learning (formerly the National Association for Outdoor Education) might be able to publish.

This volume is the result of his work and the work of all those writers whom he managed to encourage to submit articles to him. The final form has presented us with problems. The editorial group who read the collection felt that in many ways the articles are so diverse that perhaps we ought to attempt to collect them into two volumes. The dilemma which then faced us was - how to make the division. Theory and Practice volumes was an obvious possibility, as were one or two other possible ways of collating the rich variety of the contributions. In the end it was decided to keep them together in one volume. One of the practical constraints for us of course is the funding problem - two volumes would be twice as expensive to put on the shelves and tie up what small capital we have for a long time.

Perhaps ultimately the very diversity of the articles enhances the book. Readers will be able to find something which exactly chimes with their own concerns, and are perfectly capable of choosing not to read an article which does not impinge upon their concerns.

The collection offered here does not pretend to cover all the possible ground - nor does it include contributions from all those in the field who have something of value to say to us. We do however hope that the volume raises questions and stimulates debate and further work from the readership. We will endeavour to publish further articles as they come to us - either in the Newsletter, or in one or other of our journals - please do respond to these contributions.

My personal thanks go to Peter, and to Ken Ogilvie and Roger Orgill who took the brunt of the early discussions around quite how to produce this volume, as well as to the staff in the office, whose first publication for us this is. Most of all however, our thanks to all those who have contributed to this volume.

Introduction

Peter Barnes

In a time of turmoil, in society and both in mainstream and outdoor education, the question of values has remained a fiercely debated topic. It has even been suggested by some that values have largely been abandoned in a society where consumerism is seen to be running rampant and in an education system where exam results in tightly defined subjects are more important than educating the whole person. This suggestion is, of course, a nonsense. Value judgements and moral beliefs influence everything we think and everything we do. There can not be an absence of values, there can only be a difference in values. This book, published by the Association for Outdoor Learning, is all about those differences. A number of themes emerge throughout the book. The contrast between mainstream and outdoor education is returned to by a number of the writers while the changes in values in both society and outdoor education are also a common subject. The central nature of values in outdoor education is highlighted but it is, however, the importance and efficacy of outdoor education as a tool for teaching and passing on values which is the over-riding message contained in these pages.

The book is introduced by three chapters in the section 'Setting the Scene'. Geoff Nichols offers a very personal view of the values which he sees as important within development training and more importantly, perhaps, what and why we are trying to achieve with them. John Halliday contrasts mainstream and outdoor education and questions the values inherent in each while my chapter in this section gives a brief summary of where the values we work towards originated from.

A major difficulty, however, in talking about, or writing about, values and outdoor education is in defining what we mean. Thus, we can talk about:

- the values *of* outdoor education where we examine its worth,

- the values *in* outdoor education where we examine the moral and ethical code by which it is practiced,

- the values *from* outdoor education where we examine how morals, ethics, codes of behaviour and so on can be taught from an outdoor education setting.

Each of these uses of the expression 'values' is also open to debate and contention. Thus, values *of* depends on the viewpoint of the observer, usually a 'client' while values *in* depends on the viewpoint of the participant, usually the member of staff. The biggest contention, however, is in values *from* where the questions *whose* values and *what* values must be asked. Can we truly teach values or can we merely teach the ability to ask the right questions about values? As with many difficult subjects values can mean all things to all people. The section 'Values and Questions' looks at some of these issues. The chapters by Pete Allison and Pete Higgins confront the questions which they feel outdoor educators should be asking while Simon Priest and Michael Gass present a model for the way in which outdoor staff can approach questioning their own values and ethics. Steve Deeming looks at how spirituality can be a neglected part of the outdoor education process and Chris Loynes completes the section by taking a step back to question the nature of experiential education as it is often used today.

One of the central themes of outdoor education is the environment in which it takes place; this is addressed in the third section of the book, 'Values and Environment'. Julie Rea and Michael Slavkin examine one example of how girls relate to the natural environment while Barbara Humberstone broadens the debate to cover feminine and masculine values referring not only to how we relate to the outdoors but also to research in this area. Two other approaches to the environment are given by Judy Ling-Wong who looks at the impact of multi-cultural values and Geoff Cooper who discusses how to encourage the values which lead to sustainability.

The values and beliefs in outdoor education were, for a long time, largely taken as gospel without any need to justify them. In recent times, however, a number of issues have come to impact on the values of the outdoors. Most fundamentally practitioners have started to question the impact of their work both in terms of its efficacy and in its connection to society in general. Questions revolving around topics such as consumerism, the 'Pepsi-Max' era, safety, professionalism and the role of education have all become widely debated. Consumerism is seen as a feature that is destroying the moral fabric of outdoor education. We now commonly talk of the 'outdoor industry' in much the same way as any other part of the leisure market. Courses are often sold on their attractiveness to customers rather than a belief in their content. Risk has been removed from the timetable of many outdoor programmes due to the demands of an ever more cautious society. Conflict with a client's needs is an ever present dilemma for outdoor staff. For example, should an outdoor instructor teach the doctrine of loyalty to the company that the client requires when he or she believes that there is more to life than work? In the section 'Values and Organisations' three of these current issues are specifically addressed. Maurice Dybeck looks at the dilemmas inherent in any organisation that needs to raise revenue to survive and yet wishes to operate in a philanthropic manner. My chapter looks, in turn, at how the changes in values have affected the culture and community found within outdoor centres while Ian Harris examines the changes in values within the education system.

The fifth section 'Values and Ways of Working' takes a step back from the contention and debate which figures so strongly in the previous sections. This section looks at how values are taught or passed on in a variety of styles and manners. Thus, Eric Maddern examines the importance of rites of passage as a way of passing on values while Tom Lilley and Pete Allison look at very contrasting operations, one in the city and the other in the expedition environment. Julie Rea, meanwhile, looks at the process by which moral meaning is transferred and Mac McInnes examines the value of storytelling in transferring values. In his chapter David Hopkins stresses the need for a 'Quality Culture'. The section is rounded off by Phil Woodyer who looks at outdoor education and special needs groups.

The final section, 'And Finally:', completes the book with two chapters which look to the future. In the first of these Johnna Haskell uses an attractive metaphor in celebration of learning values through outdoor education. In the final chapter Harold Drasdo, in an extract from his classic essay *Education and the Mountain Centres*, looks to the future and, at the same time, reminds us of the values at the heart of what we do.

Contained within this book are extensively referenced academically structured chapters such as those written by Mac McInnes and Barbara Humberstone. There are also a number of un-referenced chapters written 'straight from the heart' and based on years of experience; these include the chapters by Geoff Nichols, Phil Woodyer and Harold Drasdo. Outdoor Education needs both of these perspectives if we are to not only establish credibility and educational 'status' but also the passion and dedication that are cornerstone values of what we do. This book asks questions, suggests solutions and develops a picture based on this broad approach. The chapters, and subjects, within the book are relevant not just to the multi-activity outdoor centre but to outdoor education in all its guises and by whatever name it uses. We often become bogged down in the semantics and minutiae of what we do, are we trainers, facilitators, tutors or instructors? Do we work in outdoor education, adventure education, development training? Do we operate in a professional capacity or in a professional manner? Whatever the sector or the terminology, values are at the heart of everything we do - this book is just a start to thinking about what, in essence, is the most important question of all - what is outdoor education all about?

Finally, in addition to all the authors, I need to thank three people for their contributions to this book. Shirley Payne, the Chair of the Association for Outdoor Learning, who had the foresight to suggest the book and the faith to ask me to edit it and Barbara Humberstone who was always ready to offer invaluable advice and help based on her own editing experience. Perhaps most importantly however, my partner Sue Towson who, despite the need for me to earn an income, not only allowed me to lock myself away for the almost two months of unpaid work that this book entailed, but even encouraged it - a good example of values in action.

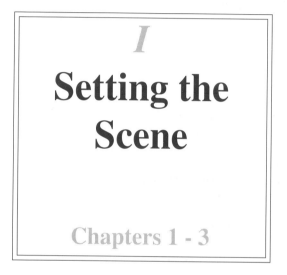

I

Setting the Scene

Chapters 1 - 3

Setting the Scene: Chapters 1 - 3

Chapter 1:   What is Development Training?

Geoff Nichols

Development Training is a glib phrase conjuring up a professional and marketable image. However, it means little unless it is qualified by answering the questions: 'development for what?' and 'development of what?' I believe that if trainers have not answered these questions in their own minds they do not know what they are doing. And if the customers buying a Development Training course have not asked these questions they do not know what they are doing. We should all think more carefully about what is meant by Development Training.

A gut reaction?

When I started work in Development Training I did not have as clear an idea of what I was doing as I had when I left. But, I had some strong gut feelings that it was the right thing to be doing. After 6 years of work in the field I was able to reflect on my experiences and work out why what I was doing was good.

I understood the people I was concerned to develop as being composed of physical, mental, emotional and spiritual dimensions. I wanted to make all these dimensions grow harmoniously towards their full potential, and I wanted to inculcate a desire to grow further. Often, the experiences of a course would enable an individual to become a more rounded individual, by starting to redress the imbalance between these aspects of the self. I thought of an individual's learning on a course as a crash course in growing up. This was achieved by a balanced but intensive bombardment of experiences selected to meet the needs of the group and the individual.

Personal Development included developing a positive attitude towards life. Problems would be perceived as opportunities and opportunities were to be grasped. With this attitude students could go on to make the most of their lives. I wanted students to develop their capacity for reflecting, appraising and learning from experiences. I wanted them to develop the ability to think for themselves. By doing this they would be able to make positive decisions about their own future development and that of the society they live in.

Growth for what?

But growth needs direction. So I had to answer 'growth for what?' This meant I had to identify the value judgments underlying what I was doing. To what sort of society did I want people with whom I was working to contribute?

I got a clearer view of the sort of society to which I wanted students to contribute by looking at the centre I was working in when it was working well. It was a place where everybody cared for each other regardless of age, sex or race. Everyone was respected as an individual. This atmosphere encouraged learning, as people were prepared to experiment and ask questions without fear of rejection or failure. People were aiming high in all aspects of their personal development. Everybody in the centre assumed responsibility for it and for each other. People were always looking for the positive contribution they could make to help others and people were the most important thing. The atmosphere in the centre engendered a lot of self-expression, creativity and fun. This state of centre nirvana did not happen all the time but it was an ideal that we knew we were aiming for.

The centre represented a small part of society as a whole. I wanted society to be characterised by the same set of values as the centre.

Understanding and better practice

This understanding of what I was doing in Development Training helped me in the doing of it. I was able to plan the students' experiences to stretch and challenge them in different ways. I was able to justify the values of compassion, respect and high achievement I was trying to inculcate by reference to the sort of society in which I wanted the students to live. As the sociologist Weber pointed out, value judgments direct all our actions. If we are clearer in what they are we have a better idea of why we are doing something.

This view of Development Training had several consequences. It helped me understand why the outdoors was such a powerful medium in which to work. This understanding should underpin the justification for including Outdoor Education in school curricula. Although I see Development Training as being contradictory to much of what occurs in the conventional school system.

I feel less committed to courses where the development of the individual is clearly of secondary importance to their contribution to the profitability of the enterprise who are the sponsor.

It gave the optimism that any student had potential far beyond what I could see - and so had I. It helped me to justify degrees of risk and danger in my work.

This is a personal view. It illustrates the importance of answering the questions 'development for what?' and 'development of what?' I am not saying that all Development Trainers should have the same answers as I have; although I must admit I would like them to have a similar answer to 'development for what?' But, whatever their answers are, having answers will make them better at what they do.

Notes

This chapter first appeared in 1988 as a guest editorial in *The Journal of Adventure Education and Outdoor Leadership*. 6(1). 2. It is reproduced here by permission of the author and with the agreement of the journal editor.

Chapter 2: Preferring to Learn Outdoors: Values and Education

John Halliday

Values are crucial to education. They affect all aspects of policy and practice from strategic considerations of what and who ought to be funded to practical considerations of what and how people should learn (Halliday 1998). It is widely believed that whatever else people learn, they should learn how values can conflict, how conflict can be resolved and most importantly how values give meaning to human experience. The term 'values education' has come to denote what can happen when people discuss, write or think about the meanings and implications of human experience in its widest sense.

Until recently interest in values in education and values education was confined mainly to schooling. It seems to have been uncritically accepted that values in all types of post or non-compulsory education are largely equivalent to what learners personally prefer. After all, these learners are either volunteers, adults or both and there might appear to be no justification for involving them in a values education that challenges their preferences. Nor might there appear to be much justification for worrying about the effect their choices might have on others. This is because, within a liberal secular culture, it is expected that people will express their personal values by choosing from a wide range of commodities that are on offer. Good instrumental relations are expected to govern the public sphere so that damaging public conflicts of value can be avoided. Within this culture, an outdoor education might be seen as just another commodity that people purchase as an alternative to an adventure holiday or a package tour which includes outdoor activities such as sailing or walking.

There is however an increasing recognition that the public-private distinction that forms part of common conceptions of liberalism is problematic and that a market in commodities is not quite as value-free as some imagine it to be (Jonathan 1997). It is recognised that private deliberations do have public consequences and that public good is best achieved when privately individuals want to work towards achieving that good. An attempt to run the public sphere according to value-free instrumental criteria is widely perceived to be impossible. Public policy is always directed towards some vision of society that is preferred. In addition the idea that schooling is something that is compulsorily done to people has been challenged from the points of view of children rights and a general expectation that learning should be inclusive and enjoyable. The opposite idea that post-schooling is something that people choose to do has been challenged through the imposition of conditions upon those trying to secure employment or unemployment benefits.

It is accepted that people learn in all kinds of situations throughout their lives and that they should be encouraged to do so. It is argued that the pace of change in and out of employment is so rapid that lifelong learning and the need to acquire so-called transferable skills should take precedence over schooling and the acquisition of fixed bodies of knowledge. If schooling is considered to be preparation for adult life, then the rate at which that life is expected to change makes it virtually impossible to plan theory-based programmes of preparation for it. Or at least that is what some promoters of lifelong learning claim (Longworth and Davies 1996).

In such a climate of change, and requirements for enjoyment and inclusion, outdoor education might be expected to flourish. It is claimed that outdoor education promotes the acquisition of transferable skills such as problem solving and team working and that it does so in a way that people enjoy (Outward Bound, 1997). Outdoor educators have considerable experience of learners who have been turned off by the kind of indoor learning experiences on offer in school but who have enjoyed and benefited from the kind of learning on offer in the outdoors. This has led some outdoor educators to make quite extravagant claims about such benefits as if it was only in the outdoors that certain types of desirable qualities and competencies could be achieved. It has led others to suggest a distinction between an academic education and an education of the whole person, the former taking place indoors, the latter outdoors (in Miles and Priest 1990). Such claims and suggestions should be treated with caution however.

People learn all kinds of practices both indoors and outdoors and it is not obvious that any one category of learning is always preferable to any other. Moreover it is worth noting that practices overlap and that they are made up of many sometimes quite different kinds of activity. For example, the practice of sailing not only involves action in the outdoors but planning, reading, collecting information and so on that generally take place inside. A key question that arises out of these observations is whether certain sorts of practice are more educationally important than others. For example, ought people to be encouraged to learn in depth philosophy or sailing? Alternatively, should they learn both more superficially? In a sense these are false dichotomies of course. To reflect upon a day's sailing can indeed involve philosophy and philosophers often use everyday examples to illustrate philosophical concepts. Philosophers sail as well as do other things. No one is exclusively a joiner or a sailor or a philosopher or a parent or whatever. Therefore people do not come to an outdoor or any learning experience devoid of any knowledge of practices more commonly associated with the indoors. Yet the question remains, even though it needs to be put slightly differently: are certain sorts of practice more educationally important than others as a prime focus for learning? Might there be no reason for preferring history or biology in school over sailing and walking however many teachers are able to link these practices in a meaningful way for students?

An obvious answer is that it depends upon the particular interests of students at any one time. A less obvious answer is that the type of practice that is the prime focus of learning is less important than the people with whom the learner learns and in particular the teacher's ability to broaden and enrich the learner's educational horizon. Nevertheless many outdoor educators do believe that the fact that learning is taking place mainly in the outdoors does offer certain unique advantages for learning certain types of things. These things and advantages are expressions of the values in outdoor education and what a values education in the outdoors might be.

It is worth recalling that within any culture there is an implicit idea of what it is to be educated – the kinds of skill knowledge qualities and attitudes that are valued. Now these things can be valued intrinsically for their own sake or extrinsically because they are the means to something else that is valued. In both cases expressions of value can never be settled once and for all but are in continual need of discussion and resolution in inclusive but independent centres of critical thinking and scholarship. Pring (1995: 110) suggests that teachers are "the mediators of different intellectual and aesthetic traditions". These traditions have authority because they have survived the critical scrutiny of previous generations. They include different voices such as poetry, history science and philosophy.

Through an induction into these traditions, people come to be able to enrich the experiences they have and their capacity to act intelligently. Pring notes however there are many voices that have been excluded from what he calls a "community of educated persons" who have been initiated into these traditions. Are outdoor educators excluded because traditionally it has been assumed that they have nothing of educational value to say? Does it matter that the activities they organise are enjoyed and appreciated by many learners previously disengaged from any kind of educational experience as such experiences are traditionally defined?

I guess that the majority of contributors to this book believe that such exclusion has taken place and that the values of and values in outdoor education ought to be more widely accepted and debated than they are. In that way outdoor education is given a chance to become sufficiently established that it too can be said to have a tradition that has withstood the critical scrutiny of previous generations and thus to have a voice in a community of educated persons. What might these values be?

Fairly obviously outdoor educators are not necessarily different from any other sorts of educator in that they can induct people into certain sorts of practice such as sailing and encourage people to extend their immediate interests into other practices such as meteorology, navigation, electronics and story telling. For certain sorts of learner, however, whose confidence is not high because of their lack of success at learning indoors at school, an outdoor education can offer the opportunity to discover that learning difficult things and personal confidence are intimately related. That is because the time between making an attempt to do something and getting clear feedback on the degree of success is relatively short in many outdoor settings. The feedback may come from the environment. For example, if map reading is inaccurate, the learner gets to know this fairly quickly without anybody needing to tell her. Where verbal feedback is given, there are often a sufficient number of things going on to draw the attention of other learners away from the nature of the feedback so that feedback is less threatening for an individual than it can be in a classroom setting. Moreover the chances are that even the most successful students in the classroom will struggle at some things in the outdoors. All of these considerations mean that people are often prepared to risk more of themselves in an outdoor setting and by so doing give themselves most chance of success. Success gives people confidence to try again and go on to learn on their own. Fear of failure leads people to devise ingenious strategies to avoid risking themselves again. Hence, they remain excluded from that community of educated persons to which Pring refers. Such considerations suggest that the values of egalitarianism and social inclusion inform outdoor education.

The landscapes within which outdoor educators often work can enhance the aesthetic and spiritual quality of the learning experience on offer. Thus, they contribute to an aesthetic and spiritual awareness of self and the other that gives meaning to intellectual endeavours in other contexts. They help to see the self against a much wider background than is usual in classroom and other contexts. They can help to build special relationships with people that enable critical reflection upon a range of issues including those relationships and the world in which they are realised. These considerations suggest that the values of aesthetics, spirituality, criticality and community also inform outdoor education.

All these values inform other types of education too however, and it is worth wondering whether outdoor educators have anything more in common with each other than with members of any other group of educators. It is also worth wondering whether outdoor education does make a special contribution to the educational meanings that these values have. What gives outdoor education special claim to have something important and unique to contribute to their meaning comes about, I think, because of the importance of authenticity to the educational enterprise (Cooper 1983).

At least two sense of authenticity may be distinguished. In the first sense, authenticity is achieved when people act in accordance with their innermost feelings. Such action may be contrasted with action that takes place according to the aims of others. In the second sense authenticity is achieved only through affirming peoples' ties to others, which is different from simply following their instructions. Charles Taylor has drawn attention to the general loss of meaning that has accompanied the rise of a narrow form of individualism that encourages people to do their own thing as if they could do that without seeing themselves against a wider background that goes beyond themselves. He seeks to recover something of the second from the first sense of authenticity which he believes to have become dominant (Taylor 1991). This dominance accompanies the dominance of the scientific worldview and rationalistic thought in general. It has become too easy to equate the quality of educatedness with just one type of voice in the educational conversation that has placed propositional knowledge on a pedestal and played down moral consideration of the uses to which that knowledge might be put. In so doing it has tended to suggest that those best able to articulate the preferred propositions from Physics, Chemistry, History and so on should be the dominant educational voices irrespective of the lack of moral courage that is often involved in such articulation. In other words, there is a tendency to value recitation over action which outdoor education might seek to counter in the interests of reclaiming an important sense of authenticity.

Thus, there is an individualism that pervades the normal educational institution and a predictability about what is expected in such institutions that tends to pass serious moral considerations by. The dominance of propositional knowledge over practical knowledge within the normal educational institution plays down the importance of moral reasoning and the values that sustain such reasoning. In contrast for most people, the outdoor experience offers something new, more communal and practical that enables what might be described as a more authentic balance between moral courage and deliberation. Experience that takes place in familiar surroundings and with familiar people encourages familiar responses and patterns. The outdoor experience may disturb those patterns. For example the correctness of responses in a classroom is largely determined by the individual application of criteria by the teacher. In the outdoors, the very criteria of correctness need to be worked out by the learners taking account of the unpredictability of the context in which they find themselves.

However artificial the nature of the task that learners are set in the outdoors, there is an unavoidable physical reality behind the task connected with weather, terrain, pain and fear which calls both for moral courage and deliberation in determining what to do. For example, group work in schools and colleges often involves the achievement of targets that make no difference to anyone's life and that are most economically completed by delegating responsibility for completion to one member of the group. That can be avoided in an outdoor setting. Physically it is not possible to complete certain tasks without committed participation by all members of a group. For most learners the outdoors provides a contrast to what they regard as normal and this unsettles routine patterns of behaviour and responses to difficulty. It calls for critical thinking that differs from the kind of manipulative cleverness that characterises thinking that is confined to the use of words divorced from a context in which those words make a difference.

It seems to me that a good reason to value outdoor education is the desire to recover a sense of authenticity that has been lost from modern education and from its associated community of educated persons. I believe that much useful work could be done by trying to elucidate further what this practically means for those teaching in the outdoors. Again however, caution is appropriate. If learners are encouraged to follow the idea that there is nothing other than 'allegiance to their own development' or 'being true to themselves' as a guide for conduct, then it becomes impossible to reason with them. That is because they can always 'trump' any reasoning with the authenticity 'card'. In effect they simply appeal to the idea that they have an innermost nature that is the final authority in determining what they ought to do. For Taylor and others however, people can only know what being 'true to themselves' might mean through the acquisition of languages, which can only be achieved through contact with others. On this view authentic self-realisation depends upon developing meaningful relations with others and reasoning with them.

In the modern world it has become too easy to conflate authenticity and honesty. As a result of a limited interpretation of liberalism in which instrumentalism is encouraged in the public sphere, there is a good deal of pressure to conform to someone else's idea of what ought to be done, irrespective of the moral worth of that idea. There is also pressure sometimes to state that their idea has been achieved when plainly it has not. A culture that demands conformity and adherence to people in positions of power may on occasions, encourage people to be dishonest. Hence there is a tendency to think that people who follow their own inner voice are somehow more honest than those who conform to the voices of others are, but this is not necessarily the case. What the outdoor experience might do is to confront people with the realisation that there must be something other than conforming to someone else's aims. What it should not do is to suggest that there is nothing other than conforming to some personal aim as if anyone could work out such an aim once and for all without taking account of the views of others. It would be a mistake too if outdoor educators themselves imagined that they were somehow more authentic or honest than some of their students merely because outdoor educators happen to work in contexts in which it is not easy for others to prescribe precisely what they ought to do. That is in contrast to those students who are constrained by the nature of the work that they do normally which demands action in conformity with the aims of others.

A common theme running through this chapter is that education is both centrally influenced by the culture in which it takes place and a central influence on the development of that culture and the kind of society that is deemed to be desirable. Hence education and value are inextricably linked. In a climate in which it is accepted that a resolution needs to be found between personal choice and public value, outdoor education may have a unique role to play in helping to recover the lost sense of authenticity that would enable such a resolution. Much work needs to be done to articulate what this might mean both in theory and in practice. I believe however that such recovery does open up a useful way of conceptualising the relationship between values and outdoor education.

References

Cooper, D.E. (1983) *Authenticity and Learning*. London: Routledge and Kegan Paul.
Halliday, J.S. (1998) *Values in Further Education*. Stoke on Trent: Trentham Publications.
Jonathan, R. (1997) *Illusory Freedoms: Liberalism, Education and the Market*. Oxford: Blackwell
Longworth, N., Davies, W.K. (1996) *Lifelong Learning*. London: Kogan Page.
Miles, J.C., Priest, S. (1990) *Adventure Education*. State College, PA 16801: Venture Publishing.
Outward Bound, (1997) *Learning that Lasts a Lifetime*. London: Outward Bound.
Pring, R. (1995) *Closing the Gap: Liberal Education and Vocational Preparation*. London: Hodder and Stoughton.
Taylor, C. (1991) *The Ethics of Authenticity*. Cambridge: Harvard University Press.

Chapter 3:   The Development of Values in Outdoor Education

Peter Barnes

Whilst it is very hard to generalise about an area as broad and diverse as outdoor education there are some common traits which lend themselves to examination. Foremost amongst these is a philosophy relating to values. This chapter examines the foundations and development of this philosophy, which in turn influences the way we approach the teaching and learning of values in an outdoor education environment. In covering so large an area, which could easily justify a book in its own right, this chapter, of necessity, can only take a selective view of its subject. Thus, it concerns itself more with trends and patterns rather than a detailed history of values.

There is no doubt that the foundation of outdoor education is strongly value based. Surprisingly these values were not always as we might see them today. Most surprisingly perhaps, is the notion that the development of an outdoor education philosophy is symbolically linked to war. The Boy Scouts of Baden-Powell, which arose from the Boer War, and, later, Outward Bound, which arose from the Second World War, were both strongly influenced by the values of their time. In particular these revolved around notions of self-denial, particularly with regard to such 'vices' as smoking and drinking and the muscular Christian ethos of *mens sana in corpore sano* or 'a healthy mind in a healthy body'. This ethos centred on the idea of physical challenge and competition against others, ones-self or nature; Kurt Hahn (1957:1), the co-founder of Outward Bound and the Duke of Edinburgh's Award spoke of the "continuity of purposeful athletic training". Such physical activity was linked directly to "the restoration of spiritual health" (*ibid*: 5) and to strong communal values, the values which Hahn saw as constituting a 'moral' character. With Britain being in the midst of a global war (Outward Bound was founded in 1941) the emphasis at the first school was very much on fitness, duty, dedication and sacrifice to the greater good.

Hahn's ideas were not, however, as original as many people might believe. To look at the true origin of values in outdoor education it is necessary to go back to the early Greek philosophers. Perhaps the greatest of these was Plato (427 - 347 BC) who in his best known work, the *Republic*, put forward the idea of young men learning virtue from taking part in risky activities. In his time the most notable risky activity was following the army to war and to learn by observing, although not participating in the fighting, war at first hand. This idea was built on much later by William James (1949) who wrote of the "moral equivalent of war" as the way to teach the military virtues such as heroism, tenacity and conscience. James was concerned only with the virtues to be found in a time of war, indeed he spoke of the need to fight a war against war. By learning the military virtues he saw a way in which people would reject war itself. In his turn Hahn developed this idea of Outward Bound as a moral equivalent of war with a carefully structured programme of activities providing the self-discipline and virtues to be found in soldiers in battle. However, Hahn, partly because of his experiences with Nazism and Fascism also emphasised the ideals of justice and compassion. In a similar way to James he saw that the learning of these virtues could provide an antidote to war. Virtue was not, however, generally seen in the context of the individual. In a similar vein to Plato before them, Hahn and Baden-Powell's concern was that each individual in society fulfilled their allotted role in life to the best of their ability - not only for their own sake but for the greater good. Virtue was seen as being central to this concern. The military virtues were needed to, first, prevent young people from becoming a menace to society and, secondly, to encourage them to play an active and worthwhile part in society's function. The history of our modern youth service (Davies, 1986) has followed a similar agenda, showing that outdoor educationalists are often more tied to society's demands than they care to think.

Carrying on from Plato, his student Aristotle (384 - 322 BC) worked on the process of education in developing virtues or, as we would say today, values. Most notably, he put forward the idea which sits at the very heart of outdoor education, that:

> *"... in our transactions with other men it is by action that some become just and others unjust, and it is by acting in the face of danger and by developing the habits of feeling fear or confidence that some become brave men and others cowards".* (cited in Wurdinger, 1994:5)

Aristotle thus lays the foundation of action, rather than ideas alone, as being the route to education. Interestingly, he also shows in the quote above how action, or experiential education, can be mis-educative just as it can be educative.

The early Greek ideal of values remained at the heart of British outdoor education for many years; indeed many would see them as still having a strong influence to this day. This links into the idea of values as being the ties, which hold a society together. These values are seen as not only legitimate but also binding. Furthermore, in a traditional society they are internalised through socialisation and form part of the moral code of that society, in other words they define what is seen as right and wrong. Unfortunately, this version of values can be taken as somewhat simplistic, it does not take into account the constraining influence of societies nor the fact that societies exist despite a discrepancy about the significance and construction of values. In modern society we are seeing more and more how hedonism and self-interest have eroded the barriers of traditional values such as those espoused by the early Outward Bound Schools.

It was a French writer, Jean Jacques Rousseau (1712 - 78) who put forward the idea of using nature as an educational tool in the way we know it today. Himself a solitary man, in his work *Emile* (1762) he suggested that experiencing nature was the most powerful form of education. Linked to this 'romantic' view of nature was one of Rousseau's most enduring legacies, that of the 'noble savage'. Although Rousseau saw the 'noble savage' idea as being flawed, the idea of 'primitive' people having higher codes of morality and values is one which still influences many people today. Where Rousseau diverted from the Greek ideals was that he saw the individual as being free and fulfilled in their own right with society being a collection of moral individuals rather than a binding force. In a similar vein one of the most influential writers of our own century Paulo Friere expanded on the importance of the individual. He saw education as "cultural action for freedom and therefore an act of knowing and not of memorisation" (1972:13). Morals and values were not, in Friere's eyes, to be learnt by rote but through a process of education where people would build their own individual moral code through understanding rather than through indoctrination.

Central to this whole process of understanding are the ideas of John Dewey. In *Democracy and Education* Dewey (1916) develops the concepts of Plato and Rousseau with his ideas of the role of the individual within society. Dewey saw the role of education as expanding ideas and celebrating a diversity of individuals. In this way society is served, as in Plato, as well as the individual, as in Rousseau. Dewey's most famous work, *Experience and Education*, expands on the Aristotelian ideas of experience as a way of education and says that "education ... must be based upon experience - which is always the life experience of some individual" (1938:89). Dewey took these ideas further by looking at the significant features of experience. Most importantly, in experiential education terms, he wrote that "experience as trying involves change, but change is meaningless transition unless it is consciously connected with the return wave of consequences which flow from it" (1916:139). In this way Dewey maintained that lessons learnt from experience could be applied to the everyday world of the student; a core belief of outdoor education today.

Modern outdoor education, while it still retains many of the Greek ideals has moved further towards the ideas of Rousseau, Friere and Dewey in its teaching. There is now a much stronger emphasis on allowing the 'student' to initiate and then to make their own discoveries. Interestingly it could be argued that this contradicts much of Outward Bound's early philosophy which was to impel students into experience (Hogan, 1968). Rousseau, and later Dewey, recognised that student learning is far more effective if it is voluntary rather than forced. The values of outdoor education may still reflect the ideas of service to a society, or community, but they are now much more centered on the individual.

Outdoor education continues to grow and develop. In recent years ideas from North America have played a strong part in shaping our ideas in Britain. These new ideas have largely centered much more around beliefs in the power of nature and the wilderness environment. The environmental movement, perhaps most notably exemplified by the John Muir Award, is largely North American in origin. The difference in the British and American approach can be seen in the structure of the solo experience. In Britain this would typically revolve around ideas of survival together with escape from the pressures of society. In America there was a much stronger emphasis on 'opening up' to nature and experiencing it rather than merely surviving it. Likewise, 'friluftsliv', the Norwegian concept of feeling at home with nature, is being recognised by more British outdoor organisations. This opening up, or interaction, with the environment is despite a mainstream move towards high adrenaline, confrontational, outdoor sports such as mountain biking and extreme skiing. This trend can be recognised in Vanreusel's (1995) 'Rambo' approach to the outdoors; a critique of how modern outdoor sport relates to nature. Further to this environmental aspect, Rousseau's 'noble savage' has been re-born in the guise of the native American and the Aborigines of Australia whose philosophy supposedly holds many of the answers to western society's problems. Eastern philosophy such as Buddhism has also started to have an impact on the thinking and values of outdoor educators. How much of this new thinking is largely a matter of trends is difficult to say but it is certain that cracks are starting to appear in the rigid Greek/ Rousseau/ Dewey tradition, which has typified outdoor education in Britain since the Second World War. Despite this, the largely white male, anglo-centric values which have traditionally dominated outdoor education in this country are only just starting to be questioned.

One major question facing outdoor education is the use of risk. An early virtue, dating back to the time of Plato and Aristotle, is that of courage. This was usually, if not always, taken to mean physical courage, which could be developed through the use of physical adventure. This did not always mean, as many believe, blind courage, indeed Aristotle saw recklessness as a great a vice as cowardice. William Unsoeld (1926 - 79), a noted American educator and philosopher wrote (1976, cited in Hunt, 1990:125) that safety should be emphasised as much as risk because true risk is always approached with safety in mind. This is not to say that the risk is negated, rather that it is not approached in a reckless manner. Dewey (1916), however, expanded on the idea that risk is not always physical and suggested that all thinking involves risk of some sort. Modern outdoor education has seized on this idea and through the use of such mediums as art and drama is now teaching the values that previously had been thought only possible to teach through physical adventure. Values such as compassion and understanding as well as self-evaluation and emotional courage are all successfully approached through these mediums.

In recent years outdoor education has also had to struggle with a number of its own core values. Central to these struggles is the notion of "the outdoor industry" (Humberstone, 1995:137). Although this term has only been used in recent years it is now widely adopted, if still contentious.

Much of this contention stems from the concept of an industry, which infers, directly or indirectly, a notion of commercialism and thus of consumerism. By working to consumerist values centres and organisations, the providers, are increasingly being forced to supply what the customer wants; even if the provider's own values disagree with what is being asked for. Consumerism has meant that large parts of the industry have been forced to take a subtle move away from being led by principles and beliefs to being led by the need to survive in a competitive market place.

Some writers have been noted for their attacks on the new face of the 'outdoor industry'. Perrin, for example, in referring to this commercialism, comments that "philosophical principles are readily forsaken and become subordinate to the profit motive" (1977:16). This view is still prevalent throughout much of the outdoor educational sector. Loynes (1996:54), in his turn, agrees with this argument and notes that the outdoor education movement has "core values ... that are not amenable to exploitation".

Strongly linked to the idea of commercialism is the idea of professionalism, which also brings with it a question of inherent values. Professionalism can be taken as synonymous with not only commercialism but with an industry driven not by social ideals but market demands. However, professionalism also implies an exemplary level of practice and the status accorded to it. In this sense the need to be professional is seen in a positive light. It is worthwhile, however, to bear in mind the underlying cause for much of this debate. Beames (1996:9), for example, writes that:

> *"Being an outdoor leader in the 1990s means being a practitioner who upholds the accepted standards of the profession, since instructing has evolved into just that - a profession, a practice. The conduct of outdoor instructors is increasingly coming under ... scrutiny".*

When this scrutiny is taken together with the debate on safety the role of the professional becomes even more problematic. In one possible scenario, the professional instructor could be expected to not only protect his or her client from harm but also to absolve that client from taking any responsibility for their own well-being. A central feature of outdoor education has always been the idea that it teaches people to take responsibility for their own actions. The authenticity involved in outdoor activities is seen as a powerful tool in this process. Professionalism is seen, by some, as removing this facility. In this manner it "disempowers the people it is intended to serve" (Reynolds, 1991, cited in Loynes, 1996:56). This is despite the ethical status given to professionals which: "involves 'central values', such as health, justice and education and is therefore of functional importance for all social groups". (Bilton, et al, 1987:383)

This chapter has shown that values develop and change over time as society changes. Even the thinkers who influence us today had different values and moral codes,

Plato and Aristotle, for example, would have had households of slaves, which would now be considered morally unacceptable. Values can also vary with the place in which societies develop Norway's friluftsliv and America's frontier wilderness can be contrasted with Britain's ordered countryside, for example. In our own times, the values of a sub-culture can be affected by the wider society; as outdoor education is currently finding in its interaction with a consumer-oriented mass culture. A notable change in the values of outdoor education has been in the move away from duty to society to concern for the individual while the value of courage has started to veer away from the act of physical courage to that of emotional courage. The role of war in the philosophy of outdoor education has begun to diminish. The values of outdoor education will continue to develop and change but it must be suspected that the core values of 'a moral character' which Hahn developed from some of history's great thinkers will continue to play a part.

References

Beames, S. (1996) 'So you want to be an outdoor adventure instructor .... ?' in *The Journal of Adventure Education and Outdoor Leadership* 13 (3), 9-10.

Bilton, T., Bonnett, Jones, P. et al. (1981) *Introductory Sociology.* London: Macmillan Education

Davies, B. (1986) *Threatening Youth.* Milton Keynes: Open University Press.

Dewey, J. (1916) *Democracy and Education.* New York: The Free Press.

Dewey, J. (1938) *Experience and Education.* New York: MacMillan Publishing Co.

Friere, P. (1972) *Cultural Action for Freedom.* Harmondsworth: Penguin Education.

Hahn, K. (1957) 'Origins of the Outward Bound Trust' in James, D. (ed.) *Outward Bound.* 1-17, London: Routledge and Kegan Paul.

Hogan, J. M. (1968) *Impelled into Experiences* Wakefield: Educational Productions Ltd.

Hunt, J. S. (1990) 'Philosophy of Adventure Education' in Miles, J. & Priest, S. *Adventure Education.* 119-128. State College, PA: Venture Publishing. inc.

Humberstone, B. (1995) 'The commercialisation of outdoor adventure - profit and loss in adventure!' in Lawrence, L. et al. *Professional & Development Issues in Leisure, Sport and Education.* LSA pub no. 56.

James, W. (1949) *Essays on Faith and Morals.* New York: Longmans, Green and Co.

Loynes, C. (1996) 'Adventure in a Bun.' in *Journal of Adventure Education and Outdoor Leadership.* 13(2), 52-57.

Perrin, J. (1997) 'Instructors, Skillmongers, Fiscal Pimps' in *Climber.* February, 1997, 16-17.

Rousseau, J. J. (1762) *Emile.* trans., Foxley, B. (1974) London: Dent Publishing.

Vanreusel, B. (1995) 'From Bambi to Rambo: Towards a Socio-Ecological Approach to the Pursuit of Outdoor Sports' in Weiss, O. and Schulz, W. (Eds.) *Sport in Space and Time.* Vienna: Vienna University Press.

Wurdinger, S. (1994) *Philosophical Issues in Adventure Education.* Dubuque, Iowa: Kendall/Hunt Publishing Company.

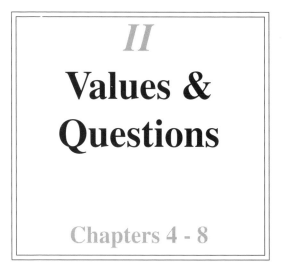

II

Values & Questions

Chapters 4 - 8

Chapter 4:   Spirituality and Living Values

Steve Deeming

I have an enduring recollection from climbing at the Dewerstone, near Plymouth, in the early 70's. I can remember stepping off grass onto the first pitch of 'Central Groove'. At that time, the National Trust was seeking to use climbing permits to 'restrict' access to the crag for environmental and other reasons. I was working with groups in that location and it was part of my very small income. 'They' did not have the right to restrict me from climbing when and where I wanted, did they? Has anyone been to the Dewerstone recently? The grass at the bottom of the Main Face and almost everywhere else has long gone.

After nearly 30 years involvement in outdoor education, this memory plugs into a growing sense of unease with the way that I have operated and the way in which the profession continues to operate. The Lyme Bay accident and its aftermath have reinforced my feelings.

Involvement, observation and reflection indicate an obvious dis-ease in our relationship with the cosmos of which we are a part. In the Northern world, we live in a post-industrial, individualistic and materially oriented society. With few exceptions, this culture does little but reinforce destructive values for all ages. Activities within an outdoor adventure setting follow the same example. The anthropocentric concepts of remoralisation, social control, commodification and an economically based desire for greater efficiency and wealth from the work place are of primary importance. Most organisations using outdoor-based activities will, by the sheer need to survive, subscribe to these concepts. Most would also say, implicitly or explicitly, that personal or social development and training are important elements of their practice. This statement is invalid unless based on a value system that puts an absolute priority on the role of human beings in the natural environment:

> *"Deep ecologists say that an ecocentric attitude is more consistent with the truth about the nature of life on Earth. Instead of regarding humans as something completely unique or chosen by God, [deep ecologists] see us as integral threads in the fabric of life. They believe we need to develop a less dominating and aggressive posture towards the Earth if we and the planet are to survive".* (Zimmerman, 1989: 24).

The above quote and other inputs, such as The Eight Points of Deep Ecology (Naess, 1989) can be more simply summarised as forms of spirituality, spiritual development or spiritual awareness. Other non-exclusive definitions include:

- the way in which we live our lives (Spretnak, 1986)

- the development of a realisation that life is greater than it appears and that a radical change/paradigm shift is needed in the way we perceive the world and our place in it, (Rees-Mogg, 1992)

The shift hinges on the concept of love, respect and awareness of self, of others and in the environment of which we are all a part (Mortlock, 1984; Sessions, 1995). The personal use and development of the tool of critical analysis has to be a vital element in the development of such a realisation. Acknowledging the process or the seeking of spiritual awareness is otherwise described as:

- Seeking the kingdom of God on Earth (Kuntze, 1994)

- Holism, or wholeness (Perls, 1969)

- The process of Self-actualisation (Maslow, 1970)

- To transcend the status quo (Rogers, 1964)

If what is written so far is accepted, it is clear that outdoor education is unable to impart a clear spiritual base to its continued existence. The reason for this omission (apart from fiscal) seems to pivot on a tacit acceptance of the process of osmosis. Why bother with spiritual development as an element of primary importance? Why not continue to see it (if seen at all) as implicit in the 'hard skills' imparted upon participants (Hunt, 1989) or communicated through subsidiary topics such as 'conservation'? (Langmuir, 1995). In the case of youth work in general, why see spiritual awareness as anything more than an aid to personal survival in a society in which change is an anathema? (National Youth Agency, 1999).

The answer is to inculcate processes that enable the individual, of their own accord, to develop the power of critical analysis and thereby build a personal value system. This would result in radical change in their lives and that of the world (Friere, 1972; Blackwell and Seabrook, 1988).

There is a fundamental obstacle to bringing about radical change (and ultimately a paradigm shift) as stated above. World history shows that there are always issues of 'power-over' rather than 'power-with' within human institutions (Rowan, 1988). These power battles manifest themselves as the replacement of one set of rules with another, even if implicit, by powerful minority groups in order to maintain authority over a tacit majority; i.e. the issues are basically political, economic, ideological or racial. Outdoor education is no different from any other form of institution. The aims and objectives of the process are often lost in a maze of organisational detail or promulgation of a stereotype. Outdoor education, as with many human-oriented organisations, surrounds itself with a cloak of professionalism to protect its participants from accident or neglect, its practitioners from litigation (Wilson, 1988) and to maintain the status quo. If spirituality is ultimately about life and death issues and an ecocentric view of creation, where can there be a role for spiritual development in such a prescriptive and proscriptive process of so-called education?

If the purpose of spiritual development is valid, it has to be accepted that spirituality is a process and not a product. Consequently, there is a need to go back to the basic premise of how outdoor education and its role in spiritual development are promulgated.

The use of the residential experience or long-distant educational trip as a format for spiritual development has to be justified and in many cases is not. The environmental audit and economic costs of travel, plus the associated on-costs, balanced against the use of 'the back-yard' and local community resources require clear and concise examination. This must not be seen as elitist or exclusive. Rural, sub-urban and urban communities have a myriad of input and stimuli that can be utilised before there is a need to travel to other areas of the environment. Where is the real wilderness if not in our own hearts and minds? In addition, what is the definition of 'need'? (Max-Neef, 1989). Why does the need to travel and to conquer seem to predominate in Western minds?

Deep and critical examination of techniques and value systems currently employed in outdoor education/outdoor adventure is required. The development of love, respect and awareness of self, others and the environment (Mortlock, 1984) offers a unique opportunity to operate in such a way that removes the desire for specialised equipment, techniques, arenas and achievements. The further use of non-invasive facilitation techniques has to allow the development of a critical personal recognition and value system. An obvious extension from this will be the further exploration, inwardly and outwardly, as a valid way forward (van Matre, 1997; Hodgkin, 1985).

Conceptually, there is a need to be clear as to what is a spiritual experience. The predominant view in outdoor education provision revolves around 'the one-off' (by either action or event). We do not know the effect of what we do/say on others. Therefore, we may as well continue a form of chaos theory, as there will be unknown effects; yet, the process will be more effective as a series of events. Having 'provided' for a spiritual experience, how do we continue it? An experience that heightens the way of the spirit and aids spiritual development need not be an 'all in one go', 'awe and wonder' peak experience. It can occur in the day-to-day and be a realisation over a period of time. (Maslow, 1964; Robinson, 1983; Hay, 1990). Consequently, it has to be a process, from cradle to grave, and not a product. The process involves individuals becoming personally empowered to bring about change for and in themselves and in their lives, rather than through the perceived needs of those individuals by others ('the professionals'). Praxis, 'the action of men (sic) upon their world in order to transform it' (Friere, 1972: 52-60) can been seen as 'community action'; e.g., resistance to environmental degradation, liberation theology movements and women's action during the 1984 UK miners strike. This is distinct from 'community development' or provision which is seen as 'Get them off the street corners!', 'Character-building!', 'Sport for All' etc. (Davies, 1986).

> *There is a view, already stated above, that established ways of working with people in the outdoors are not valid. They act to reinforce values that are set by current political, economic, ideological and race agendas. The use of the (outdoor) environment, whilst purporting to bring about change, uses limited definitions and modes of operation for a predominately white society which mimic and support dominant and destructive societal values.* (Van Matre, 1997).

Accordingly, there is a distinct need for outdoor education to develop, and universally accept, a common definition of the word 'spirituality' and its derivatives. Observation shows that current use evokes in some practitioners a distorted view of an organised religion-based practice. Yet there are clear links between spiritual development and psychological/psychotherapeutic processes - 'the inward journey' (Bugental, 1978; Davis, 1999) alongside non-organised forms of religious thought and action. To be on this 'inward journey', in the outdoors and valid through any other constructive medium, is personally threatening in a variety of ways. In the outdoors, perceived external fear and 'awe and wonder' can open many doors - some that we might not want opened. After all, we all carry 'baggage'. Hence, practitioners working with participants need skills, or access to those with the skills, to go deeper than the superficial. Without this depth, there will be no insight and ultimately no development or change. Modern schools of psychology openly acknowledge that the majority of people accept the existence of the soul - we just don't talk about it! Proponents have developed skills and practices that encompass spirituality and its global traditions alongside rigorous critical analysis. (Maslow, 1964; Davis, 1999)

The raising of spiritual awareness has to be an individual pilgrimage. Yet it cannot be of worth unless the individual person is part of an on-going, safe and nurturing community. The process is concerned with concepts of personal freedom – firmly hung on a framework of love, respect and awareness of self, others and the environment (Mortlock, 1984) or 'self', as neatly summed up by Naess in his essay 'The Deep Ecological Movement' (Sessions, 1995). The aim would be for the individual to find themselves, through their own will, questioning their actions, seeking support and validation from their companions and acting on the conclusions drawn. The journey is as close as one can get to a valid definition of personal liberty, expressed as selflessness rather than selfishness (Friere, 1972). Otherwise, the development will be egotistical, egoistical, individualistic and thereby totally anthopocentric.

Trainers/leaders/facilitators need to be clear where they are on their path of personal liberation and the development of a personal value system; i.e. their own spiritual development and awareness. Practitioners cannot be afraid to stand up and vocalise those values, or be open enough to acknowledge a lack of them or the need to find space and time to work on them. It is a community responsibility to provide a safe and secure place in which individuals can be heard (Leavitt, 1986).

Perhaps a reason why this does not happen in outdoor education provision is due to self-interest maintaining the way in which outdoor experiences and facilities continue to be provided. Might there be a fear that we, and the way the work is done, would become redundant if there were a paradigm shift? After all, much of the work is supported, even governed, by the political, ideological and economic structures that set the current rules. Yet these structures also threaten the continuation of existing work. This happens in an educational arena, ring-fenced by a distorted view of the power and value of the child, where the nation's economic interests dictate educational needs. Alternatively, might we, as individuals and practitioners, find the paradigm shift too personally threatening? Could it be that the insidious, ever-present macho element of outdoor adventure prevents me from sharing and growing in my own and others' deep personal experiences except when faced with an individualised threat to continued existence? Alternatively, could it be that we all resist change, because of the fear of the unknown? This is all the more a perturbing thought, considering the situations that we, as outdoor adventurers, deliberately seek out.

Spirituality and its development cannot be separated from political, economic, idealogical and ecological concepts of how past, current and future society operates. In light of the continuing commercialisation of adventure and the increasing degradation of holistic value systems and Creation, there need to be alternative ways of being in and being part of the natural environment.

It is time to get off the tops of the mountains, develop a sense of global and cosmic humility and not return until we have. (De Chardin, 1998, Simpson, 1997).

> *To see a World in a grain of sand,*
> *And a Heaven in a wild flower,*
> *Hold Infinity in the palm of your hand,*
> *And Eternity in an hour..*
> (William Blake)

References

Blackwell, T. & Seabrook, J. (1988) *The Politics of Hope.* London: Faber and Faber.

Bugental, J. F. T. (1978) *Psychotherapy and Process.* New York: Random House.

Davies, B. (1986) *Threatening Youth.* Milton Keynes: Oxford University Press.

Davis, J. (1999) *Introduction to Transpersonal Psychology.* Denver: Metropolitan State College.

de Chardin T. in Gallacher B. (1998) *Meditations with Teilhard de Chardin.* Santa Fe: Bear & Company.

Friere, P. (1972) *Pedagogy of the Oppressed.* Harmondsworth: Penguin.

Hay, D. (1990) *Religious Experience Today.* London; Cassell.

Hodgkin, R. (1985) *Playing and Exploring.* London: Methuen.

Hunt, J. (ed) (1989) *The Search for Adventure.* Guildford: Talbot Adair Press.

Kuntze, B. Y. (1994) *Margaret Fell and the Rise of Quakerism.* London: Constable.

Langmuir, E. (1995) *Mountaincraft and Leadership.* Scottish Sports Council/MLTB.

Leavitt, M. L. (1986) 'The Skill of Listening' in *Quaker Faith and Practice.* Section 20.74. London: Britain Yearly Meeting.

Maslow, A. (1964) *Religions, Values and Peak-Experiences.* Harmondsworth: Penguin.

Max-Neef, M. et al (1989) *Human Scale Development* in Development Dialogue 1989:1. Uppsalla: The Dag Hammarskjold Centre.

Mortlock, C. (1984). *The Adventure Alternative.* Milnthorpe: Cicerone Press.

Naess, A. (1989) *Ecology, Community and Lifestyle.* (Trans. David Rothenberg). Cambridge: Cambridge University Press.

National Youth Agency (1999) *Draft 3 National Occupational Standards for Youth Work:Unit D6.* Leicester: NYA.

Perls, F. S. (1969) *Gestalt Therapy Verbatim .* Moab: Real People Press.

Rees-Mogg, W. (1992) *Is this the end of life as I know it?* The Independent - 21.12.92.

Robinson, E. (1983) *The Original Vision.* New York: The Seabury Press.

Rogers, C. (1964) *On Becoming A Person.* Boston: Houghton Mifflin.

Rowan, J. (1988) *Ordinary Ecstasy.* London: Routledge.

Sessions, G. (ed) (1995) *Deep Ecology for the 21st Century.* Boston: Shambhala.

Simpson, J. (1997) *Dark Shadows Falling.* London: Cape.

Spretnak, C. (1986) *The Spiritual dimension of Green Politics.* Santa Fe: Bear & Company.

van Matre, S. (1997) *Earth Education - A New Beginning.* The Institute for Earth Education.

Wilson, J. (1988) *Politics and Leisure.* London: Unwin Hyman.

Zimmerman, M,. E. (1989) 'Introduction to Deep Ecology' in *Context.* 22 (Summer 1989), 24: Context Institute.

Chapter 5: Principle Ethics vs Virtue Ethics

Simon Priest & Michael Gass

As with most disciplines, certain professional actions are more appropriate than others. When these actions pertain to moral decisions and conduct, they are usually identified as ethical issues. Ethical decision making involves determining which behaviors in such issues are morally 'right' or 'correct.' How does a professional go about determining ethical conduct, particularly when there are competing ethical considerations in conflict with one another? While several writers have evolved models for ethical decision making with outdoor leadership (e.g., Hunt, 1990; Mitten, 1994), most approaches used for making ethical decisions can be grouped into one of two approaches: principle ethics and virtue ethics.

Principle ethics are guided by a proactively determined set of impartial rules. These rules are used as principles to guide ethical behavior. Outdoor leaders following principle ethics centre their attention on their actions and choices, looking to answer the questions of "What shall I do?" and "Is this situation unethical?" (Jordan & Meara, 1990: 108). Principle ethics are also based on the belief the issues being examined are somewhat similar in context and can be connected to other situations.

Virtue ethicists, however, believe that one must examine the particular factors and influences of each act, since 'correct behavior' must be determined from each specific situation and cannot be linked to other situations. Virtue ethics are also guided by the particular virtues associated with being a moral outdoor leader rather than the principles of being ethical. Virtue ethics are concerned with professional character traits, focusing on the questions of "who shall I be?" and "am I doing the best for my client?" (Jordan & Meara, 1990: 108).

The strengths of each approach are the very weaknesses of the other. Principle ethics are independent of the situation. Professional behavior, ethical for a general situation, therefore becomes the rule for all specific situations. For example, a leader notices that a group has made a navigational error and is heading the wrong way into a fragile ecosystem (Hunt, 1990). Should the leader tell the clients that they have made a mistake, or should they find out for themselves? At least three principles are in play here: client learning, client comfort, and environmental protection. Will clients learn the lesson by being told or should they experience the consequences? How far do they have to travel off route to learn? Will they damage the place they are headed into? In deciding whether clients have a right to be informed about their error, the leader would order all principles by importance and simply make an ethical decision on the basis of the guiding order. For a principle ethicist, this order would remain the same in every similar situation.

Virtue ethics are dependent on the situation. Professional behavior is contextual or subjective and may vary from one set of circumstances to another. For the navigational example, several virtues are in play: honesty, caring, and sensitivity. What would an honest person do about informing the clients? What would a caring person do about allowing them to travel out of their way? What would a sensitive person do to protect nature? Instead of deciding what to do, the leader is concerned with the type of person to be and the greatest benefit for the client and environment. Therefore, this decision for a virtue ethicist may differ from or agree with that of the principle ethicist, but this decision will also be different in any other slightly modified dilemma.

While principle ethics ask outdoor leaders to 'look outside' the situation to maintain a degree of objectively in determining ethical behavior, virtue ethics ask them to 'step inside' the dilemma to better approximate the desires and intentions of the professional's actions. Several authors (e.g., Gass & Wurdinger, 1993) have advanced the premise that the idea of using principle or virtue ethics should not be an 'either-or' decision, and that both principles and virtues need to be considered. One model where either or both elements may be used is Kitchener's (1984) model of ethical decision making.

Kitchener's model of ethical justification

Kitchener's model consists of multiple steps in a process of ethical reasoning, examining issues in a progressive sequence. If a well founded ethical decision cannot be determined at one level, outdoor leaders advance to the next one which is usually more general and abstract in its approach to the issue. The five steps of this ethical decision making model are: intuitive, option listing, ethical rules, ethical principles, and ethical theory.

Ethical responses in the intuitive level come from pre-reflective or 'gut reactions' to 'what feels right?' The ethical beliefs associated with these decisions are so well established the answer is obtained through 'ordinary moral sense.' There is little need to even consider the decision since the 'ordinary moral sense' process has already been pre-determined, usually based on the outdoor leader's "individual experience, ethical knowledge, and level of ethical development" (Zygmond & Boorhem, 1989: 271). For example, almost all outdoor leaders would intuitively claim that damaging the environment in a survival situation is acceptable. In order to save lives, they would gladly light signal fires with green wood or build stretchers by cutting down trees.

When outdoor leaders are unable to resolve ethical decisions at this level, option listing and the evaluation of these options, their outcomes, and potential ramifications needs to occur. This serves as a foundation for the ethical decision making process in whichever of the three remaining steps is used. For example, these two options could be listed for the survival and environment example: damage the environment and save lives, or protect the environment and lose lives.

Ethical rules are generally externally established codes of conduct, like the guidelines created by the psychological, medical, or legal professions. Guidelines like these are established by a profession to maintain a certain level of ethical behavior and their creation is generally considered to be a developmental benchmark in the quest for professionalism. One example of an ethical rule is: adventure programs discriminating on the basis of gender, race, or sexual orientation cannot become accredited by AEE and accredited programs found to discriminate in this manner will lose their accreditation status. (Ethical guidelines for outdoor leaders are considered later in this chapter.)

Ethical principles are "enduring beliefs about specific modes of conduct or end-states of existence that, when acted upon, protect the interests and welfare of all of the people involved" (Zygmond & Boorhem, 1989, p. 273). More general in nature than ethical rules, the five principles identified by Kitchener (1984) as being the most critical for members in the 'helping professions' include: autonomy, nonmaleficence, beneficence, fidelity, and justice. In autonomy, individuals have the right to freedom of action and choice as long as their behavior does not infringe upon the rights of others. Nonmaleficence means that, above all else, no harm will be done to people. Beneficence means that the focus of an outdoor leader's actions is to contribute to the health and welfare of others. Fidelity means be faithful, keep promises, be loyal and respectful of a person's rights. Justice means individuals will be treated as equals and implies a concept of 'fairness.' For example, Rohnke's axiom of challenge by choice (Rohnke, 1984), where people are not coerced to participate in an adventure, can be illustrative of all five of these ethical principles.

When intuitive thought, ethical codes, and ethical principles fail to resolve ethical issues, ethical theories are implemented. This is done to help determine which factors are relevant to the situation and should take precedent. Two principles used in this process are balancing and universalizability. Balancing compares options with a view toward picking the one that brings the least amount of avoidable harm to all parties involved. This is similar to the consequential theory of ethics, which suggesting that the action is ethically correct only if it produces the greatest happiness for the greatest number (Mill, 1985). Universalizability compares options with a view toward picking the one that brings the least specificity to the situation. This is similar to the nonconsequentialist theory of ethics based on the 'categorical imperative,' stating that actions should only be taken when the processes used can be fairly and broadly applied as a universal law to all similar cases (Kant, 1964). For the survival and environment example, the two options would be balanced against the measure of a human life versus the environment. In some cases, a unique and fragile environment might outweigh a human life as in the concept of rescue-free wilderness (McAvoy,

1990). If the 'save the wilderness at the cost of a life' option was chosen, perhaps because protecting wilderness might save more lives in the long run, then a universal application of this option would also have to hold true to all wilderness areas.

Application of Kitchener's model

Again, when outdoor leaders are unable to resolve a situation by determining professional or appropriate action at one level, they move to the next step. In this model, one step is not better than another, just more appropriate for providing professional guidance toward making an ethical decision. One advantage of this model is that it creates conditions for the continual evolution of outdoor leaders at all levels of ethical development. As highlighted earlier, the greater experience outdoor leaders possess in encountering certain ethical decisions, the more likely these decisions will become 'intuitive level decisions.' As they become more experienced in making ethical decisions, it is more likely that dilemmas will be resolved at this lowest level. Hence the need for outdoor leaders to practice resolving ethical dilemmas. Consider this scenario[1] as an example:

Hearing from a corporate friend in California on the positive value of adventure experiences for building teamwork in organizations, the ABC Corporation (located in Boston, Massachusetts) contacted a service provider in California (called California Adventure Training, Inc.) to provide training for them. After going over several logistical details, California Adventure Training, contacted several of the listed facilities close to Boston to ask if they could use their ropes course for part of a five day training. One of these facilities was Boston Adventures, Inc., which happened to be located near the ABC Corporation. In fact, several of the human resource professionals from the ABC Corporation had heard of the locally based Boston Adventures, Inc. programme and contacted them a few days later to find out what corporate adventure training actually entailed, how the ABC Corporation could maximize working with the California Adventure Training, Inc. programme, and how good California Adventure Training, Inc. was at providing such services. In speaking with the Corporation, Boston Adventures Inc. stated they could provide better services for the ABC Corporation and actively pursued the contract. They did not inform California Adventure Training, Inc. that they were stating this information to the ABC Corporation or that they were now negotiating for the contract that California Adventure Training, Inc. had contacted them for in order to use their ropes course. Given this information, The ABC Corporation contacted California Adventure Training, Inc. to let them know that they were no longer interested in using them for these training services and would be signing a contract with a more locally based service provider who they have been told knows their needs better.
(Gass & Wurdinger, 1993: 43)

The first step in the model is to examine the practice of attracting customers away from other organizations as an intuitive ethical decision. Based on professional experience and the belief that ethical behavior is important, outdoor leaders should ask themselves if it makes 'ordinary moral sense' to follow such behavior or decide that such behavior is unethical in all cases? They may determine that this type of behavior could lead to a wide variety of negative implications for individual programs as well as to the field and so choose not to involve themselves in this practice. They may also determine that this practice is ethically acceptable (the programme appropriately attracted customers away on the basis of safety standards or actual competence, since the staff of Boston Adventures actually did know ABC Corporation's business better than California Adventure Training). However, if outdoor leaders determine that this issue is not easily resolvable due to conflicting ideas, elements, principles or virtues, then they move to the next level of the model and list possible options of competing behavior and the consequences of such actions.

In the second step, outdoor leaders make a list of possible options that could be taken and the strengths and weaknesses of each. Four options are possible for the scenario and, in this case, they could be called: prohibitive (prohibit 'stealing' since it is unethical), open market (allow 'competition' since it is ethical), objective conditional (attracting customers is okay under certain conditions), and subjective discretional (attract customers at your own discretion). If one believes in the absoluteness of the first two options (stealing is bad; competition is good), then these are easy choices (made at an intuitive level). In the prohibitive option, stealing is wrong at all times and would not be ethically permissible under any circumstances. In the open market option, competition is right in all cases and would be ethically expected under any circumstances. If the remaining two options (under certain conditions; at your discretion) are full of conflict and lead to an ethical dilemma, then these options need to be more closely examined along with their respective strengths and weaknesses.

The objective conditional (OC) option includes establishing a proactive and objective set of standards that outline criteria as to when providers could not attract customers away from other providers. Some of these pre-identified conditions might be possession of a current contract (or in negotiation to contract) and a waiting period of a few months after an initial contact ended. At these times, other providers could not approach the customers of these 'contracted' providers. The main focus here would be a series of clearly identified conditions that were in place before a competitive situation arose. This option has its strengths. It establishes objective conditions for outdoor leaders to follow and serves to eliminate potential negative exploitation of professional interaction. It provides some degree for 'freedom of choice' among customers wishing to switch providers. It fosters the belief that outdoor leaders may freely interact on providing quality programs without fear of losing customers. It proactively identifies the 'rules' of professional interaction, as well as competition for customers. It encourages a climate of professional collaboration with the advance knowledge that losing customers in such an environment may occur. This option has several weaknesses as well. It does not remove the possibility that 'stealing' customers could still occur after the objective conditions were met. It limits, to the degree of the conditions, the customers' freedom to choose another service provider.

The subjective discretional (SD) option recognizes that there are times when attracting customers away from other businesses would be unethical and inappropriate. However, it would be up to outdoor leaders to use their own belief system in determining when this would or wouldn't be appropriate on a case by case basis. The strengths of this position are that it establishes subjective conditions for outdoor leaders to follow, serving to try and eliminate potential negative exploitation; and it provides for greater autonomy for providers and customers given that the rights of others are not being infringed upon. The weaknesses of the position are that it does not remove the possibility that negative exploitation could still occur after the subjective condition is met (e.g., beliefs by outdoor leaders that customers were 'stolen'); and it does not promote the positive development of professional collaboration without fear of losing customers.

Once various positions are outlined with strengths and weaknesses, outdoor leaders look to the third, fourth and fifth steps for guidance in deciding between both options. In the third step, they examine the ethical rules of the profession. If they see the central issue to be one of competence (where the California programme truly did not possess the competence to conduct the programme, but the Boston programme did), then the outdoor leaders can make their choice of option from this ethical rule. However, if competence is not at the heart of the issue, this step is of little use to them and they progress to the next one.

In the fourth step, outdoor leaders evaluate the major advantages and disadvantages of both options and compare them to the ethical principles of autonomy, nonmaleficence, beneficence, fidelity, and justice. The OC option establishes an impartial set of rules regarding contracts and waiting periods that block other providers from attracting customers away from the programme. The SD option recognizes that the choice of attracting customers should be made situationally by outdoor leaders considering their personal values.

Autonomy seems to be lower for both providers and customers in the OC option, because their rights to choose and their freedom to interact outside the contract are restricted by these rules. Autonomy is higher for both providers and customers in the SD option, because each are free to choose, with limited infringement on the rights of other providers.

Nonmaleficence appears to be higher for providers and moderate for customers in the OC option, because providers are protected by the rules and customers could be harmed by being unable to change their minds if 'stuck' with a poor programme. Nonmaleficence is lower for providers and moderate for customers in the SD option, because providers are open to 'attack' from other providers and customers could be harmed by the possible lack of programme quality.

Beneficence seems to be moderate for providers (depending on whether they gain or lose customers) in the OC option, because collaboration can occur and may bring increased quality or decreased motivation to improve. It is also lower for customers in the OC option, because they lose the chance to benefit from an open selection process that encourages the best programme to come to the forefront. Beneficence is moderate for providers (again depending on whether they lose or gain customers) in the SD option, because competition can bring increased quality and decreased sharing of information. It is also higher for customers in the SD option, because they benefit from a wide variety of providers and quality programs to choose from.

Fidelity appears to be high for providers and customers in the OC option, because customers remain faithful or loyal to providers, keep written promises, and respect a collaborative environment. Fidelity is low for providers and customers in the SD option, because customers switch providers, break verbal contracts, and respect only the programs' rights to compete.

Justice seems to be moderate for providers and customers in both options. In the OC option, everyone has equal knowledge of the operation rules in advance and has the fair chance to begin trusting one another in collaboration. In the SD option, everyone has fair access to discuss contracts with one another and operates in a competitive market with equal opportunity.

In this case, if the outdoor leaders believed that one of these two options possessed the highest ethical stance for addressing the issue of attracting customers away from other programs, then either the OC or SD option would be followed and the ethical decision making process would be completed. If, on the other hand, the outdoor leaders were unable to determine the ethical decision based on these principles, they would advance to the final step of using the ethical theories of balancing and universalizability to determine the appropriate ethical action.

Balancing considers both options and chooses the stance that produces the greatest benefit for the greatest number of people. Everyone would be indirectly inconvenienced (including the customer) by the inclusion of rules and the only direct benefit would go to the programme with a contract in the OC option. The only one who is inconvenienced would be the programme who loses a customer to another provider and all others (including the customer) would benefit in the SD option. Therefore, the SD option is the clear preference for balancing.

Universalizability refers to the applicability of the option to all similar cases. The OC option is the clear preference for universal generalizability: its rules suit any situation. The SD option has no universalizability, because each situation is decided on its own merits. Since one option is favored by one theory and the other by another, outdoor leaders will have to decide (at this final step) which of these two theories they hold in higher regard.

In following such a model, principle and virtue ethicists would tend to focus on different features. As highlighted earlier, principle ethicists would strive to remain objective and impartial in following the model, focusing on what outdoor leaders should do to result in the most ethical practice. Virtue ethicists, however, would examine the particular factors and influences of this particular action, attempting to interpret the intentions of Boston Adventures in the dilemma to better approximate the desires and intentions of an outdoor leader's actions.

Outdoor leaders are encouraged to use perspectives of both the principle and virtue approaches when possible to achieve a well-balanced outlook on the ethical decision. While at certain times these approaches come into conflict with one another, a combined 'objective/subjective' approach lends a balanced perspective for outdoor leaders.

Ethical guidelines for outdoor leaders

Probably one of the brightest developments of ethical decision making with outdoor leadership, in America, is the formulation of ethical guidelines by the Association of Experiential Education's Therapeutic Adventure Professional Group (AEE, 1992; Gass, 1993). A version of these guidelines can also be found in the ethics section of the programme accreditation standards identified in the *Manual of Accreditation Standards for Adventure Programs* (Williamson & Gass, 1993). These guidelines were created with the support of the American Psychological Association (APA), the American Alliance of Marriage and Family Therapists (AAMFT), Council on Outdoor Education (COE), Council of Accreditation of Services for Families and Children (CASFC), and the Worldwide Outfitters and Guides Association (WOGA). While not established as an ethical code or rules that professionals must follow or be censured from practice, these guidelines do point to the fact that the outdoor leadership field is on record for supporting certain practices. The seven guidelines relate to: competence, integrity, responsibility, respect, concern recognition, and objectivity. (Although developed for therapists, these seven guidelines are paraphrased, in appendix 1, for outdoor leaders.)

While these guidelines represent a critical and invaluable step in advancing the outdoor leadership profession, outdoor leaders should realize that following such guidelines does not release them from using ethical judgement. Just as one should not blindly follow safety protocols for a technical skill without considering the changing elements of an outdoor setting, outdoor leaders should not forgo the need to constantly examine their behavior in professional endeavors.

Ethical standards possess limitations. Ethical guidelines may conflict with the framework of certain cultures, and need to be adapted in such instances. Outdoor leaders may find themselves in a situation where a conflict exists between legal, organizational, and ethical guidelines. Conflict among ethical guidelines and their interpretation will likely arise and lead to dilemmas for many outdoor leaders. No matter what seems to be the course of action selected by the outdoor leader, the 'summum bonum' (i.e., do no harm) professionals follow to resolve dilemmas, should be guided by empathy for the client.

Notes

1. The examples are real, but names have been changed to protect the guilty.

References

Association for Experiential Education. (1992) *Ethical Guidelines of the Therapeutic Adventure Professional Group (TAPG).* Boulder, CO: Association for Experiential Education.

Corey, G., Corey, M. S., & Callahan, P. (1993) *Issues and ethics in the helping professions.* Pacific Grove, CA: Brooks/Cole Publishing Company.

Gass, M. A. & Wurdinger, S. (1993) 'Ethical decisions in experience based training and development programs.' in *Journal of Experiential Education,* 16(2), 41-47.

Hunt, J. (1990). *Ethics in experiential education.* Boulder, CO: Association for Experiential Education.

Jordan, A.E. & Meara, N.M. (1990). Ethics and the professional practices of psychologists: The role of virtues and principles. *Professional Psychology* 12(3), 43-55.

Kant, I. (1964). *Groundwork of the metaphysics of morals.* NY: Harper and Row.

Kitchener, (1984) 'Intuition, critical evaluation, and ethical principles: The foundation for ethical decisions in counseling psychology.' in *The Counseling Psychologist,* 12(3), 43-55.

Matthews, M. (1993) 'Wilderness programs offer promising alternatives for some youth: More regulation likely.' in M. A. Gass (Ed.). *Adventure therapy: Therapeutic applications of adventure programming.* Boulder, CO: Association for Experiential Education. 441-450.

McAvoy, L. (1990) 'Rescue-Free Wilderness Areas.' in Miles, J. C. & Priest, S. (Eds.) *Adventure Education* 329-334. State College, PA: Venture.

Mill, J.S. (1959). *On liberty.* NY: Penguin.

Mitten, D. (1994). Ethical considerations in adventure therapy: A feminist critique. In E. Cole, E. Erdman & E.D. Rothblum. (Eds.) *Wilderness Therapy for Women: The power of adventure.* NY: Harrington Park Press.

Rohnke, K. (1984) *Silver Bullets.* Hamilton, MA: Project Adventure.

Williamson, J. & Gass, M.A. (1993). *Manual of programme accreditation standards for adventure programs.* Boulder, CO: Association for Experiential Education.

Zygmond, M.J. & Boorhem, H. (1989). Ethical decision making in family therapy. *Family Process* 28, 269-280.

Chapter 6: Authenticity and Outdoor Education

Pete Allison

> *Not to put too fine a point on it, we live, breathe, and excrete values. No aspect of human life is unrelated to values, valuations and validations. Value orientations and value relations saturate our experiences and life practices from the smallest established microstructures of feeling, thought and behaviour to the largest established macrostructures of organisations and institutions. The history of cultures and social formations is unintelligible except in relation to a history of value orientations, value ideals, good values, value responses, and judgements, and their objectivisations, interplay, and transformations.*
> Fekete (1988: i)

One of the times when values become interesting is when they come into conflict. This can happen at numerous levels - intra and interpersonally, within departments of organisations, between organisations and politically within and between countries where differing cultural values are the cause of debate. Garrod (1993) refers to the intra personal value struggles, that we all have, between head, heart and habit. By this he means the struggles between the cognitive, emotional and behavioural domains. All people live with a certain number of contradictions in their lives and these contradictions can be seen in terms of values. These 'personal' or individual values are what many outdoor education programmes focus on. Alternatively, and sometimes in addition, programmes can work on interpersonal or group values (e.g. corporate values). This chapter raises questions pertaining to outdoor education practice and the assumptions on which it is based. It offers authenticity as a way of focusing the discussion.

At first glance, relating values and outdoor education may not appear to be particularly controversial. For example, when we are working with a youth group we may spend some time agreeing on some social norms or developing a full value contract (Schoel et al., 1988). One aspect of this may be to listen to everyone in the group and to be honest with each other but if a group also value individual freedom then what happens when one individual exercises his / her individual freedom not to tell the truth? Two values conflict (freedom and honesty) and educators make decisions which influence the values of the group.

In terms of outdoor education we can think of values in two domains. First, the values which are held by outdoor educators and outdoor education institutions and which are portrayed to the participants with whom they work. Second, we can discuss the values which participants have at various stages in the experience - the values they bring, that are discussed, that are developed consciously and subconsciously and the values that people construct and reconstruct post programme experience. It would be naive to see these two domains as mutually exclusive as, by their very nature, they are linked and connected in numerous subtle ways but this simplification can be useful. This chapter is concerned with the former - the values of educators and the values that they portray.

What values do outdoor educators portray? - Diversity? Listening? Tolerance? Individuality? Environment? This is a difficult area to explore - for what are the aims of outdoor education? Is it a tool or is it an end in itself? Which of the many fragments of outdoor education do you come from? A few brief examples in the form of questions may help to illustrate this:

What clothing do outdoor educators wear: is it bright, luminous or quiet green and merging with the environment?
What type of food is served in outdoor centres: Health food? Fast food style?
What are the environmental ethics of the organisation: do staff drive cars to work? Take buses? Drive minibuses to activities? Are ropes courses built on trees or poles?
Which skills are taught? Hard, soft, meta skills? Are literal and conceptual thinking equally supported?
How are the following aspects of outdoor education balanced: Fun and enjoyment? Teaching and Learning? Learning and Fun? Enjoyment and Teaching?
Which principles are supported and promoted and how do they reflect society - as we believe it *is* or as we desire it *to be*? Equality? Freedom? Power? Egalitarianism? Diversity? Spirituality?

From these questions it is a small step to the moral question, which of these qualities is good whilst the other bad or one better than the other? Do we require some kind of ontological vision to answer these questions? Is this a realistic objective to work towards?

For example, it is easy to see the lifestyle values which many working in outdoor education promote. These lifestyle values are not always conscious or done in order to take a moral high ground - but what do the groups that we work with think? How do they interpret the messages that are inevitably transmitted?

We all have motives, everything and everyone is selfish to some degree (Nietzsche, 1910; Baier, 1991). The terms ego and selfish unfortunately have almost exclusively negative connotations. If we follow this line of argument then we can see some of the other 'value issues' which underlie much of outdoor education. One example is the inherent contradiction in promoting teamwork (which many outdoor educators do) when individuals of the world are more interested in themselves than others. So why promote teamwork? One answer involves suggesting that teamwork is important.

It is important because 'society works better' as a cooperative unit and many outdoor education contexts offer a micro community in which this can be explored in more detail. Thus, it could be argued that by creating opportunities for people to explore and practise teamwork these behaviours are then transferred, somehow, back to society and contribute to making a 'better society'.

Perhaps we can also consider the phraseology that we use, do we work with Kids? Punters? Clients? Participants? Are we teachers? Instructors? Educators? Facilitators? Leaders? What values do these words portray? Are they a part of the commercialisation of outdoor education? If they are clients, are we, then, in a market of consumption - selling a package? Are we projecting our consumer society on to the environment that is so often carelessly used? Seeing it as an asset? A resource? Is this a symptom of adventure being presented in a bun as Loynes (1996) warned us? In his work he made the analogy of outdoor education and McDonalds. He suggested that outdoor adventure was becoming packaged and reliable to such an extent that customers were always guaranteed the same product - just like the Big Mac? Are the social responsibilities of outdoor education becoming merely a distant memory of days gone by, are we witnessing the last sunset?

To explore this, we must look further afield, to the setting of outdoor education. To the society in which it operates, to a postmodern society.

Postmodernism is a contentious and polemic term (Tappan & Brown, 1996: 101). For sociologists, philosophers, scientists and architects, to name but a few, it has different meanings. Meanings which within their own 'ist', 'ism' or 'ology' are difficult to agree upon. For some it is about Generation X, the technology revolution, for others about Nietzsche's nihilism (1910) overturning society, for others a celebration of eclecticism, pluralism and diversity. Yet for others it is about emancipation and freedom. Is it any wonder that the word postmodernism provokes so much debate when people are brave enough to mention it, never mind try to define it.

One aspect of postmodernism appears to be the theme of the fractious nature of all aspects of society. Nothing can be trusted to be what it appears; we are on permanently shifting sands in all aspects of what we see and do and who we are. Everything is a simulacra or perhaps we must merely take everything on face value and read no deeper? For some this is described by Morrison (1998) who summarises the questions:

Why am I me and why not you
Why am I here and why not there
Why did time begin and where does space end
Isn't what I see and hear and smell
Just the appearance of the world in front of the world

Isn't life under the sun just a dream
Does evil actually exist in people
Who really are evil
Why can't it be that I who am
Wasn't before I was
And that sometime I, the I, I am
No longer will be the I, I am

Douglas Rushkoff (1997) has also painted a picture of this world in *Children of Chaos*. In his work he explores the snowboard and skateboard cultures and, of course, the general surf culture of which most of us are now a part - channel surfing. Rushkoff uses this basis for a social commentary on the values of individuals and the chaotic nature of society. He concludes with the metaphor of giving birth for transformation and embracing change.

But what about the use of metaphor, that 'vogue' that has swept outdoor education? Why use metaphor? Can reality be represented AS a metaphor? Or IS reality a metaphor? Is this why it is so hard to tell what, if anything, is real? Is there any difference between what's real and what's metaphor? Are outdoor adventure educators lost in metaphors for metaphors of metaphors? So much so that we have no idea what a meta's for?

And the questions converge…what can all of this mean? The death of the meta narrative and the freedom to construct, deconstruct, reconstruct and deconstruct, over and over again, narratives as and when we please? To be whatever we want to be? The existential freedom that Sartre (1969) advocates ? Emancipation for all in every sense? The byte culture? The culture of disbelief that Carter (1993) describes?

Does postmodernism help to explain the multiplicity of faces and applications in which we see outdoor education appear? Or is the boom in experientialism and constructivist learning theory actually just a symptom of postmodernism, as Edwards (1994) has argued? Postmodernism can lead us to consider other discourses. Scruton (1999: 12) offers a cynical description of the emotivist discourse,

> *"To criticize popular taste is to invite the charge of elitism, and to defend distinctions of value - is to offend against the only value-judgement that is widely accepted, the judgement that judgements are wrong."*

If we accept the emotive discourse as dominant in society then perhaps constructivist approaches to learning (not behaviourist as it often really is, DeLay 1996) are the only way forward. Yet this is the same emotivist discourse, which MacIntyre (1981) carefully deconstructs, criticising it for presenting a 'live and let live attitude' which he sees as undermining to a moral community.

Postmodernism raises many questions. Ultimately outdoor educators must consider what values does outdoor education stand for. What about environmental values? What about the respect, love and integrity that Mortlock (1984) described? Surely these are still alive? Or are they all values that are the mistake of seeing outdoor education as an end and not as a tool with a multiplicity of applications? As Bowles (1996) reminds us, we must consider the 'maybe' and we must 'take care' with, and of, outdoor education.

Haydon (1997) and Ryan (1981) have argued that we should all grapple with such questions - not once but continually. But these questions are very far from answers or even hints of answers. Just as the disciples asked Jesus and later Schaeffer (1976) asked readers 'How should we then live?' we must ask: 'How then ought we to educate through adventure in the outdoors?'

I think we need to stop regularly and ask ourselves what we are really doing and why? Who is benefitting from what we do and what is our honest and real motivation behind what we are doing? We also need to change what we do and sometimes where we do it. As the saying goes:

Do not fall in to the trap of the teacher who has 20 years experience -
When they actually have 1 year's experience 20 times.

We need to understand more of what we do, we must try and think critically about what we do. We must act with integrity, we must respect the people who we are working *with*. We must be honest with ourselves and therefore others. We must 'question everything' that we do and the assumptions on which those actions are based.

In short we must do exactly what we so often suggest that participants in our programmes do. Yes, we must, walk the talk. Meaning, we must practise what we preach; we, as practitioners of outdoor education must continually strive to understand ourselves, understand our relationships with others and understand what we do better and better.

One way is to be always asking ourselves and others about what we do well and what we can do better. This may appear obvious but is not as simple as it first appears. Martin Heidegger (1927) was interested in the term authenticity (which was originally developed by Socrates). Socrates sought to rise beyond opinion but to attain knowledge, in particular self-knowledge which he considered essential to become true to self. Authenticity later came to be associated with Sartre's term 'good faith'.

In an earlier chapter, Halliday (1999) distinguished between two different senses of authenticity. The first sense is concerned with individuals acting in accordance with their innermost feelings. The second is concerned with affirming people's ties to others. The second sense of authenticity is more useful in this discussion. This sense is concerned with ties with others and with the acquisition of languages. These languages are required in order to know what being true to ourselves might be. We can, of course, only develop languages with others.

If we accept the second sense of authenticity and that learning a language is a part of developing this sense of authenticity then there may be a connection to outdoor education. Development of languages and development of ties with others occur on all outdoor programmes (whether as a desired outcome or as a side benefit) so outdoor education could be said to be contributing to developing a sense of authenticity.

This sense of authenticity to our essential being is difficult, not least because we all play roles of some type and to some degree. Roles in private and public life, children, adults, parents, spouses, managers, instructors, counsellors and so on. All of these roles that we *choose* to play and/or are also *asked* to play in subtle ways by the people with whom we work. We are expected so often to fulfill all sorts of stereotypes, so, to be authentic requires strength and risk.

At this stage some readers could argue that the values that outdoor education implies are inherent in the activities themselves and being an authentic educator is not important. Strength and risk are inherent in adventure to varying degrees but the influence of them as a part of outdoor education on the individual are not inherent (Smith, 1990). This leads to a further question: 'what is authentic about organised outdoor education?' To this there are two responses. First, that for many to visit these areas is expensive and impractical given their resources and knowledge. Secondly, the style and approach of the educator while in that environment is central to the experience. One educator might take a very authoritarian approach creating a clearly directed experience while another may take a very democratic approach permitting people to do as they please once they are there.

Outdoor educators take people to 'their territory', to their own comfortable environment and so have power, knowledge and power cannot be separated. It would be easy to slip away to subtle power relations, to very subtle oppression - to disempowering. But no, how can that happen? Outdoor education is empowering...isn't it? It says so in so many texts?! It is, or perhaps more accurately, it can be, with care it *can be* empowering but it is not always empowering by its nature.

Perhaps we are looking too deeply into the topic here. Maybe we should forget it all, console ourselves that what we do is somehow innately 'right', that we need not struggle with these issues. Alternatively, educators can struggle and grapple with the questions and the criticisms, they can work on them, they can find a compromise, a place where the pieces of the jigsaw all fit together? A stance to take, a stance to value on the shifting sands of postmodernism. A place where they can be authentic within themselves - to themselves and to the people with whom they work.

References

Baier, K. (1991) Egoism, in P. Singer. (ed.) *A Companion to Ethics*. Oxford: Blackwell Publishers.

Bowles, S. (1996) Techniques or Philosophy: Blending roots? Or Sewing Maybe-Seeds in Outdoor Adventure Education, *Journal of Adventure Education and Outdoor Leadership*, 13 (2): 7-19.

Carter, S.L. (1993) *The Culture of Disbelief*. London: Doubleday.

DeLay, R. (1996) Forming Knowledge: Constructivist Learning and Experiential Education, *Journal of Experiential Education*, 19 (2): 76-81.

Edwards, R. (1994) Are you Experienced? Post-modernity and Experiential Learning, *International Journal of Lifelong Education*, 13 (6), 423-439.

Fekete, J. (1988) *Life After Postmodernism: Essays on Value and Culture*. London: MacMillan.

Garrod, A. (ed.) (1993) *Approaches to Moral Development: New Research and Emerging Themes*. New York: Teachers College Press.

Halliday, J. (2000) 'Preferring To Learn Outdoors: Values And Education' (this text)

Haydon, G. (1997) *Teaching about Values: A New Approach*. London: Cassell Education Ltd.

Heidegger, M. (1927/1962) *Being & Time*. Translated by Macquarrie, J. & Robinson, E. Oxford: Blackwell.

Loynes, C. (1996) Adventure in a Bun, *Journal of Adventure Education and Outdoor Leadership*, 13 (2): 52-57.

MacIntyre, A. (1981) *After Virtue*. Kings Lynn: Duckworth.

Morrison, V. (1998) *The Philosophers Stone*. Compact Disc lyrics. London: Exile Productions.

Mortlock, C. (1984) *The Adventure Alternative*. Cumbria: Cicerone Press.

Nietzsche, F.W. (1910) *The Genealogy of Morals*. Edinburgh: Foulis.

Rushkoff, D. (1997) *Children of Chaos*. London: Harper Collins.

Ryan, K. (1981) *Questions and Answers on Moral Education*. Indiana: Phi Delta Kappa Educational Foundation.

Sartre, J. P. (1969) *Being and Nothingness*. London: Methuen & Co. Ltd.

Schaeffer, F.A. (1976) *How Then Should We Live?* Illinois: Crossway Books.

Schoel, J. Prouty, D. & Radcliffe, P. (1988) *Islands of Healing*. Massachusetts: Project Adventure.

Scruton, R. (1999) *An Intelligent Person's Guide to Philosophy*. London: Duckworth.

Smith, T. (1990) *Wilderness Beyond...Wilderness Within*. WI: Raccoon Institute.

Tappan, M.B. & Brown, L.M. (1996) Envisioning a Postmodern Moral Pedagogy, *Journal of Moral Education*. 25 (1): 101-109.

Chapter 7:   Outdoor Education and Values Education:
               Mission, Mandate or Expediency?

Peter Higgins

Introduction

In the past 10 years or so the outdoor education sector in the UK has found itself under increasing pressure to be financially self-supporting. This has spawned a wide range of stated justifications for the work of the sector and many mission statements now espouse the inculcation of values as a central purpose of the work. This overt approach is in contrast to the traditional view of 'the outdoors speaking for itself' and indeed many of the more recent approaches. At the same time, little has changed in the training of practising outdoor educators and those entering the profession. Indeed, since recent safety and licensing legislation was introduced in 1996, the focus of training in the UK has been on the gathering of National Governing Body awards in the outdoor activities. Whilst good practice undoubtedly exists, this chapter questions the premise that outdoor educators necessarily have the skills or the mandate to engage in 'values education'.

The slippery nature of values

The fact that this book focuses on 'values' does, of course, imply that 'values' and 'outdoor education' are linked. This 'received wisdom' is not new; it is implicit in the traditional utilitarian use of the outdoors for 'character building' which has been an aspect of the discipline since it became formalised in the UK in the mid-20th Century (Parker and Meldrum, 1973; Cook,1999:157).

Cook, reviewing the factors leading to, and effects of, the 1944 Education Act focuses a great deal of attention on 'the expectations of policy makers with regard to character development' (Cook, 1999:157). The Act was a milestone in British educational history as it placed a duty on Local Educational Authorities to make provision for a range of facilities and educational opportunities which eventually became formalised as 'outdoor education'. Indeed the LEAs were also required by the Act to contribute towards children's 'spiritual, moral, mental and physical development'. The question of what such values might constitute was not left to chance as the Norwood Committee produced a report to advise LEAs on what should be taught and how this might be done (Cook, 1999:157). In tracing the implementation of the Act, Cook makes clear links with the backgrounds of the individuals who influenced its development, the Norwood Report and others. Many had a background in English public (fee paying) and grammar (exam entrance) schools and were supporters of this system. For example the Norwood Committee suggested that secondary schools should promote character training through the 'infusion of values characteristic of the public schools' (Cook, 1999:162).

Much more could be said of the impact of such influences and those of Reddie (Abbotsholme School), Baden-Powell (Boy Scout movement), Hahn (Gordonstoun School and the Outward Bound movement) (see Cook, 1999:159 and Parker and Meldrum, 1973 for further historical detail). It should also be noted that much of the development of outdoor education occurred in a post-war context and that many of those involved in the 1944 Act and its implementation would have been quite comfortable with the idea that outdoor education would, in some measure, inculcate qualities in children which would serve the nation well in times of war (see Cook, 1999). Comment could also be made on the focus of opportunities for boys rather than girls in the legislation and reports of the time. The salient point for the purpose of this argument is that those who stimulated early development of outdoor education in the UK applied their own values which were 'of their time'.

This would be true of any contemporary view of outdoor education. For example, Mortlock (1984) focuses on the importance of adventurous experiences in the development of a range of personal qualities; Cooper (1991) and Nicol and Higgins (1998) place great importance on the sustainability and environmental possibilities of education outdoors; and the Board of the European Institute for Outdoor Adventure Education and Experiential Learning (Higgins et al, 1998:75) consider that 'the educational intention is to stimulate personal and social development'. None of these is right or wrong and indeed many proponents advocate inclusivity; they are simply cited here as a means of emphasising the changing and eclectic nature of 'values'.

A range of questions come to mind as a result of this. Is the role of an educator to state what values are 'right'? If so, what are they? Can values be taught? Are outdoor educators trained and qualified to do so? Does society give us the mandate to teach values?

What values, whose values?

Yaffey (1993: 9-11) is in no doubt about the answers to at least some of these questions. He speaks of outdoor education with conviction and asserts that we have a unique role to play, as nature is 'the ultimate source of all values'. He offers a list of examples of the relationship between outdoor activities and value concepts they may confer. The fact that I find myself in sympathy with aspects of Yaffey's argument illustrates my concern: he may be right or wrong but these are his values. The purpose of this chapter is not to engage in a debate on what values are, nor which ones might be 'educated' for. However, to move further a working definition must be employed and I am happy to adopt that provided by the Scottish Consultative Council on the Curriculum (SCCC, 1995:2) as:

'A set of principles which are consistent and inform and direct our thoughts, actions and activities. That is to say, a value has essentially an intellectual base, but that this base informs and has its expression in action and in life'.

I do not intend to attempt to define these principles, but the implication is that they represent a useful code for behaviour in life. Such codes might be important to an individual or to society; there may be differences or they may be identical. If we take the case of values being taught by outdoor educators (who are employed in one way or another by society) the implication is that those values should primarily be useful to society. This is of course highly normative and may or may not generate benefits for the individual beyond training to fit in with societal expectations. It may be that the outdoor educator does not agree with this role, but if 'non-normative' values are 'taught' he/she might be expected to justify the mandate for this stance.

This issue is more complex than it might seem, as the curriculum (which may include values) will itself have several dimensions. Eisner (1985) argues that schools teach three curricula. The 'explicit', 'implicit' and 'null' curricula. In the case of values education in an outdoor setting we might consider the example of an introduction to kayaking. The explicit curriculum may be the learning of appropriate technical and judgment skills to negotiate a simple river, the implicit curriculum may be values oriented (eg self-reliance/ awareness) and the null curriculum would be something left-out (eg environmental learning opportunities such as human impact on river ecology or the water cycle). If a 'values education' stance is taken by the outdoor educator the explicit curriculum might actually be the learning of the type of values mentioned above, in which case learning to kayak becomes implicit or even incidental. The degree to which emphasis is intended or given to values within these curricula is of crucial importance to the student, their family and the greater community. It is clear that the null curriculum has great relevance to the teaching of values because if some issues are given importance and others are ignored, the implication is that the latter are not relevant (eg care for the natural environment in the example above). If the outdoor educational establishment states the intention to educate for certain values, they are clearly under an obligation to say what these are and to what degree they form the focus of the curriculum as explicit, implicit or null.

Justifications for outdoor education

The original intention of outdoor education in the UK in relation to the 1944 Education Act has been noted above. In the 50 years or so since, the UK has seen growth in school and centre provision as well as in community and social work. The stated intentions and justifications have been many, and whilst these are often cloaked in philosophy, pragmatism has become an increasing feature of the field. The earliest substantial contribution was that of Harold Drasdo (1973), who did not feel the need to express justifications more forcefully than to suggest that enjoyment of outdoor experiences could have a wide range of benefits from physical to aesthetic. Such liberal views have been replaced by altogether more pragmatic arguments such as those proposed by Hopkins and Putnam (1993), Higgins (1997a) and Loynes et al (1997). The focus of the contemporary work of the latter authors is expressed in the title: 'Justifying Outdoor Education in the Formal and Informal Curriculum' and contrasts markedly with the period between 1944 and 1973 when, it seems, no-one thought it worthwhile to publish justifications or arguments at all.

During the past 50 years there has been a shift away from outdoor education being a focal element in many schools and associated outdoor centres (with an expectation that all students should have such opportunities) to much less widespread or significantly altered provision (eg Barnes, 1998 and Higgins, in press). There have been many reasons for this, but increasing curricular and financial pressures on schools and centres are high on the list. As the success of some justifications has decreased, others have been sought. For example, interest in 'outdoor management development' increased in the 1970s and '80s as did the 'therapeutic' use of the outdoors for work with young offenders. Some commentators argue that the valuable environmental learning opportunities available in the outdoors are not being made full use of (eg Crowther, 1984; Cooper, 1991; Nicol and Higgins, 1998). I do not wish to suggest that any of these are inappropriate justifications, but rather that outdoor educators have become increasingly pragmatic rather than idealistic. In terms of the teaching of values in this period the latter uses would clearly inculcate curricula which are quite different to those of an earlier period.

It is notable that in their review of research into outdoor adventure education and personal and social development Barrett and Greenaway (1995) do not appear to use the term 'values education' and make little explicit reference to values. It seems that as the old justifications are still used and 'traditional' programmes are still run, new justifications have simply been added to the list. Many of those responsible for running outdoor centres now look carefully at any new Government initiative (such as those on 'Social Inclusion', 'Citizenship' and the like) to find an opening for programme design. There appears now to be such a wide range of justifications that it is quite difficult, even for specialists, to provide a simple inclusive description of the work of the outdoor education sector.

What is special about outdoor educators?

To provide outdoor educational opportunities of the range noted above and be able to do so employing a range of technical outdoor activities within a framework of safety is, by any standards, demanding. Although there is no expectation that any individual outdoor educator would be able to provide a full range of outdoor activities and all the types of tailored courses detailed above, changes in clientele and the justifications employed require a broad and substantial initial training supported by frequent up-dates in the light of changing professional needs. This must surely be the expectation of those who place staff or students in the care of outdoor educators. Does this reflect reality?

In the UK there is no professional body, nor regulatory body dictating or advising on training and qualification (Higgins, 1997b; Barnes, 1998). Consequently outdoor educators receive their training in a variety of ways, although it is true to say that the majority now follow a general tertiary level course and also pursue a range of National Governing Body (NGB) awards in the individual outdoor activities. There are Higher and Further Education courses offering degrees or diplomas with a wide range of names, such as 'Outdoor Education', 'Outdoor Studies' and 'Outdoor Recreation'. To these, outdoor educators add NGB leadership and coaching awards at a variety of levels in mountaineering, canoeing etc. As the latter are technical by nature, one would expect the 'academic' courses to satisfy other requirements; but this inevitably generates a tension between academic and professional demands (Higgins and Morgan, in press). In terms of 'values', one would suppose that such courses would provide extensive training in such issues, or if not the selection process for prospective outdoor educators would select rigorously for a solid personal grounding in values. It seems logical to suggest that, if this individual wishes to be adaptable in the workplace, then he/she should be able to offer both the 'technical' and 'educational' qualities and therefore must receive appropriate training. Is this the case?

A brief survey of advertisements (eg in Horizons - The journal of the Association for Outdoor Learning and the Association of Heads of Outdoor Education Centres) for 'outdoor' courses at Further and Higher Education institutes gives little indication of a strong 'values education' focus. If it does take place it does not seem to be a priority in advertising. These show a preference for stressing outdoor activities (as, incidentally do those for outdoor centres).

There is evidence to suggest that the impact of the deaths of four young people on an activity holiday in Devon in 1993 has been highly significant for the outdoor sector. The subsequent enquiry led to the conviction of the company manager for manslaughter and eventually to the Activity Centres (Young Persons Safety) Act, 1995. This Act legislated for an inspectorate and tight controls on the supervision of outdoor providers. The upshot has been an even greater focus on the gathering of National Governing Body Awards, which are seen as a form of assurance of technical competence and therefore safety. Evidence for this comes from the directors of training of the National Governing Bodies and the Principals of the National Outdoor Training Centres (where much of such training and assessment is carried out) who report an increase in the number of those coming forward for assessment in recent years.

The situation for those who are maturing in their career in the outdoors raises questions about their training opportunities. Where it exists, in service training opportunities in the brochures of Local Education Authorities reflect an NGB focus, as do the requests for course attendance from staff in centres (Nicol, in prep). If further evidence were needed, one might point to the total UK memberships of most of the individual NGBs which run to many thousands versus the sector associations such as the 'Association for Outdoor Learning' and 'Outdoor Scotland' (hundreds). The preference or perceived need for NGB awards is obvious.

A survey of the agendas of the meetings of the Scottish Advisory Panel for Outdoor Education and the Association of Heads of Outdoor Education Centres over recent years also shows no example of discussion on 'values education' or its synonyms, whereas there appears to be considerable appetite for debate on changes to the fine detail of NGB awards.

This situation contrasts sharply with the technical level at which many outdoor educators operate (frequently an introductory level) and the stated personal, social, educational intentions of most programmes. In summary there appears to be a disproportionate emphasis on technical and safety aspects, which provide the framework within which we operate, at the expense of other critical professional skills. Job advertisements reflect this focus, often stating the minimum NGB awards applicants should hold.

What values should outdoor educators have?

The nature of the present discourse on values education in outdoor education implies that the discussion has not really taken place in the past, or that there are now particular opportunities for values education in the outdoors which could be capitalised on. If we are to be 'values educators' (and I am not sure the case has yet been made) we should explain our own philosophical position and what educational perspectives we can offer.

Values education is engaged in (explicit, implicit or null) in the home, school and community. An outdoor educator is part of this community and can support this in a number of ways. By accepting and promoting these values (normative); by challenging these values; or by encouraging questioning of these values and the process by which they are arrived at.

A normative approach presents some difficulties as there may be many approaches and many values expressed or implied in the wider community. For an educator to promote certain values he/she must be confident that these are absolute (eg honesty, self-control, courage, justice, charity, compassion?). I would argue that these could, and must be disputed in values education. Other values (eg environmental) may be less clear-cut, and indeed in the case of outdoor education, the environmental behaviour of many individuals and institutions seems to contradict espoused values. This poses a problem for the learner. Adopt the values the educator displays or those they say they have! There is substantial evidence to suggest that learners pick up on and adopt the former much more readily than the latter (eg Elliott, 1993; Posch,1993). Lilley (in press) makes a case for the adoption (in outdoor adventure education with young people 'at-risk') of the advice of the Schools Curriculum and Assessment Authority's 'National Forum for Values in Education and the Community'. This contains statements on Society, Relationships, Self and Environment which emphasise the 'common good of society', the value of families etc. Whilst many would consider these to be worthy aims, they are clearly 'normative' and this is in itself a good reason for questioning them. I take a similar view to the arguments (and the list of virtues and vices) Mortlock (1998) has constructed.

A challenging approach implies that the educator adopts an adversarial approach to values issues. This too is beleaguered by the problems noted above as there may well be confusion over the personal stance of the educator and their relationship to the broader community.

A questioning approach requires sensitivity, but I believe has several major benefits. It does not imply that there is always a 'right value' and that this is the same 'right value' in all circumstances. It encourages the student to learn and apply critical thinking to all such issues and this will lead to confidence in the values they arrive at (robustness), and the value of critical thinking in other circumstances (adaptability). It does not place the educator in the role of one who delivers the answers (humility). The process is an application of longstanding experiential tradition of outdoor education (consistency). This also requires the educator to be particularly aware that the approach itself promotes certain values such as those noted above.

Concluding comments

My purpose in this chapter is to challenge the assumption that outdoor educators can move easily into the territory of values education. Those who work in the closely related field of environmental education have been wrestling with such difficulties for some time. Many would be of the view that there is a pressing need for 'education for sustainability' but as Jickling (1994) argues, educating for something is really just a form of instrumental training. I believe he gets to the essence of the values issue by asking 'is it the job of education to make people behave in a particular way?' (Jickling, 1994:7).

I suggest that in order to seek 'answers' we have to engage in several debates on the motivation and mechanisms for our work in this field. Only by addressing such questions openly will we reach a point where, as individuals and as a profession, we can say we have the integrity and consistency to work in this area. I believe that if we do so, outdoor education can make a significant and substantial contribution to values education. The following comments constitute a summary:

A question of definitions and the definitions of questions. In attempting to engage with 'values' we are moving into the home territory of generations of philosophers who have wrestled with three connected issues: 'first, on what sort of property or characteristic of something its 'having value' or 'being of value' is; second, on whether having value is an objective or subjective matter; third, on trying to say what things have value, are valuable' (Dent, 1995:895). In the context of 'values education' further definitional questions arise which are associated with the degree to which we are really dealing with an ethical code, moral philosophy or the nature of 'goodness'. It should be clear then that this issue is fraught with ontological and epistemological difficulties and we would do well to inform our debate through consultation with those who work in mainstream education and philosophy.

Social and cultural influences play a central role in determining what values are acceptable and what might be 'taught' in outdoor education. In a recent analysis of the development of outdoor education in the UK, Nicol (in prep) makes the point that 'social values of any particular period provide an historical framework of reference to contextualise the forming and changing of developments'. Further, he suggests that 'in order to understand outdoor education it is necessary to disentangle the philosophy which underpins it, the methods adopted by its practitioners and the objectives it is intended to meet'. All of these imply that individual and establishment values will, inescapably, have an effect on the whole outdoor educational process.

Wysiwyg - What you see is what you get. The values we display in everyday actions are those which define us (and hence are educationally most powerful) rather than those we say we hold. Any process which purports to help students to develop their own values, but which is, even covertly directed towards certain values is disingenuous and will be seen by students to be what it is (Posch, 1993:29).

Values education, like outdoor education is a process rather than an outcome. The process of deciding on a set of values and putting these forward as those which should be encouraged is prescriptive. This can be seen as antithetical to the preferred methodology of outdoor education which is to encourage learning through experience and to develop confidence in self-directed learning and critical reflection (eg Hopkins and Putnam, 1993; Dahlgren and Szczepanski, 1998). Friere (1998) expresses the centrality of this notion to emotional and spiritual learning in the 'Pedagogy of the Heart'. 'The important thing is to educate the curiosity through which knowledge is constituted as it grows and redefines itself through the very exercise of knowing' (Friere, 1998:31).

Working to our strengths. I do not wish to suggest that I view the issue of values education in outdoor education as pointless or sterile. In fact there are good arguments in favour of engaging in values education in an outdoor context. The outdoors provides a different framework for addressing such issues than say a school and can offer opportunities for young people to 'confront themselves' (Martinez, pers com). Another strength is that outdoor education can be used to present a broad range of issues in an interdisciplinary manner (Nicol and Higgins, 1998). In discussing the difficulties in handling values in environmental education, Elliott (1993) asserts that values education is only likely to become a

> *'significant pedagogical issue in schools when there is a serious attempt at adopting an interdisciplinary approach. A uni-disciplinary approach is an excellent way of reducing the awareness of complexity and of promoting a particular value stance to the exclusion of others'* (Elliott, 1993:19).

So here, it seems we may be on home ground. If we are to engage with this issue, and I believe we should, we must be cautious about the influence of our own values and the great potential in approaching the issue by working to the strengths of outdoor education.

A garden of a thousand flowers? Carr (1999:302-3) suggests that 'the garden of values education might be seen as one in which a thousand flowers bloom (and ... a few weeds also)'. His intention is to assert that a 'general problem with the current spate of values education ... lies with the extraordinary diversity of educational and other aims which seem to be entertained within its overall compass'. He also stresses that 'unwillingness to co-ordinate a set of diverse practical activities to bring them in line with some overall strategic plan is liable to become a serious logistical problem' in the light of differing normative and evaluative underpinnings (Carr, 1999:302-3). Although he is careful to avoid a prescriptive approach, essentially Carr argues that values education should be clear in its aims and methods and that an attempt should be made to be consistent. In claiming a role for outdoor education in this arena we must ask ourselves why we are doing it at all (see Carr, 1999 for a challenging analysis) and, if we are to do it how we ensure that those who engage in such a difficult area of education are properly trained to do so. Despite (or perhaps because of) the enthusiasm the outdoor education sector is showing for this new role I would suggest that we need to remind ourselves that we are just at the beginning of this process; the perfect time for a thoughtful debate, informed by consultation with a wide range of professionals in other fields.

References

Barnes, P. (1998) What is Going On in the Outdoor Industry? *Horizons* , 1:10-13.

Barrett, J. and Greenaway, R. (1995) *Why Adventure? The Role and Value of Outdoor Adventure in Young People's Personal and Social Development.* Coventry: Foundation for Outdoor Adventure.

Carr, D. (1999) Values Education in Scotland. In: T. Bryce and W. Humes (eds) *Scottish Education*. Edinburgh: Edinburgh University Press. 296-303.

Cook, L. (1999) The 1944 Education Act and Outdoor Education: From Policy to Practice. History of Education, 28(2) 157-172.

Cooper, G. (1991) The Role of Outdoor and Field Study Centres in Educating for the Environment. *Journal of Adventure Education and Outdoor Leadership*, 8(2):10-11.

Crowther, N. (1984) The Role of Outdoor Education Teachers in Providing for the Needs of Tomorrows Society: A Philosophy and a Justification. *Journal of Adventure Education and Outdoor Leadership*, 1(6):12-15.

Dahlgren, L. and Szczepanski, A. (1998) *Outdoor Education: Literary Education and Sensory Experience*. Sweden: Linkoping University.

Dent, N. (1995) Values. In: T. Honderich (ed) The Oxford Companion to Philosophy. Oxford: Oxford University Press. p895.

Drasdo, H. (1973) *Education and the Mountain Centres.* Llanrwst: Tyddyn Gabriel.

Eisner, E. (1985) The Three Curricula that All Schools Teach. In: E.Eisner, *The Educational Imagination*. New York: Macmillan. p87-108.

Elliott, J. (1993) Handling Values in Environmental Education. In: *Values in Environmental Education*. OECD/ENSI Conference Report. Edinburgh: SCCC. p18-24.

Friere, P. (1998) *Pedagogy of the Heart*. New York: Continuum.

Higgins, P. (1997a)   Why Educate Out of Doors? In: P Higgins, C Loynes and N Crowther (Editors) *A Guide for Outdoor Educators in Scotland*. Penrith: Adventure Education and Perth: Scottish Natural Heritage. p9-14.

Higgins, P. (1997b) 'Too Many Singers and Not Enough Songs': Towards Professionalism in Outdoor Education. *Journal of Adventure Education and Outdoor Leadership*, 14(4), 17-20.

Higgins, P. and Morgan, A. (1999) Training Outdoor Educators: Integrating Academic and Professional Demands. In: P. Higgins and B. Humberstone (Editors) *Outdoor Education and Experiential Learning in the UK*. Luneberg: University of Luneberg Press.

Higgins, P; Amesberger, G; Bowles, S; Becker, P; Humberstone, B; Keus, B; Neumann, J; and Schirp, J. (1998) Outdoor Adventure Education: Learning by Sharing Cultural Differences. In: P Higgins & B Humberstone (Editors) *Celebrating Diversity: Sharing Cultural Differences in Outdoor Education*. Buckinghamshire: European Institute for Outdoor Adventure Education. p74-79.

Higgins, P. (in press) Outdoor Education in Scotland. In: J. Bailey and S. Priest (Editors) *Outdoor Education from an International Comparative Perspective*.

Hopkins, D. and Putnam, R. (1993) *Personal Growth Through Adventure*. London: David Fulton Pubs.

Jickling, B. (1994) Why I Don't Want my Children to be Educated for Sustainable Development. *Journal of Environmental Education*, 23(4), 5-8.

Lilley, T. (in press) Outdoor Adventure Education with Young People At-Risk. In: P. Higgins and B. Humberstone (Editors) *Outdoor Education and Experiential Learning in the UK*. Luneberg: University of Luneberg Press.

Loynes, C., Michie, D. and Smith, C. (1997) Justifying Outdoor Education in the Formal and Informal Curriculum. In: P Higgins, C Loynes and N Crowther. Outdoor Education and Values Education: Mission, Mandate or Expediency?

Mortlock, C. (1984) *The Adventure Alternative*. Cumbria: Cicerone Press.

Mortlock, C. (1998) Chasing Rainbows. In: Pathway to Learning. *Proceedings of the Third National Outdoor Education Conference*. Auckland College of Education, New Zealand. p39-52.

Nicol, R. and Higgins, P. (1998) A Sense of Place: A Context for Environmental Outdoor Education. In: P Higgins & B Humberstone (Editors) *Celebrating Diversity: Sharing Cultural Differences in Outdoor Education*. Buckinghamshire: European Institute for Outdoor Adventure Education. p 50-55.

Nicol, R. (in prep) *A Conceptual Analysis of the Contribution of Outdoor Education to Sustainability Education*. PhD Thesis. University of Edinburgh.

Parker, T. and Meldrum, K. (1973) *Outdoor Education*. London: Dent.

Posch, P (1993) Approaches to Values in Environmental Education. In: *Values in Environmental Education*. OECD/ENSI Conference Report. Edinburgh: SCCC. p27-35.

Scottish Consultative Council on the Curriculum (1995) *The Heart of the Matter: A Paper for Discussion and Development*. Edinburgh: SCCC.

Yaffey, D. (1993) The Value Base of Activity Experience in the Outdoors. *Journal of Adventure Education and Outdoor Leadership*, 10 (3), 9-11.

Chapter 8:   The Values of Life and Living: 'After all, life is right in any case'.

Chris Loynes

Some things are of value whether we know it or not. Try holding your breath for a while. We take the air we breathe for granted much of the time but we can't do without it for long. It is of intrinsic value to us. When we consciously give it value it is often through the rational process of science assuming it's role of explaining our biochemistry. Experiential learning gathered through the senses and often non conscious taught us a long time ago the value of the air we breathe. This understanding is so ingrained in us it is often left unarticulated only to appear in an emotional and aesthetic response to the feel of the wind on our skin, movement in the trees, the sight of scudding clouds, the scent of ozone - fresh air. Yet we draw on this knowledge all the time. It influences the very sounds and rhythms of our words, it provides a rich source of metaphor for our language, our rituals and our myths.

If you find those sentences a little poetic it's not surprising. When we have something of intrinsic value to explain and we are in touch with our experiential selves it is hard to use words in a logical form. Instead we choose to use words loosely and to suggest more than the words by their rhythm and sound. The listener, if listening well, will also respond differently, at a deeper level, intuitively some might say, perhaps from a subtly altered state of consciousness created by the form of communication.

The sensual in experiential learning

The romantics knew this and are rightly recognised as an important influence on experiential and outdoor learning. Harold Drasdo (1998) wrote about the aesthetic heart of outdoor education over 20 years ago. Indigenous people knew it better without always 'knowing' in the modern sense of the word. By definition indigenous people are still intimately connected to their place and in their community in a way that 'civilised' people are not. We have become separated by our urbanisation, our rationality, our division of labour and our capitalist economics. We talk about rather than live in nature and community and increasingly experience it vicariously through the media.

Of course this is an over simplification. We are still a part of nature if only through such simple acts as breathing. Experiences of the air and of our breathing also remain an intimate part of our understanding of the modern idea of outdoor learning. We struggle with the terrain noticed in our laboured breathing and measured by our increased pulse rate. We are exhilarated at the top when we stop and the oxygen rush floods through our system. Our 'red blooded' response to life, our delight in the wind in our hair and on our faces needs no biology or ecology lesson to tell us of its importance. Our senses and our emotional responses are enough.

One definition of experiential learning is that it is a process of attaching meaning and value to our experiences. As with the value of breathing this is often so intimate and sensual that we are not normally aware of this process in everyday life. Nevertheless the experience has influenced our values and so our actions. We have learned in a natural sense.

Experiential learning becomes conscious

We can, however, become aware of our breathing. When some aspect of its quality is altered our attention is soon caught. Perhaps a throat infection causes laboured breathing or coughing. We are embarrassed by an unexpected yawn in public. I'm sure you can all remember playing 'dragon's breath' as a child on frosty mornings. The air as it thins at altitude or the smell of a flower or a polluted street all capture our conscious minds. Our bodies can tell us things, for example through our breathing when it becomes laboured during heavy exertion or gasping at moments of panic and fear. We gasp at a surprise view. We hold our breath at the moment we let ourselves fall into the arms of the group during a trust fall.

Attention to our breathing can also be deliberately called by another person. For example 'take a deep breath to gather yourself' said to steady us before a leap for the trapeze or a delicate move across a rock face. Breathing exercises might be used to pump us up before a physically demanding challenge or calm us down before a meditation or solo.

It will be useful for this chapter to separate these two sources of stimulation of our awareness into two sets of experiences, natural and cultural. The natural experiences are those in which the quality of the air or of our breathing captures our attention. Cultural experiences are those in which someone else draws our attention to our breathing.

This 'attention drawing' can be as simple as having been taught the name of something so that you 'know' it by name and talk about it with others. By this means your valuing enters the social domain. The value of certain things is illuminated by others or debated between people. Whilst the people involved in this process are also a part of the experience and so sharing the same context, like a group together on an outdoor journey, the truth, both personally discovered through 'natural' experiences and socially determined can be said to be authentic. However, it can only be authentic to that group of people. This 'truth' also remains mutable. It is negotiated and changes; 'you know, that rock climb was tremendous after all, even though I was cursing the hard part at the time!'

Attaching value to experience

Giving an experience a value is our first and a constant creative act. By giving something in the outer world a form, by recognising it's shape, colour, texture, pattern, ways of moving, sound, smell we build a concept and, later, we are taught the name of this concept. It is both a personal and a social creation. We do the same thing with abstract ideas to which we subscribe feelings, images, words and a name. Breath is one such physical concept and 'red blooded' one such abstract idea. At first this valuing may be for utilitarian reasons. It is something we need or need to avoid - the warmth of mother, the cold of night air. Curiosity also plays its part as we poke about the world around us and discover interesting things to play with or admire.

Good and bad

Valuing, then, takes several forms. We notice something and give it an identity and perhaps learn its name. We also add values of worth to this concept - it's a good thing to take a deep breath of fresh air - we relish it; it's a bad thing to breathe in the smog and we mask ourselves from it. We develop an aesthetic sense. A wilderness journey can therefore be understood as more than simply an aesthetic experience but as a work of art created by the traveller to integrate a set of 'good' experiences.

We not only value the world around us but also ourselves. In Yungian terms we come to know the 'dark' and the 'light'. A great deal of our language, and so our ideas, about our inner landscapes draw on metaphors from nature. Simon Schama (1996) shows how this two way projection of ourselves onto nature and nature onto ourselves has intimately informed our personal and social concepts of ourselves throughout European history. Jung, among others, argued that it was necessary to have healthy natural experiences in order to fully understand these rich archetypes of the mind. The words alone are a poor substitute without the meaning that is attached to them through experience.

It could therefore be said that we imagine ourselves and the world around us. This created world is then influenced by the imagination of others. A social group have or, if they are newly formed, soon develop a dominant world view or paradigm. As individuals in the group we learn how to relate to this cultural norm. In an egalitarian group we have the power to influence the norm as well as be influenced by it. I am doing this with you now as you read this chapter in the group of English speaking outdoor educators.

Right and wrong

Not only do we discriminate by attaching 'good' and 'bad' to our experiences, we learn to overlay them with another set of values, 'right' and 'wrong' - 'you might enjoy soloing on the climbing wall but it's the wrong thing to do in front of the group. It might give them bad ideas.'

Attaching meaning to experience

So far I have described a way of understanding the processes by which we attach values to our experiences. I have argued that this is, first and foremost, a intuitive process involving the emotional and aesthetic self. However, the process of meaning making is also occurring. For the purposes of this chapter I understand meaning to be the abstract understanding of our experiences that is created personally and socially. This is a cognitive and rational process that involves the use of language but in a different way to the loose, metaphoric and poetic forms discussed before. It is a language intended to be more literal and specific and which builds models and theories.

We all build personal theories of our experience, making sense of, rather than sensing, our experiences. These theories are heavily influenced by the dominant theories of the social world. We use the abstract ideas of our culture to make sense of our personal worlds. It is hard to imagine a world without a concept of zero. What would such a world understand by the idea of nothing? But such a world existed.

We can get some idea of what it must have been like if we consider an area for which our language is deficient. We often find ourselves in confusion over the word 'love.' It has many closely related and potent meanings which, when misunderstood or used incorrectly cause much embarrassment. It would seem sensible if our language developed a richer vocabulary for these ideas but we struggle on without. Sanskrit, on the other hand, had over 20 words for love. In a similar vein the reader could reflect on the number of times I have used the word 'experience' in this chapter. German is a much better language for discussing experience as it has a rich vocabulary around this idea which is inaccessible to us.

In outdoor learning we use accepted meanings to help people on our courses understand the processes they are engaged in such as concepts of ecology or teamwork. We are also aware that there are alternative or complimentary meanings available. We tend to draw on the most appropriate 'view' of the world to help the group at the time.

Experiential learning and indigenous learning

So far I have described a process of valuing our experiences that builds a set of concepts of our inner and outer worlds. We identify objects, processes and ideas and we develop a sense of worth in relation to these concepts - it's a good thing or a bad thing. We also come to realise that this may depend on the context we are in and that others may share our views or differ from them. Through this social interaction we develop a sense of right and wrong. The whole process is possible through lived natural and social experiences.

Charlene Spretnak (1997) called this approach and the trend towards understanding our relationships with nature and with each other in this way the resurgence of the real. By this she means the building of our worlds on the foundations of natural, personal and so authentic experiences.

Mary Midgley (1995) discusses whether the development of values is a natural or cultural, nature or nurture, process. She concludes that we have a genetic predisposition to develop values and a morality but that this trait is what she describes as having an open genetic propensity. The predisposition is not deterministic but lends itself to influence by experience. Learning, she argues, is also a natural and open trait that creates the urge to seek such experiences from which to learn and so evolve our personal world views.

I could identify more natural human tendencies for which we have a genetic predisposition and which are developed by experience, developmental processes that we have learned to value. So far, in this chapter, I have referred to learning, socialising, exploring, valuing, moralising and meaning making as human attributes valued as a part of human nature. Colin Mortlock (1979), in his book The Adventure Alternative, proposed a list of six virtues that he believed were developed by adventure experiences.

Like Graham Ellis-Smith (1999), who has studied the personal, communal and natural relations of the indigenous people of south west Australia, I would like to call this authentic development of personal and social values 'indigenous'. Indeed, like Ellis-Smith, I would argue that much of our attraction to outdoor experiences is a desire to return to indigenous learning situations.

Facilitating experience

Experiential and outdoor education are both founded on the belief that the natural or indigenous process of learning can be enhanced and accelerated by facilitation much as elders or shamans would have steered the development of people in their communities. As an outdoor facilitator I both orchestrate the experiences on which people are drawing and influence the conversations about these experiences. Just as shamans might have chosen dramatic and novel experiences to aid development during a rite of passage for example, so I use unusual and adventurous experiences to enhance and accelerate the events I design.

Even our theories are based on models and ideas about the natural processes researchers find, for example: learning - Kolb's learning cycle, groups - Bion's group development and leadership - Adair's action centred leadership.

Detaching meaning from experience: the politics and institutions of experience

This ability to influence a natural process is powerful. It also allows other approaches to education and training to disturb or interrupt the indigenous learning process so that it is no longer experiential. This can occur accidentally or it can be deliberate for some ulterior purpose.

The process of acquiring a body of meaning in our field is relatively new. Most of this knowledge has been introduced from the related fields of psychology and ecology. When the fit is 'good enough' the theory has become established. Several books illustrate this eclectic process for example Ken Ogilvie's (1993) *Leading and Managing Groups in the Outdoors* and Peter Barnes' (1997) *Outdoor Education: Theory and Practice*.

Every leader has been on a steep learning curve applying these theories in their own particular context. One result of this professional evolution has been a loss of value attached to the personal or indigenous knowing developed through the experience. These understandings are suppressed by the provision of readily applicable abstract alternatives. The facilitator listens less attentively to the group whilst the group listen more attentively to the facilitator instead of to their experiences and to each others interpretations of those experiences. The creative and imaginative process of value and meaning making are essentially switched off and the experience is no longer interpreted authentically. This tendency is supported by the fact that it is easier to market the outcome of predetermined ideas than it is to sell an experience with no predictable outcome.

The use of experience as the carrier for an idea has occurred before in the evolution of outdoor experiential learning although from different motives. The power of outdoor and other sensual group experiences was tapped very successfully by the leaders of the Hitler Youth Movement to carry their messages of fascism. The processes of imparting and indoctrination are on a continuum. This might seem an extreme point to make. However, the power of outdoor experiences to carry established messages about the right way to behave has not gone unnoticed whether the context be fitting employees to organisations, young people to society or people to nature.

My argument is not that such applications are necessarily a bad thing. It depends. Provided the participants are connected to the context of a place and a culture, they are, as in the words of my title, necessarily doing the right thing or at least following the right process. It becomes a problem when some authority is attached to established and abstract ideas that are not authentic to the experience of the group. This can be justified as part of the development of young people emerging into adulthood and exploring the context of their culture. It is more like oppression when it is applied to an adult. Such an approach needs a more rigorous defence such as a therapeutic or corrective situation before it is used in this context.

Real experiential learning

The approach of using experiences to impart abstract ideas is not, I believe, experiential education. In this situation experience is being used as a proving ground of a fixed idea. As I have explained above experiential learning is, by it's nature, a source of emerging ideas rather than a place to demonstrate them.

An example will illustrate the difference. Team working is a common theme of outdoor and experiential learning programmes. Outdoor experiences provide many and varied team work opportunities. It is also a topic, which is rich in abstract ideas such as models and theories of team roles, group dynamics and group development familiar to most outdoor and experiential educators. It is common to use one or more of these theories to help a group understand its process. This is a valid approach but not I would argue an experiential one.

How would an experiential approach be different? For a start I have argued that, for learning to have occurred from an experience, it does not need to be articulated. Much of value is learned sensually. But, we are social animals and team work is a social process. Conversations considering teamwork are inevitable and provide another opportunity for important learning to occur. However, instead of providing a ready made theory with which to understand the experience the experiential facilitator would work with the group to build a theory in action based on their own experience. The participants already have an understanding of what it feels like to belong to groups and to this group in particular. By facilitating a discussion it is possible to build their own language and concepts about groups based on their experience and specific, and so functional, to their context. This would, by my definition, be an indigenous approach to learning and I believe much more likely to have an impact on values and behaviours than the simple acquisition of abstract knowledge informed by an experience.

The value of outdoor experiential learning

Many people believe that outdoor learning is a good thing. In a world that is increasingly disconnected from the real and that relies on vicarious and abstract ideas I believe that outdoor learning, when it can be recognised as truly experiential in it's indigenous form, is not only a good thing but a better thing. It develops our natural learning tendencies and allows the emergence of a personal moral framework in a way that restores the connection to the real in nature and culture. It is a sustainable way to a participative democracy and a fulfilling life. Instead of creating an audience holding it's breath we can create participants breathing deeply.

References

Barnes, P. (1997) *Outdoor Education: Theory and Practice*. Glasgow: Stathclyde University.

Drasdo, H. (1998) *Education and the Mountain Centres*. 2nd Edition. Penrith: Adventure Education.

Ellis-Smith, G. (1999) 'Restoring the Indigenous Heart' in *Proceedings of the 10th Australian National Outdoor Education Conference*. Perth: WAOEA.

Midgley, M. (1995) *Beast and Man: The Roots of Human Nature*. London: Routledge.

Mortlock, C. (1979) *The Adventure Alternative*. Milnthorpe: Cicerone.

Ogilvie, K. (1993) *Leading and Managing Groups in the Outdoors*. Penrith: NAOE.

Schama, S. (1996) *Landscape and Memory*. London: Fontana Press.

Spretnak, C. (1997) *The Resurgence of the Real*. USA: Addison-Wesley.

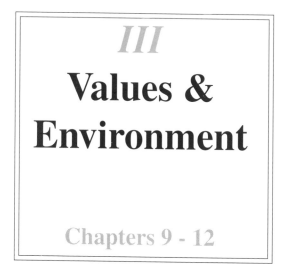

III

Values & Environment

Chapters 9 - 12

Values & Environment: Chapters 9 - 12

Chapter 9: Added and Contested Values: Femininity, Masculinity and the Environment

Barbara Humberstone

Introduction

This text explores the relationship between 'nature', outdoor education, gender and the environment. It is surprising that the relations between 'nature', gender and women have received little consideration in environmental-ecological discourses around 'outdoor pursuits' and outdoor education, given the historical Western European hegemonic woman-nature connections. This is less surprising when one finds there is frequently a general lack of analysis of the contexts and environments in which outdoor adventure education occurs. It is also significant that critical analyses of, or critical research into aspects of, outdoor education from schools of thought informed by social theory or critiques of traditional social theory are largely missing. What we do find is a small amount of research/analyses of what has been termed 'sport in nature' or 'nature-based sport' or simplistically around the outdoor pursuits themselves such as climbing, skiing etc. by researchers/analysts informed usually, but not always, by positivistic schools of thought. Similarly, there has been little research and analysis into outdoor education or outdoor learning that is informed by or engages with current critical social thought[1]. This text engages with various theoretical explanations to explore the added and contested values associated with different gender constructions in 'sport in nature' and outdoor education.

'Nature', 'values' and gender

Environmental questions around human society's links with the physical and natural worlds now feature in the arguments of many prominent social theorists such as Giddens, Gorz, Habermas and Beck. Goldblatt (1996) attempts a critical analysis of the theories of these significant European male social theorists drawing out and linking their main ideas around society's relations with the environment. But, as Dickens (1997:374) points out, this analysis has omitted to take account of important discourses around environmental issues given by other work, notably ecological feminisms. Likewise there has been a small, but increasing, genre of sports and leisure literature that takes seriously the increasing mass participation in 'sport' into 'nature' but which has been equally neglectful of arguments proffered by ecological feminism(s). Furthermore, with notable exceptions (see Vanreusel, 1995), much of this discourse has adopted positivistic perspectives on nature. Consequently, important questions such as what constitutes 'nature'?, whose interests do particular definitions support?, how and why appeals to 'nature' have legitimated women's and minority group's subordinate positions in society? And, what values are embedded in or contested within the processes and ideologies underpinning outdoor adventure education?, can not easily be raised from within such perspectives. Further, such realist perspectives may be objectivist in orientation and so ignore or dismiss important subjectivities such as values and identities (Demeritt, 1997).

'Nature', as Williams (1976:184) has remarked, "is perhaps the most complex word in the language". He draws our attention to its complexity and its use as an ideological metaphor in legitimating particular world views:

> "*What is usually apparent (when reference is made to nature) is that it is selective, according to the speaker's general purpose. 'Nature is...'- What? red in tooth and claw; a ruthlessly competitive struggle for existence; an extraordinary interlocking system of mutual advantage; a paradigm of interdependence and co-operation.*"(Williams, 1980:70).

Vanreusel (1995), who uses the term 'sport in nature', suggests that the meaning of 'nature' has shifted as a consequence of the increasing number of participants, the diversity of activities and a gradual transformation over time in the values attached to aspects of these activities. He infers that this shift in representation of 'nature' is a consequence of the shift in values underpinning the 'democratisation' of 'sport' into 'nature' which influences the general public's image of what constitutes 'nature'.

Although questioning notions of 'nature' and drawing attention to its complexity, its amenability to social construction and its shifting definitions, Vanreusel and other sociologists concerned with such human activities as skiing, climbing, sailing and so forth that rely largely upon the natural environment, do not explicitly question the concept of 'sport' as it is applied to these particular activities. Nor do we see discussions around or analyses of outdoor education but for a few notable exceptions (see Higgins and Humberstone 1998; Pilz 1996; Journal Adventure Education and Outdoor Leadership, 1996) adopting critical sociological or cultural studies approaches. Vanreusel's (1995) analysis of 'sport' in 'nature' provides a useful starting point by which the notion of values as they emerge in relation to gender and to environmental understandings in outdoor education may be considered. Vanreusel (1995) argues that the image of the outdoor participant has changed from that seen to be an ecological friend, immortalised in the 'Bambi' type, to that perceived as an ecological foe, or 'Rambo' type. However, he implicitly problematises 'sport' in this context through identifying the generalised changing values and actions of those engaged in these 'sports'. What constitutes 'sport' appears to stay the same. But it is the values, actions and relations with 'nature' that underpin these 'sports' in 'nature' which are seen to have changed over time. These values and actions change from those which we might impute to be 'caring', 'loving' (frequently seen as feminine attributes) to those that are 'destructive' and 'aggressive' which are perceived as particularly masculine, as embodied in the 'Rambo' image called upon by Vanreusel.

Likewise sports feminism(s) provide fruitful schools of thought upon which we may critically draw in considering gender and values in outdoor education and outdoor learning. These critiques have drawn attention to the significance of 'sport' as a culture conveying and legitimating ideologies and symbols of particular dominant forms of masculinity and by exclusion and opposition, particular ideologies of femininity. These ideologies of masculinity or femininity inform our thinking on what it is to be a male or female and embed images of appropriate (dominant) gender behaviours. Such ideologies espouse particular 'valued' ways of being and doing, differentiating masculinity from femininity in different social, cultural and environmental contexts. And as Hargreaves (1994:43) points out historically in Western cultures, "sports constituted a unique form of cultural life: they were overwhelmingly symbols of masculinity and chauvinism, embodying aggressive displays of physical power and competitiveness". Hargreaves further reminds us of the ideological link between woman and Nature and the ways in which calls of 'naturalness' have been used to identify men with culture and in particular the culture of sport. Sport then was perceived as, "the 'natural' domain of men ...Whereas men were identified with Culture...(and the public sphere), women were symbolically aligned to Nature and to their reproductive roles and positions as wives and mothers in the home". Despite much sport feminist analyses which recognise and question dominant images of femininity (and to a lesser extent masculinity) and their calls to 'naturalness', rarely is the non-human an issue or 'nature' itself considered. That is 'nature' for sport's feminism is pointed to as legitimating 'symbol' or signifier but not as material substance. Moreover, sport and leisure feminists have largely neglected the physical and natural environments in which 'sport' is realised. Questions around agency and structure have focused almost exclusively around the social and political context and although much of this discourse has been located in an historical framework, spatial and physical environments have largely been ignored. Consequently, with notable exceptions that have emerged from outdoor education perspectives, (Henderson, 1996; Henderson and Bialeschki, 1992 in North America; Humberstone 1991,1992; Humberstone and Collins, 1997 in UK: Pedersen, 1993, 1998 in North Scandinavia), feminist critique has been all but silent on environmental issues in 'sport'.

Nevertheless, we might turn to feminisms that draw attention not only to the symbolisation of 'nature' as a legitimator of various forms of oppression, but also to its material reality which is also subjected to domination and exploitation. These ideas emerge from the eco-feminist analysis as exemplified in such works as Diamond and Orenstein, (1990) and Soper, (1995). They highlight the strong links between 'nature' and gender in Western thought and the common oppression of *both* 'nature' and women. Historically, according to much ecofeminist argument, Nature (aligned with woman) is devalued compared with Culture (associated with man) and underpinning ecofeminist perspectives is a recognition of this common oppression of both woman and nature and the concern to transform this double subjugation (Harding, 1986; Merchant, 1980).

From ecofeminist perspectives, explanations that recognise the symbolism of Nature as signifier but not its material substance, albeit shaped and constructed by human hand and hegemonic ideologies, are inadequate as *transformative* explanatory frameworks. For it is in the interests of both dominated humans (woman and man) and exploited Nature to challenge all forms of domination. Feminist critiques of outdoor education need to take seriously the call for a fundamental re-conceptualisations of the woman/nature; man/ culture binaries *and* non-human exploitation. Current environmental feminism argues that this re-conceptualisation is premised upon the acknowledgement and understanding of the significance of the connections between the oppression of women and other subalterns (oppressions as a consequence of race, class, sexuality and so forth) *and* the exploitation of 'nature'. Consequently, it is argued that to challenge and change these webs of unequal power relations requires a synthesis of feminist and ecological approaches (Naismith and Radcliffe, 1997; Warren, 1987, 1990). These ideas are important in attempts to understanding not only 'sport in nature' but also they help us to explore more deeply the differences that the philosophical underpinnings, and environmental contexts, of outdoor education and outdoor learning may engender in terms of gendered values.

Socio-ecological approaches

The development of philosophical feminisms of the environment has been concerned largely with addressing the conceptual issues around dualism, hierarchy and domination, which underlie Western notions of 'nature', environment and gender difference. According to deep ecologist Michael Zimmerman (1990:142), although there are commonalities, there is also a fundamental criticism proffered by ecofeminists that needs to be addressed by deep ecologists:

> *"Both are critical of atomism, dualism, hierarchalism, rigid autonomy, and abstract rationality ... because deep ecology has been formulated almost entirely by men, it is characterised by unintended patriarchal prejudices. Whereas the deep ecologist speaks of the drawbacks of anthropocentrism or* human-*centredness, the ecofeminist speaks of the drawbacks of an androcentrism or* man-*centredness.*

> *This insensitivity to gender differences and androcentricity in the majority of deep ecological perspectives is problematic since it is the relations between women and men and other groups which are rendered invisible in prevailing environmental perspectives and practice. For Warren (1990:144), without this feminist critique, "one presents environmental ethics as if it has no bias, including male-gender bias,...: failure to notice the connection between the twin oppressions of women and nature* is *male -gender bias".*

Such criticisms can be addressed at much of the ethical considerations around environmental issues and 'sport in nature' and outdoor education. Socio-ecological developments that draw attention to ethical approaches to nature-based activities like much deep ecology or radical environmentalism also appear gender blind. Vanreusel (1995:281) points to a four stage model as an ethical basis for a socio-ecological approach addressing the pursuit of outdoor 'sport' versus environmental protection debate. However, despite reference to the 'Rambo' image of the outdoor pursuits participant, this model is androcentric and thus so is the proposed socio-ecological approach toward which it leads. For example, the fourth stage of ecological consciousness is ecological sensibility, or deep ecology that sees impending biospheric degradation as a symptom of anthropocentrism. Further, according to Norwegian philosopher and naturalist, Naess (1984), living according to deep ecological principles, in oneness with nature, would bring about fulfilment of human existence as well as liberating 'nature' from human exploitation. But Pedersen's (1993;1998) feminist research and critique of the romanticized ideology of Friluftsliv (Norwegian outdoor nature life) points to both its elitism and male centredness.

The socio-ecological approach to outdoor sports highlighted by Vanreusel (1995) is underpinned by these notions of ecological sensibility or deep ecology. Vanreusel (1995:281) reveals the fourth stage of the ethical stance for 'sport' in 'nature' as:

The ethics of the environment as given

The highest ethical level is no longer centred on *man*, or on the view that the environment is there to serve *man*, eg for recreational ends. It is now based instead on an indissoluble interdependency between *man* and *his* environment....The individual no longer lives and plays *in* the natural environment but *with* an environment of which *he himself* is part and which *he himself* should therefore respect as *he* respects *himself*. (Vanreusel, 1995:281) (non-underlined italics added)

This advocation of an ecologically sensitive approach, like much comparable deep ecology, sensitive to environmental ethics, is clearly androcentric, reflecting the male dominant social relations within which ecofeminists argue many environmentalists work and within which traditionally many sociologists of sport or outdoor educators have worked. Until the fundamental aspects of Western dualistic thought patterns and patriarchal relations are acknowledged as historically integral to this degradation, we can not hope to alter the deep structures underpinning relations or transform hierarchical relations of power between humans and between human and non-human.

As King (1990:111) points out in arguing against a radical cultural feminist standpoint to ecological theory,

> "The connecting of woman and nature has lent itself to a romanticisation of woman as good, and as apart from the dastardly deeds of men and culture. The problem is that history, power, women, and nature are a lot more complicated".

And it should be said that man's relations with 'nature' are made the more complex as a consequence of man's historically dominant alignment with culture and Natures' traditional coding as 'female' (Soper, 1995). These traditional gender codings, I would suggest, may be problematic for men and women engaged in outdoor education and outdoor learning. In a sense, the outdoor education and learning environment provides the context in which such coding can be challenged. Men have the opportunity to align themselves with nature, arguably problematically needing still to identify themselves as 'not woman'. Whilst women have the opportunity to be and be seen as competently able in traditionally male physical activities ('sport in nature').

Gender identities, counter-cultures and outdoor education

Clearly, gender identities are complex, contested and changeable. Sports feminists such as Gilroy, (1997); Hall, (1996) and Hargreaves (1994) point to the female body as a site of struggle in resisting conventional images of 'sports' and femininity. Likewise, physical activities and 'sport' based in 'nature' historically and currently constitute arenas of struggle and tension through which challenges are being enacted to dominant images of 'sport' and forms of both femininity and masculinity. Evidence suggests that 'sport' in 'nature' may provide spaces not only for the reaffirmation of hegemonic masculinities (the 'Rambos') but also, in certain conditions, *transformative* contexts in which the masculine body, as well as the feminine, is being redefined/reconstituted (Humberstone, 1990,1993; Wheaton, 1998). Such conditions may constitute 'sport' with much of the characteristics of physical skill, power and exertion ascribed to dominant images of 'sport' but without the *excessive* aggressive competitiveness underpinning much 'sport' and with the added value of co-operation in and sensitivity to the environment.

Examination of the writings of some of those women (e.g. Dann and Lynch, 1989; Tullis, 1987) and men (eg. Bowles, 1996; Higgins 1996: Mortlock, 1984) who themselves participate(d) in 'sport' in 'nature' and are/were involved in aspects of outdoor education provision, uncover, in some of these texts, what appears as a counter 'sport' culture in which the physical activities in 'nature' are perceived as underpinned by values absent from much of mainstream sport. One such texts asks,

> *Is Mountaineering anything to do with sport? Despite some affinities , the answer is no. It is impossible to find a definition of sport which will include all the values of mountaineering without also including all manner of activities which are manifestly not of a sporting nature.* (Drasdo, 1972:33)

Drasdo's text describes these added values which include, amongst others, reference to aesthetic and ecological sensibilities. Androcentric and largely uncritical in character, this early text represents something of the 'Bambi' culture to which Vanreusel (1995) alludes and which it is suggested is perceived to be loosing ground to the 'Rambo' culture of mass participation of 'sport' in 'nature'. However, there is evidence to suggest that Drasdo's text conveys something of the values forming a basis of one of the contemporary counter-cultures running contrary to the macho competitive ideology, the 'conquer the mountain' syndrome, portrayed in much media coverage of men and women involved in 'outdoor pursuits' today.

These are complex issues around gender relations and particular constructions of masculinity and femininity in 'sport in nature' and outdoor education which need exploring and analysing further if we are to understand the machismo inherent in 'Rambo' representations or make sense of other more 'gentle' identities of the outdoor 'sport' enthusiast, male or female, mass 'produced' or counter-cultured, and their relations with and constitution of 'sport' in 'nature' and within the outdoor education context.

Consequently, in order to appreciate the ways in which men and women 'operate' in outdoor education, we need to understand the ways in which both the female and male body are differently and similarly constituted in diverse physical, social and organisational arrangements in Nature. This clearly draws attention to the ways in which individuals may be shaped by particular cultures and ideologies, but also it allows for the corporeality and autonomy of female and male bodies within material Nature that can act on account of individual and collective values to influence decision making. These decisions may be immediate in relation to the place and time in 'nature' or they may be made through reflection on experiences with and in 'nature' at later times and places, perhaps to influence policy at local, regional and global levels. Since, as Naismith and Radcliffe (1997:202) point out from an ecofeminist perspective, "Grounded in physical bodies, people's social relations with environments are mediated through these same bodies". Furthermore, many ecologically sensitive organisations, rather than taking a view of organised retreat by 'sport' from 'nature' advocated in Digel (1992), argue that particular forms of outdoor education bring the physical body into close contact with 'natural' environments and it is through these very interactions with 'nature' and the elements, in all their forms, that sow the seeds for environmental awareness and ethical sensibilities. An exemplary case is that of the surfers and windsurfers in the UK who, concerned about the pollution of the waters, have instigated an action group, Surfers Against Sewerage, to lobby against the sea's use as an arbitrary dumping ground. Consequently, as one male outdoor educator/environmentalist reflects:

> We must help people to experience directly and to become aware of their practical and spiritual connections to the 'natural' world. I am not against outdoor activities, nor am I against the idea of adventure. Far from it. My own first love of the outdoors came from uncomplicated forays into the hills, onto rivers or sea, and this love exists to this day....We have to have a love for a place (whether it be an old quarry with a few rock climbs, or the planet itself!) first, before we will take an interest in caring for it. (Higgins, 1996:38)

Such reflexive accounts and alternative movements from which they emerge should not be ignored. It is important to examine if and how alternative identities to the Rambo images are constructed in various contexts. But, in the process, critical/feminist/

ecological sociologists need to continue to question the invisibility of women and their voices (and those of other subalterns) and the persistence of the use of generic man, as is evident in much environmental discourse (Humberstone, 1996; Warren, 1996). They also need to explore the many paradoxes which lie within alternative cultures or movements (see Becker, 1996; Bowles, 1996; Humphreys, 1997; Piltz, 1996; Suoranta, 1996).

Furthermore, unlike Digel (1992:266) who considers "Education-a doubtful instrument", evidence suggests that particular forms of outdoor education can provide opportunities for females and males to challenge hegemonic masculinities and forms of femininity and the values that shape them and so begin to understand their individual, collective and global responsibilities to nature (Cooper, 1994; Higgins 1996; Humberstone and Collins 1998; Maxted, 1996; Repp 1996). For as Soper (1995:209) succinctly reminds us, "A community too sorely deprived of the joys of nature may come to care less for long term human survival and well-being".

Conclusion: connecting theory and practice

On surveying the works of Giddens, Gorz, Habermas and Beck for analysis of their discourses on environmental degradation and environmental politics, Goldblatt (1996:200) is of the opinion that,

> *social theory, for all its strengths, is not an idiom or discipline that is well suited to the elaboration or discussion of this kind of political problem. It requires closer attention to the minutiae of social institutions and their operations than the overarching structural themes that are social theory's speciality.*

This view has direct implications for the orthodox structuralist social theory that has been deployed on much research on sport, leisure and the environment. Examinations of the values and ethics underpinning individual actions, together with the ideologies that both shape identities in context and also influence movements and institutions involved in outdoor adventure education are imperative. Social research that is based on an interpretative-hermeneutic paradigm such as ethnography may inform our understanding of beliefs and values underpinning particular (counter-) cultures and ideologies and the ways in which identities are created and challenged (Humberstone 1997). But, it is a giant leap from social research and social explanation to generating large scale *democratic* political movements needed to halt environmental (human and non-human) degradation of global dimensions and to replace this with sustainable lifestyles and politics. For as Goldblatt (1996:203) remarks,

> *"We know that we cannot go on as before. But how to go on, how to live individually and collectively, how to make the transition soon and how to persuade the intransigent, the selfish, the powerful and the uninterested?"*

Vanreusel (1995) has called for socio-ecological approaches to nature-based sport to be underpinned by ethical and moral debates. Likewise the ideologies and values associated with outdoor adventure education and outdoor learning need to be explored in light of these explanations. In so doing, outdoor education may, in some sense, inform these approaches and explanations presented in this text. This must not mean that issues around the relations and ideologies of *gendered* environments are ignored. Rather, they should be central to any new research agendas and discourses in the field. Such approaches would analyse gender identities in practice, the practices of groups that have appropriated the natural environment as place in which to convey dominant sport's values, and groups with alternative values, which are arguably those espoused within outdoor education. This means opening up the dialogue to all groups concerned at practical and theoretical levels, whilst refusing to grant any of them *the* truth. For as Demerit (1997:223) argues, "Exclusive knowledge claims serve only to divide, to empower a few anointed experts, and to exclude the many different voices that can and should speak".

This text calls for a new approach to the social study of outdoor education that is based on the premises of critical feminism and socio-ecology. However, the perspective that I advocate, not only synthesises feminist and ecological approaches, but also takes grounded interpretative research seriously, and is underpinned by concern for social as well as environmental justice.

Notes

This paper is a revised version of ,'Re-creation and Connections in and with Nature: Synthesising Ecological and Feminist Discourses and Praxis?', *International Review for the Sociology of Sport, Special Issue: Sport and the Environment.* 33 (4): 381-392. 1998
1. However, this now is taken more seriously in the recent research and publications concerned with outdoor adventure education (see, for example, Higgins and Humberstone, 1998, 1999; Warren, 1996)

References

Beck, U. (1991) *Risk Society: Towards a New Modernity* London: Sage.
Becker, P. (1996) In Quest of Paradise. Comments on the Current Attraction of Excitement and Adventure, *Journal of Adventure Education and Outdoor Leadership* 13 (2): 67-70.
Bowles, S. (1996) Techniques and Philosophy. Blending Roots? Or Sowing Maybe-Seeds in Outdoor Adventure Educations, *Journal of Adventure Education and Outdoor Leadership* 13 (2): 7-19.
Cooper, G. (1994) The Role of Outdoor Education in Education for the 21 st Century, *Journal of Adventure Education and Outdoor Leadership* 11 (2): 9-12.
Dann, C. and Lynch, P. (1989) *Wilderness Women, Stories of New Zealand Women at Home in the Wilderness.* New Zealand : Penguin Books.
Demeritt, D. (1997) 'Ecology, Objectivity and Critique in Writings on Nature and Human Sciences', in T. Barnes and D. Gregory (Eds.) *Reading Human Geography. The Poetics and Politics of Inquiry.* London: Arnold.

Diamond, I. and Orenstein, G. (Eds.)(1990) *Reweaving the World. The Emergence of Ecofeminism.* San Francisco: Sierra Club Books.

Dickens, P. (1997) David Goldblatt, Social Theory and the Environment in *Sociology, the Journal of the British Sociological Association* 31(2):372-374.

Digel, H. (1992) Sports in a Risk Society, *International Review for the Sociology of Sport.* 27 (3): 257-273.

Drasdo, H. (1972) *Education and the Mountain Centres.* Tyddyn Gabriel: Welsh Universal Press.

Gilroy, S. (1997) Working on the Body: Links between Physical Activity and Social Power, in G. Clarke and B. Humberstone (Eds.) *Researching Women and Sport.* London: Macmillan.

Goldblatt, D. (1996) *Social Theory and the Environment.* Cambridge: Polity.

Hall, A.M. (1996) *Feminism and Sporting Bodies: Essays on Theory and Practice.* Leeds: Human Kinetics.

Harding, S. (1986) *The Science Question in Feminism.* Milton Keynes: Open University Press.

Hargreaves, J. (1994) *Sporting Females: Critical issues in the history and sociology of women's sports.* London: Routledge.

Henderson, K.A. (1996) Women and the Outdoors: Toward Spiritual Empowerment, in K. Warren (Ed.) *Women's Voices in Experiential Education.* Iowa: Kendall/Hunt Pub. Co.

Henderson, K. and Bialeschki, M. (1992) Ecofeminism: Recreation as if nature and women mattered, *Leisure Information Quarterly* 17 (1): 1 - 5.

Higgins, P. (1996) Connection and Consequence in Outdoor Education, *Adventure Education and Outdoor Leadership* 13 (2): 34-39.

Higgins, P. and Humberstone, B.(Eds.) (1998) *Celebrating Diversity: Learning by Sharing Cultural Difference.* Third European Congress for Outdoor Adventure *Education and Experiential Learning.* BCUC:EIOAEEL.

Higgins, P. and Humberstone, B. (Eds.)(1999) *Outdoor Education and Experiential Learning in the UK* Luneburg, Germany: Verlag Erlebnispadagogik (German and English publication).

Humberstone, B. (1990) 'Warriors or Wimps? Creating Alternative Physical Education, in M. Messner and D. Sabo (Eds.) *Sport, Men and the Gender Order.* Champaign, Il.: Human Kinetics.

Humberstone, B. (1991) Rethinking Sport and the Environment. The Challenge of Ecofeminism to the Use of Natural Assets. *Commission d'Etude du Sport Universitaire: The Challenging Patterns of Recreation and* Leisure. FISU/CESU.

Humberstone, B. (1992) The web of Connections - Patriarchal Relations and the Abuse of the Environment, in *Leisure and New Citizenship. Conference Proceedings of the VIII European Leisure and Recreation Association.* Bilboa: Universidad de Duesto.

Humberstone, B. (1993) Equality, Physical Education and Outdoor Education - Ideological Struggles and Transformative Structures? in J. Evans (Ed.) *Equality, Education and Physical Education.* London: Falmer Press.

Humberstone, B. (1995) Bringing Outdoor Education into the Physical Education Agenda: Gender Identities and Social Change, *Quest. The Journal of the National Association for Physical Education in Higher Education* 47 : 144-157.

Humberstone, B. (1996) Others Voices: Many Meanings? Technique and Philosophy for Outdoor Adventure. The Case for Women, *Adventure Education and Outdoor Leadership* 13 (2): 47-52.

Humberstone, B. (1997) Perspectives in Research in Outdoor Education: Values and Ethics, *Journal of Adventure and Outdoor Leadership* 14 (1) 7-9.

Humberstone, B. and Collins, D. (1997) *Ecofeminism, 'Risk' and Women's Experiences of Landscape*. Paper presented at the LSA Conference, Leisure, Culture and Commerce. Roehampton, London 9-11 September.

Humphreys, D. (1997) 'Shredheads go Mainstream'? Snowboarding and Alternative Youth, *International Review for the Sociology of Sport* 32 (2) 147-160.

The Journal of Adventure Education and Outdoor Leadership (1996),*Finland Welcomes Europe and the World,* 13 ,(2) April.

King, Y. (1990) Healing the Wounds. in I. Diamond and G. Orenstein (eds.) *Reweaving the World. The Emergence of Ecofeminism.* San Francisco: Sierra Club Books.

Maxted, J. (1996) *Fostering an Ecological Consciousness through Adventure*. Paper presented at the 'From Mystery to Mastery' Conference. New Zealand 7-9 December.

Merchant, C. (1990) Ecofeminism and Feminist Theory. in I. Diamond and G. Orenstein (Eds.) *Reweaving the World. The Emergence of Ecofeminism.* San Francisco: Sierra Club Books.

Mortlock, C. (1984) *The Adventure Alternative*. Milnthorpe, Cumbria: Cicerone Press.

Naess, A. (1984) 'Identification as a Source of Deep Ecological Attitudes', in M. Tobias (Ed.) *The Ecologist* 14: 194-204.

Naismith, C. and Radcliffe, S.A. (1997) (Re)mapping Mother Earth: A Geographical Perspective on Environmental Feminisms in T. Barnes and D. Gregory (Eds.) *Reading Human Geography: The Poetics and Politics of Inquiry.* London: Arnold.

Pedersen, K. (1993) Gender, Nature and Technology: Changing Trends in 'Wilderness Life", in J. Oakes and R. Riewe (eds) *Human Ecology: Issues in the North, Volume 11. The Canadian Circumpolar Institute,* University of Alberta.

Pedersen, K. (1998) Doing Feminist Ethnography in the 'Wilderness' around my Hometown, *International Review for the Sociology of Sport* 33, (4): 393-402.

Pilz, S. (1996) *'Experiential Learning and Outdoor Activities for the Benefit of Young People? A Critical Analysis'.* Keynote presented at the 2nd International Conference: Youth and Social Work on the Move. Spital, Austria.

Repp, G. (1996) Outdoor Adventure Education and 'Friluftsliv' seen from a Sociology of Knowledge Perspective, *Adventure Education and Outdoor Leadership* 13 (2): 63-66.

Soper, K. (1995) *What is Nature? Culture, Politics and the non-Human.* Oxford: Blackwell.

Souranta, J. (1996) The Possibilities of Education in the Culture of Violence, *Adventure Education and Outdoor Leadership* 13 (2): 40-46.

Tullis, J. (1987) *Clouds from Both Sides.* London : Grafton Books.

Vanreusel, B. (1995) From Bambi to Rambo: Towards a Socio-Ecological Approach to the Pursuit of Outdoor Sports, in O. Weiss and W. Schulz (Eds.) *Sport in Space and Time.* Vienna: Vienna University Press.

Warren, K.J. (1987) 'Feminism and ecology: making connections', *Environmental Ethics* 9: 3-20.

Warren, K. J.(1990) 'The power and promise of ecological feminism', *Environmental Ethics* 12: 125-146.

Warren, K. (Ed.) (1996) *Women's Voices in Experiential Education.* Iowa: Kendall/ Hunt Pub. Co.

Wheaton, B. (1998) New Lads?: Masculinities and the 'New Sport' Participation , Paper presented at the LSA Conference, ' *The Big Getto'*, Leeds, July.

Williams, R. (1976) *Nature.Keywords: A Vocabulary of Society and Nature.* London:Fontana.

Williams, R. (1980) *Problems of Materialism and Culture.* London:Verso.

Zimmerman, M. (1990) Deep Ecology and Ecofeminism. in I. Diamond and G. Orenstein (Eds.) *Reweaving the World. The Emergence of Ecofeminism.* San Francisco: Sierra Club Books.

Chapter 10: Working Towards Multi-Cultural Values In Environmental Participation

Judy Ling Wong

Majority goodwill

Black Environment Network (BEN) is established to promote ethnic environmental participation. It exists because it is optimistic. It believes that the majority of British people are people of goodwill, not racists. However, we also realise that goodwill is not enough.

The power of this goodwill as a force against racism can be released only when it is expressed in practice. All organisations are powerbases, which can choose whether they wish to pull their weight with respect to social change.

BEN defines environmental participation as:

- Access to the use and enjoyment of the environment

- Access to information, activities and resources enabling an informed view of the environment

- Participation in the protection, preservation and development of the environment

BEN works on two principal fronts to create a climate within which full ethnic environmental participation can take place. We work to represent issues and concerns of ethnic groups with regard to the lack of equal opportunity for ethnic participation in the environmental sectors. At the same time we work, through raising awareness and the provision of training, to enable organisational personnel to acquire the necessary understanding and skills to work effectively with ethnic groups.

Ethnic persons as full British citizens

But, why should organisations feel they should reach out to involve ethnic communities? What is the context that makes people committed to take action to enable ethnic participation in British society ?

Nowadays, everyone uses the term multi-cultural society. Too often it seems simply to mean that we are trapped on these islands with a lot of people whose origins stem from different cultures, and it is a matter of coping with these alien intrusions. It is a scenario which says ethnic persons do not belong here. We are told that British people need to be tolerant to ethnic groups. Tolerance is neither adequate nor appropriate for settled ethnic communities.

The presence of settled ethnic communities in Britain is viewed as a consequence of past history. Rather it is a fact of an inextricable relationship of mutual engagement that extends into the present and the future. Unless this is recognised, we have a scenario which says that there is no need to think about ethnic communities. Working with us is seen as doing us a favour, rather than making amends for the consequences of long term neglect, and putting into place the rights which have been denied to us for too long.

To arrive at equality, we need to be seen as full legitimate members of British society. Only then will action taken to enable ethnic persons to fully participate in the future of Britain be seen as an overdue central social theme.

Taking care of our own

Because of everything that has happened around the murder of Stephen Lawrence, we have at the present time an open atmosphere for social change in the context of a multi-cultural society. We should make a push for an analysis of how we can forge new and appropriate multi-cultural values.

We need to recognise that we are a long way from the ideal. The sympathies aroused are still in the main perceived as 'what is happening to *them* - black communities' rather than what is happening to *one of us*, to part of *our community*. Ultimately it is about taking care of our own.

Ways forward towards a sea change in the context of inclusiveness

No amount of reaching out will encourage ethnic communities to emerge into an atmosphere tinged not only by the unpleasantness of racist abuse and inequality, but by what is perceived as real physical danger. Like everyone else, ethnic persons need to be convinced that to be in Britain is to be held within the safety of our own home.

The nature of the recent awakenings around the case of Stephen Lawrence has exposed the severe lack of understanding of central concepts to underpin the interpretation of events. It has shown that even a basic vocabulary is not in place to enable proper discussion. Vital terms such as ethnic, racial, and cultural are used interchangeably as if they were the same. The term institutionalised racism finally arrived, albeit half understood and half accepted. Popularised misinformation distorted perceptions. A deepening of understanding and a continuing learning debate is urgent. A sea change in attitudes and working practices will ultimately be consciously expressed through the re-positioning of the social context.

We need social and political leadership to inspire commitment at senior level within organisations to equal opportunities for full participation by ethnic groups, against the context that ethnic persons are full members of British society who have been disadvantaged through a social framework that bred wrongful exclusion.

The debate has also mostly revolved around controlling the situation. But, a crucial development is to jump the gap to the wish to connect with and enjoy engagement with a part of society that is part of ourselves. A lot of work needs to be done around facilitating the enjoyment and valuing the excitement of a multi-cultural society. Much of this will touch on revelatory experience, discovery and personal transformation - a shift of vision about what being a multi-cultural society means. The arts have a significant role to play in this.

Deprivation

Deprivation is often measured mechanistically by, for example, levels of income of a particular social group. But more importantly, there are more serious deprivations which destroy the spirit to engage with life.

BEN has forged the definition : 'Deprivation is the loss of access to the variety that is life'. In this area, outdoor activity and contact with the wider environment has a lot to offer.

The needs of vulnerable groups

Within the environmental sector, and the outdoor activity and education sectors are huge networks providing a comprehensive range of activities, developmental opportunities, training, and social and leisure opportunities. These can significantly enhance the quality of life of disadvantaged and vulnerable groups, including ethnic groups. It is also a positive setting for the engagement of mainstream groups with ethnic groups.

Environmental engagement and outdoor activity can contribute through providing:

- the opportunity to enter a supportive framework
- exposure to a widened range of roles and values which assist self-determination
- exposure to a widened range of stimulation
- opportunities to participate in activities which enhance the quality of life
- the widened availability of guidance

- opportunities to engage in activities which give direct control over aspects of one's life and immediate surroundings, thereby nurturing a sense of personal power

Dreaming for real

Opening out opportunities for participation in a wide variety of activities affect vulnerable persons at the core of their being. Gradually they are enabled to arrive at something which all of us take for granted in our everyday life - the ability to work towards the fulfilment of ordinary life goals, and therefore 'dreaming for real'.

What is it that we all have that enables us to be motivated, to feel we can make choices, shape and direct our lives and therefore dream for real?

- A sense of personal potential
- A sense of personal power
- Resources and access to resources
- Above all, a social framework which convinces us that we are included in its future plans

Working for equal opportunities in organisations

Many aspects of inclusiveness can be attended to within organisations under the banner of Equal Opportunities. Creating a setting for equal opportunities within organisations can be summarised as :

- Arriving at organisational commitment to the involvement of ethnic groups

- Awareness of the context of exclusion of ethnic groups in relation to a particular organisation or field of activities

- Acquiring understanding and skills to design and undertake effective positive action

A structure for change within organisations

The following proposes an ideal situation within which senior commitment releases resources and supports personnel through a developmental programme. However, change can proceed through individuals within organisations as well. Individual workers interested in working with ethnic groups can join external networks such as BEN, and enable their organisation to come into contact with an inclusive way of thinking. They can, through their own pieces of work, inspire change by example within an organisation.

- • Commitment to equal opportunities at a senior level
- - Putting Policy and Strategy into place

- • Commitment of resources
- - Monetary resources and personnel time

- • Commitment to organisational cultural change
- - Awareness raising and the promotion of understanding at all levels of the organisation
- - An atmosphere and framework within which equal opportunities can be implemented
- - Facilitation of contact between personnel and ethnic groups

- • Commitment to personnel development
- - Training and developmental programme to enable personnel to acquire the understanding and skills to work effectively

- • Commitment to a framework for action
- - Allocating personnel time within work programmes
- - Identifying and setting targets
- - Provision of personnel support
- - Undertaking analysis and research which enable input by ethnic groups, with a view to identifying the focus for effective input by a participation organisation

A unifying vision of multi-culturalism

BEN proposes a particular view of multi-culturalism. It is a vision which sees diverse cultures as an illustration of the range of potential of the human personality.

Unique cultures are cultures which once upon a time evolved in isolation. Isolated groups, through the impact of their particular environment combined with the human potential of the group, produced solutions to living as unique cultures. But, as soon as we meet with other cultural groups, we become multi-cultural.

All cultures belong to us as the human race. Being in touch with them awakens aspects of ourselves and gives us the choice of how we wish to be even when many of the elements are mutually exclusive. World cultures show us what we can all be in particular circumstances - humanity in all its glory, as well as in all its cruelty. It is a great lesson.

Once upon a time we used to have cultural isolation through the simple fact that we could not cross a river, a mountain, or the sea. But in a world of mass travel and mass media, we live in a world which opens us to multiple cultural influences with no escape.

Some people feel that multi-culturalism is a vision of boringly flattening out everyone. But, fortunately, we actually have no time within a single lifetime even to begin to encompass all the cultural aspects on offer. We are actually doomed to uniqueness. A contemporary definition of a unique culture at particular points in time would be 'a unique combination of multi-cultural elements'. In that sense we are always unique.

We are always unique

We have come too far in time for cultures not to be multi-cultural. History has been a story of the meeting and interaction of cultures. We can think that our culture is completely unique only because we do not know of the origin of the cultural aspects we hold so dear.

Food certainly is something which each nation parades with pride as a strong component of cultural identity. Think of Italy, what did they do for cultural identity before tomatoes, from North America? And before Marco Polo went to China and brought back noodles? No Spaghetti Bolognaise! What did Holland do for a national image and a state-wide industry before tulips - from Turkey and beyond! Did you know that the idea of the three course meal came from the Arabic nations, through the Black Moors in Spain? And, can life go on in Britain without millions of cups of tea and coffee, and turkey for Christmas?

When I was talking about Italy, tomatoes and noodles at a conference, everyone laughed. There was a young Italian lady in the front role getting increasingly angry. She stood up and said, "Italian food is nothing like Chinese food !" "But", I said to her, "that is the whole point, we take what we like from each other and we make it our own, transformed. There is no cultural threat, only fear. Culture has always been and always will be about creativity. We will all always be unique."

A shift in vision - the power of ways of seeing

Once we are open to the idea that all cultures are now intrinsically multi-cultural and that all cultures belong to us, our perception of everything that is around us is transformed. BEN promotes a particular community project called "The cultural garden".

When I was developing the first cultural garden at Walnut Tree Walk School in London, I talked to a friend who trained in horticulture at Windsor about identifying plants which came from the countries of origin of the inner city children. She laughed and said, "The typical British Garden is but a collection of glorified foreign weeds!"

Indeed, to create a garden with plants from different parts of the world, we can get only what can grow here and what is already here. And, what is already here is astonishing. Dahlias from Mexico, Magnolias from China, Gladiolus and Red Hot

Poker from Africa, Bergenia from Siberia, the Indian Bean Tree from South America, Peach Trees from Iran, Oriental Poppy from Armenia and so on. Through taking part in the creation of the cultural garden, the children at Walnut Tree were amazed to find that all the 'English' gardens they see on their way to school are full of plants connecting them to all parts of the world. They came into school shouting, "I have Chinese plants in my garden." Finding out created a shift in vision - a discovery that multi-cultural elements are all around us that plants from their countries of origin have been here and loved for a long time! And, all of this is here because of inter-cultural engagement.

Such an example of the shift in vision leads us to the proposal that the most appropriate interpretation of the environment is multi-cultural interpretation.

The multi-cultural interpretation of activities and sites

Access to engagement with the environment is not only about physical access. Yes, due to prevalent poverty among many ethnic groups it is fundamental to aim to fund transport to enable environmental experience and facilitate inclusion in programmes of activity. But, we also need to address intellectual access - the generation of activities, heritage resources and site-interpretation which reflect and draw from diverse cultures.

Multi-cultural interpretation is interpretation within a framework, which recognises that all cultures are multi-cultural and that culture is in evolution. We are all recipients of culture as well as the creators of culture.

Of course it is of utmost importance that local, national and international history are presented, but we must acknowledge that the values which frame their presentation are our own. We may aim to make known the values of the past, but the tone and presentation of this material communicates the values and judgement of the present. It is one thing to examine the values of aristocrats within a National Trust property, another to glorify them. All of us, individuals or organisations, if we pledge to be open to everyone, then we need to work consciously at positioning ourselves socially and culturally, and be aware of the personal impact of interpretation on our visitors. Do we tell working class folk that it is all right to ignore the contribution of their ancestors? Do we condone the piracy of works of arts from other nations?

When one enters a site or engages in activities of any kind, messages are everywhere. One is immediately confronted by interpretive resources that begin to draw boundaries. Those of us who are in charge of public sites and who run public programmes of activities, with the remit to serve all sections of society, need to examine how we make our special contribution through the expertise of our field of work, but at the same time engage those we serve in a relevant way. We should always attempt to go beyond ourselves and ask some vital questions:

Do we value the interaction and creativity that is essential for building a cohesive vibrant and progressive culture that involves everyone in working together for a better future?

Does our work acknowledge the common ownership of knowledge and skills?

Do we strategically contribute to access to our organisation by everyone?

Who are we providing for when we present our work in the way we do?

What do we offer as a special resource and how can we develop resources which are socially and culturally relevant to those we serve?

Are we stimulating participation and inter-action which benefit different social and cultural groups?

Are we inviting the creativity of others to spur the progress of our work?

Who are the key partners that we need to work with in order to facilitate organisational culture change and deepen understanding of those we have traditionally excluded?

Besides enjoyment and entertainment, do we enrich and inspire?

In a country dominated by a peacetime interpretation of people and nature, how can we consciously strengthen values which protect world peoples and the world environment within an unstable world?

Moving forward with the momentum

Beyond being touched by what has happened around Stephen Lawrence's murder, we need to be moved beyond all the unresolved feelings of pity, outrage, anger, helplessness to the motivation to wish to know more about our relationship to ethnic communities and arrive at situating ourselves as one.

Ethnic communities are part and parcel of British society. The facts of Britain is a multi-cultural history. We are inextricably linked to the fact of Britain. The denial of the full status of being British persons to ethnic communities has caused enormous suffering and damaged the lives of many ethnic persons. The denial of the role ethnic persons have played has caused much anguish. We have laid down our lives and fought wars in the name of Britain. There is a social and human debt to be paid.

Beyond that, we wish to be able to look forward to participating within British society within a framework that allows us to make our full contribution to multi-cultural Britain.

Chapter 11: The Gender Based Relationships of Girls to their Natural Environment

Julie Rea and Michael Slavkin

Girls and nature

People learn how to behave and what to value through the socialization process of their culture. Consequently, it is important to understand the impact of socially constructed meaning on later social interaction. It is not a new idea that self-concept is a result of socialized interaction (Rogoff, 1990; Wertsch, 1985). Our notion of gender is one of the key components of our self-concept (Strayer & Trudel, 1984).

The Biophilia Hypothesis has been employed in recent studies attempting to further understand the development of self-concept (Kahn, 1999). This theory essentially states that there exists a developmental need for people to be exposed to the life process, and the element of diversity that exists within that process, as found in nature. Interactions with nature are related to development, and are influenced by the interactions within socialization experiences (Kahn, 1998; Kellert, 1997). Furthermore, people's experiences with nature are impacted by their understanding of their gender roles (Warren, 1996).

Gender role identity is defined as an individual's perception of self in terms of socially dominant stereotypes of masculinity and femininity (Bem, 1981). The gender role identity of each girl in the study discussed in this chapter, conducted at a residential summer girl scout camp in a Midwestern state in the United States, was determined with the Bem Sex-Role Inventory, BSRI (Bem, 1978). The BSRI, determines two scores, one indicating a feminine, and one a masculine score. There are four possible outcomes from these two scores: masculine, feminine, androgynous (high masculine and high feminine), and undifferentiated (low masculine and low feminine).

A girl's gender role identity is related to her interaction with the natural environment. For example, there may be a relation between a feminine gender role identity and expressed discomfort with dirt, bugs and bones that are involved in the activity and are frequent components of nature. In contrast, a girl with a high masculine identity score may express less discomfort with these same elements of the natural environment.

Language and social semiotics

In order to consider the above questions, the field of social semiotics was deemed an appropriate lens through which to interpret the data. The underlying assumption of social semiotics is that action and meaning are not separate. Rather action and meaning are intertwined as a system of social meanings and interactions. The very nature of learning itself is social and not individual (Thibault, 1990).

The principles of social linguistics have made their contribution to the field as well (Lemke, 1990). The important contribution of social semiotics to the study of human behavior is that it focuses on the meaning making process. It does not assume meaning apart from the meaning made in use (Lemke, 1987). By not imposing a meaning, but rather noting that meaning is socially constructed, the inquirer begins to observe a process of social semiosis, that of culture, which contains and communicates the meaning of that evolving culture in which that social interaction occurs.

Beliefs and motivation to learn

Motivation to engage in an activity is tied to this ability to envision oneself involved in certain actions (Brophy, 1999). So follows the idea that based on gender stereotypes, roles in group behavior are linked to the pre-existing selves that one can identify oneself with. If a girl is heavily self-identified with a feminine nature and can reference no place in her understanding of feminine as assertive and directive oriented, then it is much less likely that she will be motivated to act in a directive or assertive role in a group activity. If, however, she has an association for feminine that allows for assertive and directive behavior, then she would be more likely to feel motivated and act in an assertive or directive manner in an environment or activity that offered that opportunity.

While it cannot be said that the girls in the study described here would act in directive or assertive roles should they have been placed in a group which included boys, it can be said that as a result of their engagement in this activity, they have observed, and been part of a group which models females in directive and assertive leadership roles, thus introducing models of such behavior as feminine.

The naturally-occurring environment

Ecological systems and naturally occurring settings are environments which have certain distinct properties that have an influence on those within the system independent from those things imposed by an individual or structural form. They are dynamic systems wherein all participants make meaning through their interaction within that environment.

The premise of this chapter is that there are indicators in the community, which make apparent to the members of that community, the meaningful relationships being addressed as well as the systems of addressing those relationships which are being utilized (Thibault, 1990). If the girls are to become meaningfully engaged in their interactions with nature and the elements of nature which they are socialized to respond to, then they must be able to discern which global systems of meaning will be employed in the current activity.

Procedure

The twenty-four study participants interacted in three group problem-solving activities. No adult involvement occurred during the activities. First, each group of six was asked to exhume a set of horse bones for examination. The skeleton was buried in loose wood chips, and rope was used to mark off the six sections. Group members were free to collaborate with the others in the group as they discovered, uncovered, and reconstructed a skeleton. Group members were to remove parts of the skeleton and place them at site two, a grid of the same dimensions located next to site one. Participants knew that their work at site two would be complete when a finished skeleton was constructed. At the third site participants were asked to re-form the skeleton with the use of steel hooks and pins. Girls worked together to identify the most appropriate methods for completion of the task.

Three graduate-student experimenters, two women and a man, observed the activities. Field notes were taken in an attempt to identify the meaning making process between group members as it occurred. These phenomena were observed in their naturally occurring environment to capture descriptions of group members interacting as well as sharing their respective beliefs about the leadership roles of group members, girls their age, girls their race, and so on.

Results

Three significant areas of meaning were identified from the data. First, there was a relationship with nature, as an element of life, with which one could interact in some meaningful manner. Second, there was the normative set of verbal responses from which the girls verbally expressed themselves upon their initial contact with the bones, bugs, and dirt. Finally, there was the nature of the group process itself and the meaningful interactions within that process, which indicate what these girls see as appropriate behavior for them as females in a problem solving activity.

The relationship between the nature and life

Clearly, the girls quickly and aptly built a "relationship" with the natural environment contained within this activity. It is perhaps obvious that the elements of a group of bones capable of being structured into a single skeleton indexes life directly. However, it is also deemed symbolic that the bones themselves and the life process represented by them bespeaks a larger context of what "life" or "being alive" means. This would include all elements of nature, plants, rivers, etc.

Not a single one of the four groups failed to identify with the particular questions they raised in their efforts to know their tools, the bones, as a form of life. They posed questions related to the age, gender, name, cause of death, condition of body, quality and character of life experienced by the horse, issues related to the proper use and care of a horse. The girls even showed concern for the feelings and comfort of this horse, even though it was obviously long since deceased and its remains were in an unrecognizable form when the activity began.

Girls even contrasted their own skeletal structure to that of the horse, and interacted with the bones on a personal level, in their efforts to know and draw similarities between themselves and the horse. They raised questions prior to their identification of it as a horse, as to whether it had been a dinosaur or Girl Scout. They named the skeleton. After it was identified as a horse, they questioned the potential familiarity of this particular horse.

There was no indication that the life represented by this skeleton was unimportant or separate from the activity process of their group or themselves. There were over thirty distinct comments made regarding this story of life. These questions were found throughout the data and appear to represent a natural process congruent with the interactions of these girls while interacting with the elements of nature posed in this activity.

Words as defining structure of action

The words used by the girls as they approached the activity reveal the predominant theme worthy of note in this study. The polarity between what the girls' words were (gross, dirty, ugh), upon first discovering a bone in the mulch, and their simultaneous behavior and affect created a consistent pattern, or theme. Upon all but two occasions when an exclamation was made upon discovering a bone, it was negative. However, in all but a few instances at the completion of their group work, the girls' behavior and/or affect contradicted these exclamations. On several occasions there was a mockery made of the exclaimed aversion. It was as though these girls were verbally complying with the culturally imposed norm of how they *should* respond to interaction with the dirt, bugs, and bones involved in the first phase of the activity.

This would be explained as evidence of the role pre-existing meaning plays in the ongoing meaning making process, and as evidence of semiosis. An example of these incongruent reactions is an exclamation such as "Is this real? Ooooh yuck!" complimented with tone and affective cues that the girl was being sarcastic. Questions such as "These have been cleaned, right?" were also presented as though the girl who was actively engaged in the activity, and showed no non-verbal indication of hesitance, was attempting to verbally qualify a feminine concern so that she would be socially appropriate in her behavior. While smiling, and actively digging or placing bones, girls would make comments such as "This is a gross foot I am digging up," or "bones are disgusting."

At the same time, the girls all posed as a group, proud of their work and endeavor, for a picture with the completed and standing skeleton. This is not a displeased or distant looking group of girls in the photos. They smile and hug, hold, and position themselves in front of and all around the horse skeleton. Clearly there was an incongruence which transcended the data. Throughout the findings this dichotomy appears to indicate an awareness of, but unwillingness to endorse, the cultural norms of feminine response to such things as dirt, bones, and bugs as frightening or disgusting. It can be seen in the roughly eight hours of data represented by this study, that in fact, the girls were involved in redefining what acceptable responses would be to such elements of nature. Their actions and behaviors were clear signs of a more positive and approachable reaction set that became normative throughout the course of the activity.

The meaning of cooperative group process

The third area, supportive and cooperative group process while interacting within nature, was supported through language and behavior as well. There was a multitude of supportive phrases wherein the girls asked for or offered assistance. There were many occasions wherein they simply looked to determine assistance and support from the modeling opportunities made available in the other girls' actions. The role of consensus was apparent, and dominated the findings. While there was not a need to all agree there was a norm of consensus of the group in both determining goals and carrying them out. Often there would be a quality control type of statement offered by a member of the group if the group task appeared to be getting off track.

The importance of setting in defining human behaviors

Dominance in our society is gender-specific, being identified as a masculine-oriented, managerial role. However, in this collaborative setting, dominance was found from the feminine-typed leaders, who commanded some authority over the masculine-typed girls. It was because these girls were engaging in a collaborative environment that they were found to be somewhat hierarchical and confrontational.

Though the group activity at site two appeared to work best with collaboration, interaction, and equal member participation, the masculine-typed girls went through the activity as individuals. The girls were unsure whether this is part of who they were (independent, self-reliant, limited group orientation) or a result of the expectations provided by the natural setting.

The literature is filled with examples of masculine-typed, managerial girl leaders that challenged feminine-typed, empathetic girl leaders (Edwards, 1994; Jordan,

1992). The results from site two revealed that masculine-typed girls were more apt to act independently of others, and that feminine-type girls were more apt to dominate and demand some collaboration. Though masculinity is valued in our society, it is not easily accepted in certain environments. Problem-solving settings like those at site two provided opportunities for both masculine and feminine models to succeed.

A critical result that differs from the previous literature on this subject was identified by observations of the girls engaging in the naturalistic setting. Without an understanding of what occurred between the sites, an accurate understanding of their leadership styles would not have emerged. Future studies of gender roles should include some observational component, so that a better understanding of the intersection between individual and context can result.

In examining these girls engaging in a variety of problem-solving tasks, it became clear that, at this site, the needs mandated by the situation were stronger in moving the activity than the self-described gender roles identified by participants. Gender role patterns were difficult to identify without knowledge of their BSRI typology. BSRI information was helpful in identifying whether girls may have difficulty in interacting with specific tasks mandated by the environment.

Importance for future studies and activities set in nature

Environments and problem-solving strategies need to be examined for the impact they place on the behaviors of their inhabitants (Barker & Wright, 1955; Barker et al, 1978). Future observations need to be performed to identify if similar patterns exist in other problem-solving arenas. It would be valuable to identify whether similar girls' leadership styles would be identified in traditional classrooms, alternative classrooms, male-only small groups, or mixed gender environments.

It is noted in current research that the role of socially constructed meanings are significant in the individual construction of mind:

> *If learning is best conceived, not as learning and remembering*
> *information, but as connections with and within communities of practice,*
> *then we will come to give full value to the collaborative nature of*
> *cognition, investigate the role of culture and community more thoroughly,*
> *and provide better opportunities for nurturing these connections.*
> (Cunningham, 1998).

In this study, the role of group membership in determining a girl's perception of her ability and identity was apparent. It is highlighted well in the following episode. One subject, upon sitting down to take the first gender identity scale, began to cry. This was prior to the group activity and she stated that she felt she could not do well on any kind of paper "test", even when it was explained to her that there were no right or wrong answers. After completing the group activity it was assumed by the researchers that she would not wish to take the follow up scale. However, she came and asked for one, and when questioned as to whether or not she was comfortable taking it indicated clearly, "I can do it now, I can do this because I am part of the group and the group is doing it."

Issues related to experiential and outdoor programming

Lakoff and Johnson (1999) have presented the basis of cognition and learning as a metaphorical process. Definitively, we know that communities of learners utilize metaphors not only to understand themselves, but to teach. It is the nature of socially constructed meaning to be encapsulated in the metaphorical process itself. The semiotic perspective enables focusing on the metaphor as it transfers meaning from one sign to another, and to hold the capacity to alter existing beliefs.

Quinby (1992) provides one example, in regards to the interaction between the feminine gender role and nature, he says a fundamental ecofeminist concept is that of the web of life. Plumwood (1993) on a basis of feminine relationships to nature, alludes to the web of life metaphor. She points out that western society has taken such a deeply entrenched view of nature being "no more than a resource for human ends," and having "its significance and value conferred by or through human interests." The metaphor of humanity as part of an inter-connective, web-like, system is essentially lost to western society. It is useful to note that the very elements that Plumwood (1993) cites are indeed closely related to those (relationship with nature, cooperative interaction within nature endeavors, and positive, engaging interest inspired by that interaction) which arose from the data which we collected in our study.

Facilitators need to be attentive in their work with participants in natural environments. They should also identify that there is an ongoing evolution of meaning that is made regarding the relationship basis of human interaction with and in nature for both feminine and masculine identities. This awareness can become an intentional element of that facilitation process. Questions and concerns this awareness raises which need to be further explored by professionals in the field and research include: Does the set up of an activity assume and bias the process of the participants in their approach to elements of nature? In what manner might the interaction which is addressed in that processing become valuable in the structuring of social meaning about the nature of human relationships to nature?

The impact of the group meaning making process and the role of the gender specific contributions is an important focus for the training of facilitators. Cognizant, intentional implementation of this factor is essential in the competent work of the outdoor professional.

References

Barker, R.G. et al. (1978) *Habitats, Environments, and Human Behavior.* San Francisco, CA: Jossey-Bass.

Barker, R.G. & Wright, H.F. (1955) *Midwest and its children.* San Francisco, CA: Jossey-Bass.

Bem, S.L. (1978) *Bem Sex-Role Inventory: Manual.* Palo Alto, CA: Consulting Psychology Press.

Bem, S.L. (1981) 'Gender schema theory: A cognitive account of sex typing' *Psychological Review,* 88, 354-364.

Brophy, Jere (1999) 'A model of values aspects of motivation.' *Educational Psychologist.* Mahwah, NJ: Lawrence Erlbaum Assoc.

Cunningham, D. J. (1998) 'Cognition as semiosis: The role of inference.' *Theory and Psychology,* 8, 827-840.

Edwards, C.A. (1994) 'Leadership in-groups of school-age girls.' *Developmental Psychology,* 30, 920-927.

Jordan, D.J. (1992) 'Effective leadership for girls and women in outdoor recreation.' *Journal of Physical Education and Research Development,* 2, 61-64.

Kahn, P.H. (1999) *The human relationship with nature.* Boston, MA: MIT Press.

Kellert, S.R. (1997) *Kinship to mastery: Biophilia in human evolution and development.* Washington, DC: Island Press.

Lakoff, G. & Johnson, M. (1999) *Philosophy in the flesh.* New York, NY: Basic Books.

Lemke, J.L. (1987) Social semiotics and science education. *The American Journal of Semiotics.* 5(2), 217-232.

Lemke, J.L. (1990) *Talking science: language learning and values.* Ablex: NY.

Plumwood, Val. (1993). *Feminism and the mastery of nature.* London and New York: Routledge.

Quinby, Lee. (1992) *'Ecofeminism: saving the earth from patriarchy.'* *Guardian,* March 18, 1992, 10-11.

Rogoff, Barbara (1990) *Apprenticeship in thinking.* New York: Oxford University Press.

Strayer, F.F. & Trudel, M. (1984). 'Developmental changes in the nature of social dominance among young children.' *Ethology and Sociobiology,* 5, 279-295.

Thibault, P. J. (1990) 'The making of meaning on talking science, language, learning and values.' *The Semiotic Review of Books.* 4(3).

Warren, Karen J. (Editor) (1996) *Ecological feminist philosophies: an overview of the issues.* Bloomington and Indianapolis: Indiana University Press.

Wertsch, James V. (1985) *Vygotsky and the social formation of mind.* Cambridge, MA: Harvard University Press.

Chapter 12: Encouraging Values for Sustainable Living

Geoff Cooper

There is something chilling in the idea of the majority of young people today believing that the future (their future) is going to be a worse time to live in than the present.
(Jonathon Porritt, in Huckle and Sterling, 1996: xi)

Young people, society and the planet

We live in a society divided by education and wealth. An increasing number of young people fail in our education system and find themselves on the outside, dispossessed. Our prevailing culture measures success in terms of material possessions. The growth of unemployment, homelessness and crime and the break-up of family life are some of the obvious signs of social disintegration. Many sections of the population are disaffected, they are failures in the present system, they are not valued and often they gain recognition only by confronting the system which has dispossessed them.

Young people leaving school face many uncertainties. They are encouraged to consume; to strive for glamour, speed, excitement. These can only be achieved through well-paid jobs. Yet for many these jobs are not available. Does our education system address any of these issues? Are we educating young people to feel at home in a society where there are fewer opportunities for work? Are we challenging an economic system based on greed and growth and which is failing to support the basic needs of a section of our people and others on the same planet?

The same process that has produced these social and economic upheavals in Britain is provoking ecological uncertainty at a global level. We are consuming the Earth's resources at an unsustainable rate and through our greed and waste we are threatening the global systems we depend upon. Our abuse of the rainforest and the oceans arises from the same system that disregards global poverty and the needs of the under-privileged in our own society.

There is a lack of purpose in many people's lives. We have become removed from the natural processes of living. We insulate ourselves from the rhythms of nature, from the seasons, from day and night, from the land and sea, from other life. We surround ourselves with surrogates, second-hand experiences, vicarious pleasures.

These are poor compensations for feeling part of the planet, for having a spiritual connection, a kinship with the Earth. There is a need to reconsider our lives, to look for ways of living which are not to the detriment of other people or harmful to ecosystems. We need to redefine 'quality of life' and adopt more sustainable lifestyles. At a time when formal education is doing little to promote values, outdoor education has a vital role to play in creating a new vision for the future.

Towards sustainability

The term 'sustainability' dates from the publication of The World Conservation Strategy (IUCN 1980). It has become increasingly important as a concept since the United Nations Earth Summit in Rio in 1992, when governments throughout the world drew up priorities for action on environment and development. There have been many attempts to define sustainability. An early definition and one often quoted is:

development that meets the needs of the present without compromising the ability of future generations to meet their needs (World Commission for Environment and Development, 1987)

This definition was a starting point but is now considered to be too narrowly centred on the needs of people. More recent definitions have stressed the importance of improving the quality of our lives without harming the ecosystems we depend upon.

Sustainability is not just about environmental protection but also includes sharing resources more equitably and improving the quality of our lives in terms of access to health care, education, justice, work, leisure and democracy. Sustainability relates to people from all sections of society and countries of the world. It is concerned with both present and future generations. It implies the need for a new ethic based on co-operation rather than competition, quality of life rather than standard of living and community rather than individual interest.

Educating for sustainability

Governments have recognised the role of education in this process and many have signed up to Agenda 21 of the 1992 Rio Summit which states that education is critical for promoting sustainable development and improving the capacity of people to address sustainable development issues (UNCED, 1992). The introduction of the National Curriculum in schools in England and Wales created few opportunities for this new education in a system overburdened with knowledge-based learning and the values of the free market. It was proposed that environmental education could be taught as a cross-curricular theme through the ten foundation subjects. Although it was possible to teach aspects of knowledge and understanding, little attention was given to the development of the appropriate skills and values which are fundamental to encouraging a more sustainable lifestyle. In Scotland environmental education has a more central place in the 5-14 Curriculum. Although it is largely knowledge and skills based it also aims to develop informed attitudes and values relating to the care and conservation of the environment (Scottish Office, Education Department, 1991). There are now more hopeful signs in England. A Panel for Education for Sustainable Development was set up by the Government in 1998 and it has prepared a report as a contribution to the current National Curriculum Review (Panel for Education for Sustainable Development, 1998). In the report the panel suggests that "education for sustainable development enables people to develop the knowledge, values and skills to participate in decisions about the way we do things individually and collectively, both locally and globally, that will improve the quality of life now without damaging the planet for the future".

The report proposes that education for sustainable development should follow seven principles:

1. Interdependence - of society, economy and the natural environment, from local to global.
2. Citizenship and stewardship - rights and responsibilities, participation and co-operation.

3. Needs and rights of future generations.

4. Diversity - cultural, social, economic and biological.

5. Quality of life, equity and justice.

6. Sustainable change - development and carrying capacity.

7. Uncertainty, and precaution in action.

Underlying these seven concepts are sets of values, skills and understandings. Although the report places more emphasis on values than an earlier UNEP-UK document on education for sustainability (Sterling and EDET, 1992) many are expressed in terms of 'appreciating' a concept or situation. For example, appreciating that the quality of life of future generations is endangered or enhanced by actions we take now, rather than exploring a broad set of values.

The significance of values in educating for sustainability

Education for sustainability is a broad concept which includes aspects of personal and social education, citizenship, economic understanding and moral and spiritual considerations. To assess the importance of developing values for sustainability it is helpful to introduce a model (Cooper, 1998):

Figure 1. The process of educating for sustainability.

This framework is based on the three simple considerations:

(i) I recognise the need to act - *Awareness*.
(ii) I know how to act - *Empowerment*.
(iii) I will act - *Commitment*.

Let's consider these a little further:

(i) Awareness.
There are two aspects of awareness. It is important to have a knowledge and understanding of issues influencing the environment and our quality of life. For example, it is necessary to have some ecological understanding to appreciate the intricate relationships between plants, animals and ourselves. But it is also vital to have knowledge of political structures to appreciate how and why decisions are made which influence these relationships. So we can understand that the removal of hedgerows means a loss of habitats for a range of insects, birds and small mammals but we also need to understand that this environmental issue has been produced by underlying economic considerations such as the need to obtain higher crop yields from greater mechanisation allowed by large fields.

The second aspect of awareness is concerned with feelings and having a personal connection with the environment. We have become separated from nature, we think of ourselves as apart from, rather than a part of, nature yet our minds and bodies still respond to rhythms of day and night, lunar cycles and the changes of the seasons. There is an urgency to develop this biological awareness through encouraging a personal response to the environment. Understanding comes through feelings as much as knowledge. This aspect of awareness could be the key to influencing values and attitudes.

(ii) Empowerment.
People often feel cut off from the decisions that affect their lives. There is a need to encourage greater responsibility. Such empowerment is based on developing self esteem, confidence and motivation. Many people have poor self worth, they have failed in a school system designed to measure a particular type of intelligence and academic learning. They are given little responsibility in this system, there is a lack of identity and motivation is low. The first step is to reverse this process, to develop self esteem and to improve confidence.

Empowerment also involves encouraging a range of skills and competencies. Effective communication is essential and for many oral literacy may be more important than the written word. Interpersonal skills are increasingly important in an age when knowledge can be acquired at the press of a button. Problem solving, lateral and critical thinking and negotiation will be valuable to those involved in decision making. Creativity and vision for the future are also required to inspire positive change. These skills are often underdeveloped at school. Knowledge of ecological and political systems also forms a prerequisite for empowerment.

(iii) Commitment.
Sometimes we are aware of an issue that needs addressing, we have the ability and confidence to take action but we still do not do anything about it. Our commitment to act is strongly related to our value system. Values are the key to encouraging changes leading to more sustainable lifestyles. What are these values that underpin a more sustainable existence?

Core values

Values can be considered as underlying beliefs and principles that shape our attitudes and behaviour. The dominant value system in Western countries is based on material possessions, social position and external appearance. There are, however, higher 'core' values recognised by many different cultures throughout the world which form the basis for a more peaceful and spiritual life. I believe that these same values underpin the concept of sustainability.

Brahma Kumaris World Spiritual University, a non-governmental organisation affiliated to the United Nations, has developed an international education programme called "Living Values". This programme (Brahma Kumaris, 1995) describes twelve higher values: co-operation, freedom, happiness, honesty, humility, love, peace, respect, responsibility, simplicity, tolerance and unity - which are common to all people. It is believed that these values are the basis of human dignity and self worth and their adoption leads to deeper understanding, a better quality of life and a more peaceful and sustainable world.

Writers from the time of the ancient philosophers have considered the importance of higher values in guiding our lives. Plato, for example, argued that the three deepest values were goodness, truth and beauty and that by adopting these values people can transcend self interest. In Buddhist teachings nature and people are inseparable, a decline in morality leads to a deterioration in the environment. The condition of people and the earth are determined largely by our values, priorities and choices (Lily de Silva 1992). Other writers suggest that we can learn from direct experience of nature. David Orr (1994), for example, believes that the earth can teach us essential values such as silence, humility, holiness, connectedness, courtesy, celebration, giving, restoration, obligation and wildness.

The importance of these underlying values is not to provide a code or ideology but to show alternatives to our dominant value system based on possessiveness, greed and selfishness. These values provide a structure or guidance for us to explore our own beliefs and principles. Most outdoor leaders will be more comfortable in providing opportunities for young people to reflect on and clarify their own values (Burns and Lamont 1995) than to present a creed to be followed.

Contribution of outdoor leaders

Outdoor leaders have several advantages when working with young people. They often work with small, well-motivated groups in informal situations. Unlike classroom teachers they do not face the constraints of the formal curriculum, exams, timetables or the bell. They have a good image, enthusiasm and work in interesting and challenging environments. As a result their teaching can be influential and inspiring.

In the model of education for sustainability presented earlier leaders have an important role in raising environmental, social and political awareness and also in encouraging the skills and knowledge that help to empower young people. Outdoor leaders have for many years recognised the value of their work in personal and social development. These skills are fundamental and form the basis of good citizenship. However, there may be an even more important area of work concerned with encouraging young people to explore their own values. This may lead to commitment in changing personal and social behaviour towards more sustainable lifestyles.

It should be possible for leaders to address all the core values through their work but clearly some may be easier to explore in outdoor education. I would like to suggest a few examples:

1. Reconnection.

The outdoors provides opportunities to experience *freedom, happiness and humility* through contact with the natural world. We can respond to the elements - wind, water, rock, sky - and the natural rhythms and begin to appreciate the interdependency of life on the planet. This may help to re-build our connections with the earth and for some could be the key to gaining commitment for the environment.

2. Co-operation.

Learning in schools is usually based on competition. This may be appropriate to train a top class athlete or a Mastermind contestant but it is totally inadequate for educating for community living in a rapidly changing society. Teamwork and co-operation can be developed in many ways in the outdoors, for example through problem solving activities, group fieldwork and mountain expeditions. *Trust and empathy* can result from living and working closely together in a small group. Such values are transferable and of fundamental importance to sustainable living.

3. Responsibility.

Outdoor education often places young people in situations where they have to take responsibility for their own actions. They may experience real situations where failure to act responsibly will have unfortunate consequences for themselves and others in their group.

4. Tolerance.

Moving through the outdoors we confront real issues, for example there may be land use conflicts such as the need to protect an ancient woodland threatened by a new road or the impact of a wind farm on a small rural community weighed against the benefits of renewable energy. Through activities such as fieldwork and drama we can begin to explore the complexities of such issues, appreciate the underlying social, economic and political pressures and make our own judgements. Exploring real issues helps to clarify our own values and may lead to more tolerant attitudes to other points of view.

5. Simplicity.

Chris Loynes (1996) has argued that outdoor adventure is being packaged and commercialised and this process dissociates people from their experience of community and place. There is, however, the opportunity in the outdoors to experience a simpler, healthier and uncommercialised existence. Wild or quiet places can provide an antidote to mass culture with its 5five minute soundbites. There is time to reflect, to put our lives into perspective, to consider our values. Outdoor leaders are in a position to introduce young people to the concept of *quality of life* and to encourage them to assess their basic needs and values.

6. Reflection.

Experiences in the outdoors provide many opportunities for reflection. In a culture based on constant noise and action this is of fundamental importance to the development of core values. Reflection is relevant to all aspects of our lives and constant reviewing and planning helps us to cope with change.

These are just a few examples of how outdoor leaders can help young people address their own values and encourage appropriate values for sustainability. It should be stressed, however, that the actions of the leaders themselves and how they demonstrate their own values may be as important as the outdoor activities and programmes in changing young people.

References

Brahma Kumaris (1995) *Living Values: A Guidebook,* London: Brahma Kumaris.

Burns, S. and Lamont, G. (1995) *Values and Visions: A Handbook for Spiritual Development and Global Awareness,* London: Hodder and Stoughton.

Cooper, G. (1998) *Outdoors with Young People: A Leader's guide to Outdoor Activities, the Environment and Sustainability,* Dorset: Russell House.

de Silva, L. (1992) 'The hills wherein my soul delights', in Batchelor, M. & Brown, K. *Buddhism and Ecology,* 18-30 London: Cassell.

Huckle, J. & Sterling, S. (eds) (1996) *Education for Sustainability.* London: Earthscan Publications.

IUCN (1980) *World Conservation Strategy,* IUCN/UNEP/WWF, Gland.

Loynes, C. (1996) 'Adventure in a Bun', *Journal of Adventure Education and Outdoor Leadership,* 13 (2), 52-57.

Orr, D. (1994) *Earth in Mind: On Education, Environment and the Human Prospect,* Washington DC: Island Press.

Panel for Education for Sustainable Development (1998) *Education for Sustainable Development in the Schools Sector,* CEE/DEA/RSPB/WWF-UK.

Scottish Office, Education Department (1991) *5-14 Working Paper No.13, Environmental Studies,* Edinburgh: HMSO.

Sterling, S. and EDET (1992) *Good Earth-Keeping: Education, Training and Awareness for a Sustainable Future,* London: UNEP-UK.

UNCED (1992) 'Promoting Education, Public Awareness and Training', *Chapter 36, Agenda 21,* London: Regency Press.

World Commission for Environment and Development (1987) *Our Common Future,* (The Bruntland Report), Oxford: Oxford University Press.

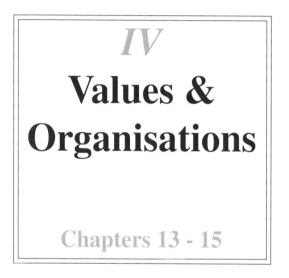

IV
Values &
Organisations

Chapters 13 - 15

Values & Organisations: Chapters 13 - 15

Chapter 13: Shared Values: Culture, Community and Centre Management

Peter Barnes

It is often heard that the outdoor industry consists of a community of like minded people (Barnes, 1999a). This reaches its zenith in the community of an outdoor centre, particularly one with residential staff. Given the implied power of the residential experience, it would be expected that the community of the outdoor centre must play an important part in the overall client experience. But what makes an outdoor centre community and what part does management play in its evolution and maintenance? Paramount to answering these questions is the identification of outdoor staff with their work.

This identification does not, however, happen in isolation. Identification, organisational culture and community are all important parts of a larger equation. To a large extent the two inter-linked factors of culture and community are both a cause and a result of outdoor instructor's identifying with the work they do.

Organisational culture has always been a somewhat tenuous concept to describe. Indeed Williams (1987:87) describes culture itself as being "one of the two or three most complicated words in the English Language". In the context used here, however, it can be simply described as the "particular way of life ... of a people [or] group" (Williams, ibid:90). Given this definition of culture it follows that organisational culture can be described as:

> *the sum of accepted norms and modes of behaviour in an organisation. Staff attitudes and embedded organisational structures combine to create unique cultures in every [organisation]* (O'Leary, 1996:75).

Handy (1997:157-158) expands on this idea when, rather than using the term culture, he talks instead of the American idea of the "soul and personality of an organisation". This he describes as one of those concepts which is largely indefinable but is instantly recognizable when it is met. Positive soul, he says is noticeable for a belief that the organisation is on "some sort of a crusade, not just to make money, but something grander, something worthy of one's commitment, skills and time". In the case of the outdoor industry this sense of a crusade is manifested in a number of ways but most typically through the values of an organisation and critically through a community of shared values. South (1986:1) highlighted this a decade ago when he said that

... one of the greatest impacts on a participant arriving for an adventure programme was ... the vitality of the community of staff living fully to a set of values.

If we accept that outdoor staff bring their own agenda to working in the outdoors and, furthermore, that this agenda is based around ideas of altruism and education as much as about activities it is clear there is a values based paradigm at the heart of the outdoor community (Barnes, 1999a). As with culture, however, community as an ideal is also hard to define. The term has been used in so many different ways that is has become devoid of any real meaning. One aspect about community that is clear is that it carries "warm and favourable connotations" (Newby, 1987:37). This aspect of community can be seen, particularly given the supposed ideals and ethos of many outdoor centres, as the antithesis of a modern, commerce and hedonist oriented, society. Modern society is generally considered to be a community moving away from traditional values and beliefs. The expression 'postmodernism' is increasingly used in an attempt to describe this phenomenon.

Postmodernity is a contentious and often poorly defined, or understood, concept which, despite its ambiguous nature, still manages to form a cornerstone of current philosophical thought (Lyon, 1994; Morgan, 1998). A key feature of postmodernity is that it manages to be both a celebration of, and a reaction against, the relentless onslaught of technology. It is this technology that can be argued to be largely responsible for society's alienation from traditional values and tradition. The postmodern world is one of multiple realities where traditions and values are all ripe for re-negotiation. It is the television commercial and Hollywood movie which now define reality for many in the western world. This mass culture, usually commercial in origin, has bought about a "levelling" (Stewart, 1997:121), or homogeneity, of society on a worldwide scale. The twin foundations of reality and truth, the church and state, have both undergone dramatic changes over recent years. The political structure of western society has largely lost its credibility through the cynicism which started with Watergate and progressed through the Falkland and Gulf wars to the 'sleaze' scandals of the last decade. Populist, 'sound-bite', politics, exemplified by Kennedy and developed by 'New' Labour, have, if anything, compounded this cynicism. Religion, in its turn, has moved away from the traditional centre path and entered an age dominated by the alternatives of fanaticism and fundamentalism or the mysticism of a 'new age'. In the place of these traditional foundations there has evolved an obsession with self, narcissism and open displays of emotion which recently reached its zenith at the death of Diana, Princess of Wales. A feature of this obsession with self has been an unbridled growth of the consumerist society at the cost of productive society. Running through all these changes is the common thread of technology and, in particular, mass communication. The shrinking attention span of a postmodern populace must be grabbed by sound-bite statements and electronic propaganda. If the modern world brought in the age of the three minute pop song then the postmodern world is the age of the advertisement.

In the postmodern world identification of self is manifested through the influence of advertising. Shopping is a prime leisure activity and corporate logos are worn with pride as a way of saying 'I belong'. Although postmodern society can be seen to be eclectic, pluralist and diverse in composition it can also be seen as being bound together by a single, albeit ambiguous, world-wide culture. Even in remote areas of the third world the culture of the 'Coca-Cola generation' is based around Hollywood images and a lifestyle defined by the logos of Levi jeans and the Colours of Benetton. Simmel (1858-1918) pre-empted the concerns of many people when he observed this attachment to the world of consumerism as devaluing the human condition.

How, then, do the conflicts of an age of postmodernity affect the outdoor education industry? In the first instance, to use an example which exemplifies the age of the commercial, the "Pepsi-Max" era is upon us. Courses are shorter, activities need to be ever more exciting; the adrenaline buzz rules in the battle to attract 'customers'. Centres and organisations which for decades preached the value of the expedition and the 'solo' experience are introducing activities such as snow-boarding, mountain biking and ever higher rope courses. Commercialism has become ever more pervasive. Even more than this, however, traditional values are being held up to examination and questions are being asked about the effectiveness of truths that have long been held as sacrosanct (Wurdinger, 1997). The outdoor industry is asking itself if it can continue to exist in its present form. At the time of writing, the outdoor community in the UK is struggling with the concept and meaning of professionalism and ever encroaching legislation is seen by many as threatening the very nature of outdoor education itself. Even more fundamentally, Furedi (1997) reflects Simmel's concern and asserts that society is now so obsessed with safety that our fundamental development and growth as human beings is endangered. This obsession with safety, paradoxically, has reached its zenith in the field of outdoor education. Excitement in safety[1] is the new watchword, risk is rapidly becoming the forbidden subject. In the nihilist version of a postmodern world the values of Kurt Hahn (Barnes, 1999b) are evolving into the consumerist values of the theme park.

It is against this background of change and commercialism that the outdoor community must be examined. Relating this aspect of the outdoor centre community to the values mentioned by South (1986) it is clear that community can be regarded as being much more than the simple dictionary definition of "the people living in one locality" (Collins English Dictionary, 1990:320). The outdoor centre community implies that staff not only live together but also share common values, beliefs and goals. Frequently, these values and beliefs are at odds with the society in which the outdoor industry must function. Communities in tightly knit outdoor centres often protect themselves by traditions which defy the commercial environment. Certainly the argument put forward by Emile Durkheim (1961, cited in Rollinson et al, 1998:533) that myths and rituals, in a sociological setting, are symptomatic of underlying beliefs and values would support this implication. Often, these myths and rituals are seen most clearly in the role of morning meetings/gatherings, whether amongst the staff or with clients. An observer seeing a morning meeting for the first time can usually get a fairly good snapshot of the underlying values of a centre. Questions such as: are all the staff involved; are the senior staff involved; is the meeting a two-way process; is there a 'positive feel' to the meeting; what information is given out and do clients have a role in the meeting are all valuable clues.

The importance and relevance of organisational culture to staff motivation can not be underestimated. The ethos and goals of an organisation are reciprocal and closely inter-twined with the culture of that organisation. Hersey and Blanchard (cited in Teschner and Wolter, 1990:279) observe that:

the closer ... the individual's goals and objectives to the organisation's goals, the greater will be the organisational performance.

The implications are, that in an industry where it is often assumed that staff motivation is largely intrinsic, a shared sense of communal ideals and vocation is of much greater significance than extrinsic motivators such as salary. Hopkins and Putnam (1993:221) agree with the significance of organisational culture and point out that:

Managers need to pay careful attention to the culture of their organisations; and to focus on 'culture' as an explicit part of their work.

A major impact on organisational culture can occur when the financial direction of the organisation is changed through such events as the employment of new management, organisational take-over or financial crisis. One way in which financial difficulty is often handled is an increase in formal structures, less egalitarianism and greater psychological distance between managers and employees. In such cases there may arise a sub-culture within an organisation which is at odds with the culture being imposed, or suggested, by the senior staff (Morgan, 1997). Gossip, always a potent force in outdoor centres, can play a major function in such sub-cultures. It is, however, possible that sub-cultures are not always negative, in the case of large departmentalised organisations they can even be positive (Rollinson et al, 1998). However, sub-cultures formed through unwelcome change imposed upon a workforce can be very divisive to an organisation's development and certainly to its internal harmony.

It is important to remember that organisational culture is "an active, living phenomenon through which people jointly create and recreate the worlds in which they live" (Morgan, 1997:141). As such, it can clearly be seen as a phenomenon which is constantly in flux and subject to change. This aspect of organisational culture is sometimes referred to as organisational climate (Rollinson et al, 1998) with culture being relatively stable and climate being subject to change. Organisational climate also has a more direct bearing on the lives of the workforce with culture being less tangible. A good example of this in recent times has been the increased emphasis on safety in many outdoor centres which has led, in some cases, to a reduction in staff autonomy and an increase in centralised control (Jesset, 1995; cited in Barnes, 1999a:60). Thus, combining an increased amount of centralised control over safety issues with a period of financial difficulty and restructuring would have an almost inevitable impact on the managerial/employer - staff/employee relationship. Sadly, such a situation has become almost routine at many outdoor centres in recent years. In this example it can be seen that the culture of a typical outdoor centre, usually revolving around ideals of personal development, has remained relatively stable but the climate, the move to greater safety and financial controls has changed.

In addition to these fluctuations in organisational climate it must be considered that employment, in modern western societies, has largely developed as a result of industrialisation and capitalism. A major feature of capitalism is that work, or labour, is generally regarded as one half of a wage-labour relationship. Even in 'enlightened' companies which utilise maximum employee involvement, the essential structure of a capitalist based organisation is oriented around profit. Part of the effect of this need for profit is that the wage-labour element of the organisation becomes subject to the labour market. This means, in effect, recruiting and employing staff in the most effective way for the benefit of the capitalist aims of the employer. One of the major results of this has been the creation of the employer-employee relationship, the well known 'them and us' situation. Despite this it appears, almost as an axiomatic truth, that people are defined by what they do. As Handy (1997:92) writes, "work has always been a major strand in people's self-description, and, therefore, a major component of their identity". This is even more so in cases, such as the outdoor industry, where people are not only identified *by* their jobs but also, on a personal level, identify *with* their jobs. Allied to this is the unusual vocational element of outdoor work where, even when the capitalist, or economic, imperative applies, there is usually a sense of shared purpose. Moreover, many outdoor organisations, even in the commercial sector, work on a largely 'not for profit' basis which leads to a greater staff identification with the goals of the organisation. The identification of outdoor staff with their employer's aims is, however, not absolute. It is still possible that the "dominance of the economic imperative" (Handy, ibid:4) which governs the working environment can cause alienation and subsequent strain on the employer-employee relationship.

As already discussed, in recent times the sense of community in many outdoor centres has been under attack from a number of sources, many financial in nature. Amongst these has been the cost-cutting measures of making staff live out of the centre (thus realising valuable client space) and an increased use of freelance staff throughout the industry. In addition, professional managers have often failed to bridge the gap between vocationally-motivated staff and financially minded employers. It is in the implementation of financial constraints and a different ethos "that managers have the power to corrupt the sense of community amongst [teaching staff] necessary for the successful flourishing of a practice" (Halliday, 1990:49).

Managers do not, of course, only have the power to corrupt, they also have the power to create. As Morgan (1997:147) writes, "the fundamental task facing managers rests in creating appropriate systems of shared meaning that can mobilize the efforts of people in pursuit of desired aims and objectives". The critical element of this statement is that the meanings, which underpin organisational culture, are "shared". It is where there is a breakdown in the understanding between employers and employees as to what is being shared that tension arises. An example in the outdoor industry would be where staff believe themselves to be in sympathy with the aims of the organisation and working on a 'vocational' basis but the management adopts a more organisational approach and treats the staff as employees rather than kindred workers.

This critical management-employee relationship is reflected at the core of two opposing views of management philosophy; unitarist and pluralist (Fox, 1974, cited in Rollinson et al, 1998:682). Unitarist management revolves around the idea of the organisation as an harmonious entity in which there is a common purpose and aim at all levels of the organisation. This is contrasted to the pluralist approach which recognises that organisations are made up of groups of people which, while they may follow the company line in public, have their own agendas. It might be thought that outdoor centres being, typically, quite small would have little room to accommodate a pluralist agenda. It is recognised, however, that outdoor staff may have their own purposes in working for a centre, which might have little to do with the aims of that particular organisation (Jesset, 1995 cited in Barnes 1999a:62). Typically these aims tend to revolve around the opportunities to gain experience and qualifications. Pluralist managers recognise that conflicts may exist because of staff having private, legitimate, purposes to pursue. They also recognise, however, that these private aims can be used to the companies' benefit (Rollinson et al, 1998). In-house training would be a good example of this mutual satisfaction of separate aims.

It is only when there is harmony between an employers expectations, the goals of an organisation and the agenda of the staff that a positive sense of community can flourish. It needs to be recognised that there may be pluralist agendas held by different staff within a single organisation and there may also be active sub-cultures. Often, for example, there is a strong anti-commercial sub-culture in an outdoor centre. Despite this the centre manager must balance the beliefs and values of the staff with the needs and demands of the organisation. Even if conflicting values need to be accommodated there must be accordance, or at least acceptance, of the fundamental core of the community, the values and ethos of the organisation as a whole. Without this, at best the organisation will fail to function harmoniously and, at worst, it will tear itself apart.

Notes

1. David Jamieson MP, in an open letter to the Fifth Outdoor Forum (1997) wrote that "Activities should be challenging without being hazardous and should provide excitement without danger". Interestingly, Sir Chris Bonington in his opening address to the Fourth Outdoor Forum (1996) argued for exactly the opposite case and maintained that hazard and danger are central to the true outdoor experience.

References

Barnes, P. (1999a) 'The Motivation of Staff in the Outdoor Education Industry.'
    Unpublished Ph.D. thesis, Glasgow: University of Strathclyde.
Barnes, P. (1999b) 'The Development of Values in Outdoor Education.' in this text.
Furedi, F. (1997) *Culture of Fear.* London: Cassell.
Halliday, J. (1990) *Markets, Managers and Theory in Education.* London: The Falmer Press.
Handy, C. (1997) *The Hungry Spirit.* London: Hutchinson.
Hopkins, D. and Putnam, R. (1993) *Personal Growth Through Adventure.*
    London: David Fulton Publishers.
Lyon, D. (1994) *Postmodernity.* Milton Keynes: Open University Press.
Morgan, G. (1997) *Images of Organisation.* Sage Publications: Thousand Oaks.
Morgan, D. (1998) 'How leading sociologists evaluate the contribution of
    postmodernism.' in *BSA Network.* Oct '98, 6-7.
Newby, H. (1987) *Comparison and Change: Community.* Open University course:
    An introduction to sociology (block 3:20). Milton Keynes:
    Open University Press.
O'Leary, T. (1996) 'Nae fur the likes of us - Poverty, Agenda 21 and Scotland's
    environmental non-governmental organisations' in *Scottish Affairs.* 16, 62-80.
Rollinson, D., Broadfield, A., Edwards, D. (1998) *Organisational Behaviour and Analysis.*
    Harlow: Addison-Wesley.
South, G. (1986) Editorial, *Journal of Adventure Education and Outdoor Leadership,* 3(1),
    15.
Stewart, R. (ed) (1997) *Ideas That Shaped Our World.* London: Marshall Publishing.
Teschner, D. P. and Wolter, J. J. (1990) 'Beyond minimum competencies: Toward
    an integrated model of staff development.' in Miles, J. & Priest, S. (1990)
    Adventure Education. State College, PA: Venture Publishing. 275-284.
Williams, R. (1987) *Keywords.* London: Flamingo Books.
Wurdinger, S. (1997) *Philosophical Issues in Adventure Education.* Iowa: Kendall/Hunt.

Chapter 14: Commercial Considerations

Maurice Dybeck

Any value-based project, from helping the homeless to running a playgroup, will involve commercial considerations: the cost, the level of the activity, who is to pay for it, and the ability of the providers to deliver what is required. The experience of the Brathay Hall Trust, over the past 50 years exemplifies the need to recognise, and to keep a realistic balance between, commercialism and altruism. This chapter[1] examines a particular period in Brathay's history - the 1980s and the early 1990s - when commercial pressures were such that it became very difficult to maintain the programme of youth development for which the place had been founded in the early post-war years. But first we must examine altruism and the idealism of the founder.

Francis Scott was a highly successful businessman. He followed his father in developing the Provincial Insurance Company into a major national institution. In one field, car insurance, he was astute enough to develop policies in the early days of motoring and to ride on the expansion of motoring in the subsequent fifty years. His friend and business advisor was John Maynard Keynes. When the firm moved to Kendal in 1920 Scott became interested in youth work. He was already in love with the outdoors, though a leg injury meant that it was sailing, rather than walking, that was his main sport. He founded Brathay in 1946 stating:

"The idea that ... good fortune called for a share of the family wealth to be allocated for charitable purposes has no doubt been the origin of most of the existing Charitable Trusts..." (Scott, 1967)

Brathay's sole aim and purpose was:

... the opening up of young people's minds to the possibilities of living adventurously in the world of physical activity as well as in the world of the spirit. (ibid.)

The residential centre at Brathay Hall had, for its first 25 years, a staple four-week course for boys mainly from industry, an Exploration Group running up to 17 expeditions a year and, in the middle years, a very active Field Study Centre. The success of these activities is well documented and their influence on other developments nationally and internationally is widely accepted (Dybeck, 1996). But none of the work could have taken place in the way it did without the substantial 'commercial' backing of the Francis Scott Trust. For the first 20 years that underwrite amounted to around 50% of the total running costs.

With his business experience no one could have been more aware than Scott of the need for an enterprise to be adequately costed. But budgeting for education or youth work is very different from selling insurance and, to promote some new cause in this area, beliefs may have to be backed up with not only salesmanship, but also with some external source of money. Scott was particularly keen to see that industrialists were persuaded of the value of Brathay courses for their young apprentices, whose own work environment was so different from that of the Lake District. He knew they would only come if the price was right. In other words, if the price was subsidised. The approach worked and Brathay thrived. In modern parlance, Scott was seeking to provide what would be seen by industrialists as 'value for money', with the 'value' to the industrialists being in the better-orientated employees.

Being sheltered by a 50% subsidy had many advantages. Brathay was free from a heavy constraint to make ends meet. Courses would still run even if numbers were low. Significantly, Brathay was able to experiment and develop a unique style. The courses were superficially similar to those of Outward Bound, but Brathay was able to diversify into a variety of experiences beyond the mountains: there was sailing and rowing, and also art and drama leading to exhibitions and impressive performances on every course. The attraction and relevance of such activities to shipyard steel workers may not have been obvious and, to many, would hardly be regarded as sale-able, unless offered at an attractive price. It was the value of the charitable subsidy which allowed, in the 1950s, the foundation of a variant: the six-week Brathay 'Oxfordshire' schools courses out of which, it could be argued, grew the movement towards school residentials. Similarly, the favourable seed-bed in which the Field Study Centre was planted in 1967, was one provided by Scott with help from other charitable foundations.

The extent to which, today, any organisation should be dependent upon substantial charitable backing, needs examination. At one end there are those, like Oxfam, whose whole existence is naturally dependent upon charity. Somewhere down the scale are public libraries, whose funding we expect to come, in the main, from taxes. However, it is worthwhile to remember that it was a millionaire Scot, Andrew Carnegie, with his vision of culture for the masses, who stimulated this movement. In our own time it has been successful entrepreneurs like Lord Sainsbury who have made possible extensions to our cultural resources in both city and university. Most people would aver that education is too precious to be left in the market place, and indeed it has been the recipient of more philanthropy than any other cause. Thanks to this, consumers have been sheltered from having to consider what is the true price of education.

Now, in the case of Brathay, once an experiment has got beyond its launch is it right and proper that those who benefit from it - either the sponsors or the participants themselves - should be asked to pay the full price? By the 1980s it was clear that the trustees of the Francis Scott Trust were beginning to think so. The subvention had been steadily reduced to around 11% of the annual turnover and the Scott trustees were looking to diversify the use to which they put their monies, helping local projects such as arts centres in Kendal and, later, more general social work. Brathay, they said, had come of age and should be progressively less dependent upon its parent benefactor.

For a while, the reduction in aid did not seriously affect the Brathay operations. They were successful and expanding. Well-filled courses meant that costs could more easily be covered. More importantly in the long term the capacity for innovation led to a highly significant breakthrough in the early '70s when Brathay youth training methods were adapted for use with adult managers. The logic of this expansion, in terms of its trust deed, was that such work influenced those who, through their leadership, influenced young people. The new moves meant that there could be, for this new clientele, a more realistic pricing policy. The cost benefits to firms, in terms of leadership development, increased teamwork and efficiency, were clear. However, Brathay had no monopoly on this innovation which paved the way for other organisations who entered the field of what became known as Development Training. Ironically, it was this very success that led the Scott Trust to initiate further cuts in the subvention. The trust stated that if Brathay could pay its way with adult courses then it would have less need of charitable support.

Youth courses

Against this pattern of declining charitable support but successful work with adult managers it is important to look at the changing pattern of demand in youth work. Some of these changes could be described as the 'Lancashire Cotton Mill Syndrome'. Brathay, through its opportunity to experiment, had set up new patterns of working - and then found that its work had been exported elsewhere. Unlike industry, who usually jealously guard copyright, Brathay, with Scott's encouragement, was proud to see its ideas replicated elsewhere. (This was long before the current concerns about ownership of intellectual property.) The earliest example of such an 'export' was the Oxfordshire schools courses. After a few years Oxfordshire set up their own courses in Patterdale. The Field Study Centre, one of the first to concentrate on schools, rapidly became popular and oversubscribed. As a result it was soon in competition with the new LEA centres, and even the YHA.

Traditional Brathay four-week courses declined partly because firms were building up their own 'character training' resources either in-house or with new providers, many of whom could offer a cheaper package. There was also the time factor. Perhaps the same objectives could be achieved in a shorter period. Firms no longer felt they could afford to send employees away for a whole month. Value for money became the watchword in this, as in all production plans. Even the Brathay Exploration Group, which had pioneered world-wide and helped other groups especially through the Young Explorers' Trust, was now feeling the pinch from competition. Intermediate Treatment work with young offenders had been highly successful, leading to the foundation of the Eagle Crag Centre in the Brathay grounds, funded largely by the

Rainer Foundation. But, again, this was to be replicated, more cheaply, by social workers on their home ground.

Salvation seemed to be forthcoming in 1978 through the government's Manpower Services Commission unemployment training schemes. Brathay ran courses for the Youth Opportunities Programme and for a while these restored the youth numbers enabling Brathay to make a name in this new field, particularly in training the trainers at its Accredited Training Centre. True, this was an operation in which 'commercialism' called the tune. The government wanted youngsters off the books of the unemployed and was prepared (at first) to pay generously for anyone offering a viable programme. Hopefully, Brathay, with its own altruism, was able to lift the stakes above mere fitting of trainees to (potential) jobs. As in its earliest courses back in the '40s the vision was the wider one of training for life. Ironically, it was the return of employment that led to the decline in course numbers and cessation of these 'job-schemes'.

The dilemma

So, by the mid '80s, Brathay had to face a stark choice. Previously, almost all clients had been young people. But by 1983, only 25% were from the traditional young employees field. Around 50% were from the specialised youth training field: government schemes, Intermediate Treatment and Trident Trust. Almost all of these were soon to disappear as a result of outside policy changes. However, there was the successful and growing field of adult management and, as long as this remained, Brathay would be solvent. Had altruism finally lost out to commercial pressures? Was Brathay becoming, as many perceived, just a management training centre?

The new Principal did much valuable work raising funds from charities to prop up the youth work thus enabling Brathay to persist in what it knew to be the founder's intent. Eagle Crag was expanded and bursaries were made available to underwrite work with those in need. Outward Bound had always used the bursary approach - funded through many local support committees and LEAs - to ensure a steady flow of students into its traditional courses. But with high inflation Brathay found it difficult, even with bursaries and the much-reduced Scott subsidy, to offer youth courses at an acceptable price. Was the answer to stick to the altruistic intent and seek ever more charitable aid in order to run (costly) youth courses? (Few organisations are able to make youth work of this kind self-financing.) Or should they be thoroughly commercial and go all out on the management training bandwagon providing, for these customers, an acceptable product and, for Brathay, some stability?

In 1985, amid the diversity of activities going on at Brathay, there were the seeds of a polarisation into two camps. The Principal asked for guidance: should Brathay be commercial or altruistic? 'Commercial Brathay' was running highly successful courses for businesses working mainly with adult managers. It used the better style of accommodation and wanted to expand to take larger numbers and further upgrade the place. (It was even borrowing Trust money in order to provide ensuite rooms for delegates.) It could then recycle the profits from its management courses into its own development (for managers). 'Altruistic Brathay' covered all activities with people under 25. For them life was a struggle. To quote the Principal:

> *Altruistic Brathay feels, and usually is, under pressure to behave as if it were in the market place, and to accept customers only if they can pay the price. It has little scope or time for research, enquiry and development for which, under the Trust Deed, Brathay partly exists.* (Richards, 1985)

Neither did it have the resources to set by for such research. Things were made worse by the fact that Brathay prided itself on offering (to both adults and young) a 'Rolls Royce' product, the price of which could never be cheap.

Thus, one possibility was the division of Brathay into two halves (possibly on different sites) one dealing with the commercial side and the other with the altruistic side. In 1997, Outward Bound, with similar problems but more locations, opted for this solution, converting their Eskdale School into a management training centre. After considerable debate Brathay rejected this option. Consequently it suffered for living in a world that was not prepared to pay the asking price for a high standard of youth work. Although a survey indicated that other centres, such as Outward Bound's Ullswater School and the YMCA Lakeside Centre, could provide good youth programmes at lower prices, Brathay had not exercised its marketing skills in this field, and found it very difficult to adjust to commercial realities. The management work flourished but there was a steady decline in the numbers of young people and many of the activities which Brathay had hallmarked ceased. Brathay's salvation lay in the concept that altruism can only be pursued effectively if it is backed by philanthropy while, conversely, philanthropy can only be effective if applied by altruists.

The duality

In conclusion to this chapter there are many lessons about how commercialism and altruism can live together in a duality.

First, there is not really a polarisation between commercialism and altruism. It is simplistic, untrue and unfair to talk as if businesses acted solely in the interests of profit for their shareholders. For example, a safe good quality workplace is not just a legal requirement; provision often goes far beyond what is required by law. The Royal Society of Arts, in its support for industry, has identified much that is altruistic in the ideals and values of businesses (RSA, 1995). Nevertheless, those who send employees, whether junior or senior, to Brathay do so because they want to get good value training.

Second, hard times can focus the mind wonderfully on what are the real priorities. For its first 43 years Brathay lived under the shelter of a Scott Trust subvention. This allowed it freedom to do valuable work but it did not always have to assess the real cost of each and every enterprise. The result was that, when it was eventually forced to ask customers to pay all the bills, it had priced itself out of the youth and schools market. In the '90s a much leaner, efficient, but no less effective Brathay is emerging. For example, the average working group size, which had declined to 5 in its management work, is now back to between 7 and 10 with no loss in quality. Courses are shorter, more intensive, and closely designed to customer needs. Enterprises nationally have found that charitable trusts prefer to target money at special projects rather than encouraging dependency on core funding. The Scott Trust has done just this with Brathay and while they no longer give any annual subvention they are quick to support many of the new developments with grants towards building improvements and helping young people attend particular courses.

Third, there is no need to be apologetic about a Robin Hood philosophy. Brathay now makes it a matter of pride to use surpluses from management training courses to support work with young people. Firms, in their turn are able to feel good that they are not only giving their managers a good training; by paying the full price they are helping others. In fact some firms, who are regular customers, go much further and charitably designate further funds towards particular courses for young people. All this can, with astute management, lead to the attraction of further funds from other firms, trusts and foundations. Support breeds support as long as the providers can see that it leads to success. This style of fund-raising is relatively new to Brathay. Now, Brathay itself, through its success with management courses has, since 1992, become the chief 'commercial' funder of its own youth work.

Fourth, if you have values you should proclaim them. In the past, under its Scott umbrella and when demand was strong, there seemed little need to say what you stood for. If sufficient people came to your door you just did your job. (For example the Brathay Field Study Centre regularly closed its books for the coming year in the previous December.) If you did things well, and people copied your ideas or set up rival camps, so be it. You got on and did more things well and, hopefully, kept your share of the market. Nowadays, through its high profile reports, publications, presentations and conferences Brathay seeks to be better known for what it is. In some senses it is seeking to be a 'University of Development Training'. And behind such aspirations lies the need for evaluation, assessing and proclaiming both the economic and the social 'added value' of the work. Asked 'What does a Brathay course do?' the answer is that it prepares people not narrowly for work, but more for life. This makes people work-worthy in the widest and best sense. (What could be more commercial than that?)

Fifth, it takes a special blend of leadership qualities to manage an operation in which vision and values are always to the fore. But vision and values alone are not enough. The world has seen plenty of operations where the person with the charisma has not managed the day-to-day realities. (Even Brathay has dark stories about altercations with Scott in the early days!) Today's visionaries must also have a sound business sense, a firm control on all that is going on, and the courage to take hard decisions. Brathay is fortunate in having survived a crisis with its values intact and its business on a firm foundation. The values which it seeks to sell to its customers, young and older, are those which it applies, through good teamwork, within its own operation.

Notes

1. This chapter draws from the first two references below as a general source.

References

Brathay: Annual Reports and internal documents 1946 -1999.

Dybeck, M (1996) *A Broad River. The 50 year History of Brathay*. Ambleside: Brathay Hall Trust.

Richards, D. (1985) Paper to Governors and Trustees. 15 July 1985.

RSA (1995) *Tomorrow's Company - Enquiry Report*. London: Royal Society of Arts.

Scott, F. C. (1967) Memorandum of Nov 1967 (looking back at his reasons for founding Brathay) Ambleside: Brathay Hall.

Chapter 15: Changing Values? Outdoor education and secondary schools at the end of the 1990s

Ian Harris

Introduction

When you have been at the top of a rock face with a young person, and seen real fear in their eyes and then watched them experience the mental trauma of taking the first steps of an abseil; or when you have seen these emotions overcome by a sense of achievement and excitement on reaching the bottom, you certainly do not need to question the value of outdoor education. When at the end of a weeks sailing course the roughest, toughest child, who never says thanks for anything, goes up to the instructor and says 'thanks, that was the best week of my life' you know you have achieved something.

Many of us working within the field of outdoor education do not need to question the value that such experiences provide. The value of outdoor education in the development of the whole child, particularly the personal and social aspects of their education is widely accepted (Education Select Committee 1995). However, changes brought about by the Education Reform Act (ERA) of 1988 have been dramatic. The ERA led to a very different approach to education (Simon 1988) epitomised by the new approach to curriculum planning. Head teachers are now responsible by law to deliver the National Curriculum, which is presented in a subject based format, controlled for curriculum content. There are also tests and inspections undertaken, with publication of the results to ensure that the school is performing to the required standard. However, these tests, undertaken by pupils at ages 7, 11, 14 and 16, and particularly the publication of results in the form of league tables have been strongly criticised for concentrating on very specific parts of a pupils education. This concentrates on subject knowledge with no consideration of other important aspects of their education, such as personal and social development.

During the three decades from 1950 there was a notable expansion in adventure education, particularly in terms of the number of centres offering outdoor and adventurous activities (Hopkins and Putnam 1993:35). However, outdoor education is not a subject defined in the National Curriculum. It is mentioned as a cross curricular approach that schools can adopt, and 'Outdoor and Adventurous Activities' are included within the physical education national curriculum as an option for secondary school pupils. Mitchell (1992:19) acknowledges that the inclusion of outdoor and adventurous activities within the physical education elements of the National Curriculum does provide a 'foot in the door.' If this 'foot in the door' is a significant opportunity, it could be expected that a further expansion in outdoor education would have been seen during the 1990s. Humberstone (1990:224) however, recognised that "... there was very real concern that outdoor education ... may be severely curtailed or worse still, outdoor education may be lost".

Methodology

The research addressed in this chapter adopted a case study approach, focussing on one Local Education Authority (LEA) in Southern England. Published work was initially reviewed before the primary data for the study was collected. To identify the current and future opportunities for outdoor education within the secondary school sector a questionnaire was sent to 'The Head of Outdoor Education / Head of Physical Education,' at all state run secondary schools within the geographical area of the county. This included schools with Grant Maintained Status (GMS) and also those operating under Local Management of Schools (LMS) arrangements within the control of the LEA. A total of 65 questionnaires were returned; 69% of the sample. This information was then entered into a computer for analysis using the Statistical Package for Social Sciences (SPSS). Further data was collected through eight in-depth semi structured interviews with physical education and outdoor education teachers, deputy heads, centre managers/directors and LEA officers. The interviews were transcribed and then analysed by theme.

Results

1. Timetabled provision for outdoor education
Thirteen schools (20%) indicated that in the early 1990s they had been running an outdoor education course of some description, as a specifically timetabled course, within their curriculum. The current situation shows that only three schools (4.6%) indicated that they ran an outdoor education programme as a timetabled part of their curriculum. In all of these cases this was an option at key stage four. In one school this was a GCSE in Nautical Studies, the other schools both operated a non-examination option called 'outdoor education'. At one sailing centre, the manager indicated that in the early 1990s he had eight schools regularly using the centre to undertake GCSE nautical studies, the number over a five year period has declined to just one. No schools were anticipating the introduction of outdoor education as a new subject on their curriculum.

2. Outdoor and Adventurous Activities within physical education
The National Curriculum for physical education includes six areas of activity, three of which must be included at key stage three, including games and either dance or gymnastics. The results of the questionnaire showed that all schools delivered games, gymnastics and athletics at key stage three, so meeting their National Curriculum requirements. Many schools (80%) also delivered dance to their female pupils, with only 40% offering swimming and 36% offering outdoor and adventurous activities. The curriculum experienced by boys was similar, with 65% of schools offering dance, 45% outdoor and adventurous activities and 40% swimming.

However, during interviews with some teachers who had indicated that they included outdoor and adventurous activities, it was noted that this area of activity only consisted of an orienteering type activity on the school site. It could be argued that this activity was more akin to cross country running than outdoor activities and therefore should have been categorized as an athletic activity. If this is widespread then the figures of 45% and 36% may be misleading.

3. Opportunities for outdoor education outside the timetable
Twenty three schools (35%) indicated that they offered some form of outdoor education activities as part of their extra curricular programme, after school or at lunch times. While seven schools only offered one activity within this programme, the majority offered either two or three activities, with three schools offering four different outdoor activities in this way.

Fifty seven schools (88%) indicated that they ran residential courses or out of school trips that temporarily replaced the school timetable and included outdoor education activities. Year seven was the most popular year group to take out on these experiences with the least popular being year eleven. This matches the expectations relating to the emphasis being placed on GCSE and National Curriculum testing work. Only five schools indicated that the number of pupils going on the trip was approximately equal to the number in the specified year groups and only one school indicated that every child in the year group went on their residential course. The most popular type of course undertaken was a multi-activity outdoor pursuits course with 75% of courses meeting this description.

Discussion

The ERA 1988 introduced many changes to schools. It has been suggested (Simon 1988) that these changes are part of a package to change the values set within schools. The impact of these changes on outdoor education were unknown at the time of passing the Act. However, from the results presented here, it would appear that the delivery of outdoor education has undergone a dramatic decline within the curriculum time of secondary schools during the 1990s. It could be argued, however, that the real benefit of outdoor education is through the residential experience and results show that 88% of schools provided such opportunities for some of their pupils; which some may consider to be a healthy number.

Different aspects of the ERA would be expected to impact on these different areas separately. The significant areas of the ERA that have been considered within the research are: the National Curriculum; the management and financing of schools; and regulations on charging pupils for curricular time activities. A further area in need of consideration, outside of the educational legislative framework, is the effect of safety concerns, especially following the Lyme Bay canoe tragedy of 1993.

a valuable educational tool. Further evidence of the educational outcomes achieved with young people may be necessary to convince policy makers at both central and local Government levels that these experiences are invaluable in the complete education of the young mind and body. However, Government set values in education indicate that priorities will remain with the three Rs, and schools will primarily be judged by the publication of annual league tables based on pupils performances in tests at ages 7, 11, 14 and 16. This, as already highlighted, leads to pupils performance being measured and evaluated in a limited spectrum of education. These values and the financing of education within these priorities are likely to continue to place increasing pressure on outdoor education and it is possible that a further decline in opportunities may result.

The evidence collected would indicate that there is no likelihood that outdoor education will be lost from schools. However, the delivery of these opportunities will vary between schools, but will always depend upon an enthusiastic member of staff who is convinced of the value of these activities in the full development of the young person. These enthusiasts are the greatest asset for the world of outdoor education and they will ensure outdoor education survives in schools despite the changes that have been seen in education priority at Government level.

Notes

1. Unreferenced quotes are extracted from the research data.

References

Anderson, J.; Savill, T.; Andrews, R.; Edwards, C.; Harris, I. (1996) *The National Youth Watersports Audit.* Southampton Institute.

Davies, B. & Braund, C. (1989) *Local Management of Schools.* Northcote House.

Dearing, R. (1994) *The National Curriculum and its Assessment.* SCAA.

Education Select Committee. (1995) *Safety in Outdoor Activity Centres.* HMSO.

Harris, J. (1994) Physical Education in the National Curriculum *British Journal of Physical Education.* Winter 1994.

Hopkins, D. & Putnam, R. (1993) *Personal Growth Through Adventure.* London: David Fulton Publishers.

Humberstone, B. (1990) The National Curriculum and Outdoor Education. *British Journal of Physical Education.* Spring 1990

Mitchell, S. (1992) A foot in the door Outdoor and Adventurous Activities in the National Curriculum *Journal of Adventure Education and Outdoor Leadership.* 9(3)

Simon, B. (1988) *Bending The Rules.* London: Lawrence and Wishart.

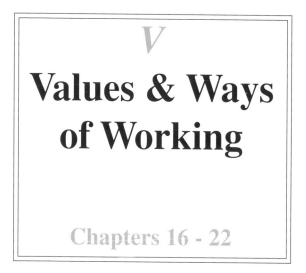

V

Values & Ways of Working

Chapters 16 - 22

Values & Ways of Working: Chapters 16 - 22

Chapter 16: The Moral Meaning Making Process of the Experiential Education Activity

Julie Rea

We make meaning out of what we experience, or more specifically what we perceive from what we experience. This perception involves our attitudes, values, and understandings of the world. All of these stem from the foundation of our beliefs. We know when beliefs are strong and stable, that they are resilient and resist change (Pierce, 1877). We know as well that they include the metaphors into which we place new meaning (Lakoff & Johnson, 1999). It is the nature of cognitive process to attempt to fit new meaning into those larger schemes or metaphors by which we function since according to Pierce, it is very uncomfortable to change our beliefs.

Pierce (1877) says that the object of reasoning is to find out, from the consideration of what we already know, something else which we do not know, indicating that the reasoning process requires us to make inference from one awareness to another. Thus, the reasoning process, the means by which we make meaning, is the ability to transfer from what is known to the unknown, so that it may become known as well. It is then the nature of this reasoning process that there must be vehicles, images or significations, which move from one instance to another. This paper will consider these images, or significations as critical to understanding the reasoning process through which we make meaning. It is through images and signs, that one becomes able to make determinations regarding the thoughts and actions that are relevant in a particular instance. From the semiotic perspective, the internal images or significations will be called signs and the process through which these signs move, from the known instance to the unknown or new instance, will be called semiosis.

The role of metaphors is significant in the meaning making process (Calvin, 1996; Lakoff & Johnson, 1999). It is by means of these metaphors that we frame our world view. We also integrate and acknowledge the schemes within that world view which are being addressed, in the continual evolution of the meaning making process (Cunningham, 1998; Lakoff & Johnson, 1999; Lemke, 1987; Thibault, 1990). The meaning making process, semiosis, involves the utilization of our pre-existing beliefs. The semiotic process is not one that functions independently of the lens through which an individual sees. The 'umwelt', or world view, engages any sign, or experience, into its ongoing and pre-existing process of semiosis. That meaning which is attributed to any sign comes then, more purely, from the ongoing attribution process within the organism than it does from the sign. The 'umwelt' is made up of all of the beliefs that are pre-existing and support efforts to make meaning of all it encounters so that new signs fit well with what is already there. Pierce (1877)

explained this as the innate resistance to change, or the fixation of beliefs. It is natural for the mind to seek continuity, and so maintain beliefs, rather than contrast, which requires altering those beliefs.

Cognitive dissonance, or disequilibrium, is a necessary step toward a new or modified belief. So then, if meaning which is contrary to pre-existing beliefs is to be made, it is important to place an individual into an environment where those pre-existing beliefs can be challenged in a significant manner. This environment also needs to facilitate a process of logic that can serve to modify or alter the pre-existing belief. This occurs as individuals and groups seek understandings by which to make meaning in this new context.

How this works in experiential education practice

What is there to the problem solving process, to the cooperative learning environment and to the very nature of human socialization and discovery that is missing from many of public school classrooms? I suggest that in the realm of moral reasoning it is often in the lack of associated experience from which to create meaning through abductive reasoning (reasoning between two theories or ideas to make sense of facts), as well as the social and overt logical processes through which new information may be processed. Cunningham (1998) notes the important role of abductive inference as we seek to make meaning from the facts provided by experience, as it is embedded in a context. It is in the abductive process as well, that we can consider the relationships between theory or ideas and the transferability of the implications of one to the other.

Johnson (1985) asserts that there is a direct link between the ability to connect the imaginative capacity found within metaphorical thinking and the ability to move between conceptual levels of moral principles (reasoning) in the case by case details of individual moral dilemmas (experience).

What is involved in moving rationally from the formulation of a supreme moral principle to specifying particular imperatives as they apply to the messy and intricate circumstances of our lives? I want to ask what Kant (1724-1804) might mean when he says that this deliberative process is rational. My suggestion will be that the notion of rationality involved here will be a very broad and rich one, involving imaginative processes that Kant only hints at in his remarks in moral judgement. I shall argue that these processes are often metaphorical and that the presence of such imaginative acts calls into question any strict interpretation of the dichotomy between imagination and reason and that between imagination and understanding.

Here Johnson (1985) takes us beyond the explicit process of moral reasoning to the implied. He argues that this indicates the connecting force of the imagination. The imagination is that which utilizes the created and housed signs, known through the various modalities of the human as those not only experienced by the mind through sight, but all the sensations of the body; auditory, tactile, olfactory, gustatory, kinesic, and emotional. Danesi (1998) notes that all of these sensations create visual signs in the mind, making semiosis an intermodality process. He cites as an example our ability to imagine, thereby creating a representation in our mind, the feel of grass that is wet or the smell of fish. Certainly, if the mind has signs for smells and feelings then we have a system through which they are imaged. And within that process of imaging, we have an ability to utilize them as representamens, interpretants, or objects in later experience and efforts at meaning making. The moral meaning making process utilizes such a dynamic model as we find in Pierce's description of the sign. His description identifies the triadic process of interpreting stimulus by the perceiver. The *representamen* is something which stands for something else, to some extent, to someone. The *interpretant* is, in form, what it stands for, and the *object* is the manifestation of that meaning. What is in one instance a representamen becomes an object in another and so forth. Our current experience is then processed as an example from the models which are provided for us in our metaphors. The meaning that we make of such experience is seen in the dynamics of placement is represented with the semiotic process. As well, we create an awareness of our own role in this cycle of meaning making as we take on the behaviors and actions which we know to be meaningful in another context. To explain how this happens in the field of Experiential Education we begin by placing ourselves in the process of what occurs there.

Imagine an environment in which those who are problem solving and engaged in the process cooperatively are encouraged to touch each other, brainstorm, cheer, jump around, try out things to see if they work without risk of criticism or negative repercussion from outside. Imagine that these problem solvers critically evaluate the process of their efforts, set their own goals, establish their own definition of success, and work together with mutual respect, support and appreciation. Imagine that in this environment the group is given increasingly more difficult problems to solve. Then as each task is resolved successfully, the group climate becomes more and more refined and exciting. The team members celebrate their accomplished goals, and own the process from beginning to end. Members realize the valuable assets and equally valuable limitations of their independent parts/members as well as the identity of the whole. Then the identities of the two blend, and merge into the team mentality that is celebrated. The celebration includes commonly felt empathy and shows of support; pats on the backs, touches of the shoulder and embraces of the whole person. The group members voice their feelings and thoughts about the process in their critical reflection, whether seemingly relevant to any outcome or not. Because, in this environment all of these thoughts and feelings are viewed as important and prioritized as though they were the key to successful outcome. Here, people as individuals with the emotional responses and thoughts that each houses, is common property of the group. Each person is seen as a value, as well as a responsibility, to that same whole.

Many of those things missing from the public education environment are exemplified above. The description is one which any facilitator of a low ropes or teams course would immediately recognize as a possible description of the regular experience of groups they work with. There is frequent and freely shown physical engagement. There is dialogue about the characteristics within the group, their value as they exist, or their potential to benefit the group better, by varying from their current state. As well, there is collective support for this process because there is collective motivation for the best end to be reached along with the most satisfying avenue to that end to be taken.

So how does all of this occur? What does the experiential education activity ask of the participants? And what does it offer that is distinct from what is normally found in educational environments? It asks that group members engage themselves collectively in its process. The group is defined as a team and while it acknowledges individuality of group members and encourages cognizance by the group of those differences, it focuses the group on the awareness of their identity as a whole, as a team.

As part of a small group working together through, for example, a low ropes, or teams course, the group is given a task. As well, they are given shared responsibility and accountability for accomplishing that task. They are told that a priority of the process is to determine group goals which they will own and work from in embracing this task. The problem solving activity is framed by the facilitator so that the group can understand the task and any imposed constraints that they must consider in their attempts to accomplish that task. Following that direction the group is free to act toward a defined end.

After the task/goal has been met, or the opportunity to meet it has expired, comes the part of the experiential education model which I want to focus on here. This is called debriefing an activity by some, processing by others, and various other things still. But the important aspects of this to consider for the purposes of this paper are as follows. First, the facilitator will begin to inquire what the group members actually experienced, asking questions such as, what happened there? or other questions of a similar nature. These are questions that get at the tangible facts of what occurred and makes them explicit by stating them for the whole group. An example would be, Sally tripped and fell down and when Mike helped her up it broke one of the rules of this activity and so we all had to start over.

The second part of the debriefing would be to inquire as to what meaning was made by those in the group as a result of what was experienced. So a question which a facilitator might pose would be, so what issues did this action of Mike's raise for those in the group? Possible responses could include, well, I really wanted to go ahead because we were almost to our goal, and it frustrated me that we had to start over, or it made me feel secure to know that getting to our goal wasn't as important as reaching out to assist someone in the group who we saw fall, etc. This line of questioning invites the group participants to share their feelings and thoughts, make overt their own awareness of themselves and their process, and highlight other things that they may be assuming or concerned with from the activity.

It is clearly a step beyond identifying tangible facts. The role of abductive reasoning begins to play a part in this second step. The line of inquiry in this step identifies the agendas, issues, and reflections of personal perception. It is in this second step that the explicit issues may be debated and reconsidered in light of the new experience which the group has engaged in through their problem solving activity, perhaps opening up the opportunity for cognitive disequilibrium in group participants. Someone who has been extremely competitive may see how that competitive tendency becomes threatening to people they work with. They are then faced with an opportunity to accept it as a potentially ineffective trait for a team member at times. A person who generally hesitates to offer suggestions, out of insecurity, may be encouraged by the group to become more vocal as they seek solutions. By doing this the person may begin to see the need and reward of asserting and sharing their opinions and ideas, and come to view them as valuable. Or a person who has always maintained that it is better to work alone may be faced with facts and experience that offer the associated awareness that by working within a group one can accomplish more than when working alone. While these examples perhaps sound simplistic, they offer a concrete explanation of what might occur in the second stage of the debriefing experience.

The third step of the debriefing process is where the most overt use of abduction comes in. Here the members are asked to transfer something which has become a newly presented or perhaps a known and expanded principle to a second setting or theoretical place and find the meaning that it makes there. The process is that of moving from an idea or principle in one location to an equal or like idea in another location. The third stage of the debriefing process is for the facilitator to lead the group members to transfer their awareness to another context, to make a conceptual meaning taken from this experience and place it into a second context and consider it there. The question a facilitator would pose at this stage would be: and now what? e.g. now what can we do with this new awareness? Often the connections are obvious to team members. Sometimes the transfer process requires quite a lot of focus and dialogue. A simple example, following the examples given above could be, it is important for me to share my ideas at work even if I feel insecure about them because I may have an idea that will assist the office in accomplishing something it couldn't without me. The part of the process can be one where juxtaposition occurs. Group members are often asked to take two, otherwise unrelated things, and juxtapose them to see where there are similarities.

A slightly more complex scenario which I wish to present as an example, is one where the facilitator frames the activity by placing two ropes out on the ground. The ropes lie straight, face each other, and are some distance apart. He/she then divides the group into two teams and asks each participant to stand side by side behind one of the lines, with their foot touching the person's foot next to them. The groups are to walk as a line towards each other until they are close enough to shake the hand of those standing opposite them without separating the side of their foot from the foot of the person next to them. The task is defined as complete when the two groups are close enough to shake hands. It is the responsibility of anyone who breaks the connection between their foot and the foot of the person next to them to let everyone know so that all can go back behind the original lines and start over. This activity generally prompts competitiveness between the two groups and often results in at least a few of the individuals withholding the information from the group that they have broken from the foot next to them.

These facts are raised in the debriefing of the activity. Issues then which are addressed often include trust within the group, the competitive frame of reference from which individuals often work, the feelings of frustration by slower members or members wishing to contribute ideas that get left behind by those quicker or more vocal. These issues are easily transferrable into other contexts and groups/individuals will transfer them to the settings quite readily. Often there will be individuals who alter their existing belief about a rule or concept of how one should behave or act in social environs based on their experience in these groups.

When using the term transfer here, regarding the movement of new knowledge from one context to another, making it apply to the second, it is important to consider the use of metaphor. In this stage the use of metaphors are most easily placed into the debriefing process. They can often be seen in the vocal efforts of participants attempting to resolve the disparity they feel by challenging their pre-existing beliefs with new or altered ones. The use of metaphor also offers the opportunity, to make a more elaborate and contextualized association within a group meaning making process. Facilitators often employ these metaphors unintentionally. It is intentionality that produces the opportunity to utilize reflective practice for professionals so that refinement of processes can be ongoing.

It is in this part of the process that so many opportunities for both abduction and genuine doubt occur. When genuine doubt arises, and abduction takes place, there are truly teachable moments produced. That is the goal of experiential activities, reaching the point of disequilibrium where a belief can be modified, altered, grounded, or otherwise enhanced, so that individuals can function in a more productive manner in other areas of their lives.

The semiotic perspective offers a most valuable lens for observing this meaning making process because of the distinct and complex process of the social semiosis that occurs. The same frame/activity/experience will often be used to create varied, and in some cases, opposing meaning depending on the individual make up of the group. As well, the group dialogue seems to be quite influential on the individuals within the group. This highlights the fact that the meaning making process occurs, at least in part, outside of the individual, between group members.

We know that genuine doubt arises from our experience. So then it is naturally embedded, or anchored, in a relevant context and will first be processed there. Being in a state of genuine doubt is unpleasant - the world does not make obvious sense - so it is necessary to create or alter beliefs so as to move to some new state of belief, a process that Peierce (1877) labeled the fixation of belief. That new belief/learning can be best seen as it becomes transferrable to other and differing contexts. If learning is best conceived, not as learning and remembering information, but as connections with and within communities of practice, then we will come to give full value to the collaborative nature of cognition, investigate the role of culture and community more thoroughly, and provide better opportunities for nurturing these connections (Cunningham, 1998). The context within which the experiential education model teaches, or facilitates learning, is such a context. It creates a community and makes explicit this process of meaning making. It is a context which can offer a unique perspective on the social semiotic process. And the social semiotic perspective can enlighten us more fully as to the value inherent within that learning context.

Recognizing the powerful nature of the experiential educational model raises significant questions of intentionality and ethical guidance by facilitators within groups. First, the questions of intentionality have to do with competence. Are facilitators trained to have a sufficient awareness of the powerful process that is occurring within this arena? Second, there is the component of ethical concern. Is the facilitator able to encourage groups and individuals to process toward their own ends, and construct their own meanings or is he/she leading and directing the process based on the values and beliefs that he/she wishes to have the group members adopt? These questions are both complex and pure. While they are detail ridden, they are pure as they hold a core position in the foundation of the fields philosophy. They are perhaps some of the most important questions which can be addressed as the significance of the experiential activity as a learning environment becomes overtly considered.

References

Calvin, W. (1996) *The Cerebral Code.* Cambridge, MA: MIT Press.

Cunningham, D. J. (1998) 'Cognition as semiosis: The role of inference.' *Theory and Psychology.* 8, 827-840.

Danesi, M. (1998) *Sign, Thought & Culture.* Toronto, Ontario: Canadian Scholar's Press.

Johnson, M. (1985) 'Imagination in moral judgment.' *Philosophy and Phenomenological Research.* 46(2), 265-280.

Lakoff, G. & Johnson, M. (1999) *Philosophy In The Flesh.* New York, NY: Basic Books.

Lemke, J.L. (1987) 'Social semiotics and science education. *The American Journal of Semiotics.* 5(2) 217-232.

Lemke, J.L. (1990) *Talking Science: Language Learning And Values.* Ablex: NY.

Pierce, C. (1877) 'The fixation of belief.' *Popular Science Monthly.* 12 Nov.

Thibault, P, J. (1990) 'The making of meaning on talking science, language, learning and values.' *The Semiotic Review of Books.* 4(3).

Chapter 17: Pathways To Manhood - Tackling the problems of boys growing up

Eric Maddern

Conflict between the generations is not new. 4000 years ago in Babylon a story carved in stone told how the Creator's offspring were "loathsome, overbearing and unsavoury in their ways, troubling the mood of heaven by their hilarity". And so, some say, are the youth of today.

But now the problems of youth are greatly compounded. The twentieth century has been a time of extremely rapid social, cultural and technological change. The rates of growth in population, speed of travel, information, invention, consumption and communication have been exponential and unprecedented. Alongside this has been a dramatic erosion of social norms and moral values. The relative certainties of the past have disappeared. The security traditionally offered by work and family, home and community no longer exists. Whilst we seem to be freer than ever before - potentially with a huge array of life style choices at our fingertips - we are simultaneously and ironically more burdened.

Nowhere does this burden show up more vividly than in the difficulties faced by boys growing into men. This transformation from childhood to adulthood is never easy and, with high levels of testosterone flooding their bodies, adolescence for boys is naturally a time of manic and depressive extremes. This instability is increased today because, not only are boys falling behind girls in most aspects of education, but also there are fewer traditional male work roles, so many young men are faced with uncertain job futures. They are surrounded by consumer desirables and a culture that measures worth by material possessions. Unable to legitimately acquire these symbols of value there is a build up of frustration and anger which eventually either explodes or implodes. If fuelled by hanging out in street gangs it may come out in manic aggression, violence, delinquency and crime. The highest crime rate of any age group is among 15 and 16 year olds (Phillips, 1992). Or if suffered alone this pent up emotion will be turned inward and result in a downward spiral of despair the end point of which is all too often suicide. (Male teenage suicide has escalated in the last two decades and is now the second biggest killer after road accidents). And, of course, alcohol and drugs (and for some, perhaps, cyberspace) often provide a ready escape route from life's hard realities (Katz, 1999). As a result of all this many young men, charged up with anger or anxiety, are 'accidents waiting to happen'. Unfortunately it is often only when the accidents do happen that the attention of adults is finally attracted.

For many boys it is especially hard for them to feel truly valued. Take the discussion on whether teenage mothers should give up their children for adoption. Rarely is mention made of the fathers. Should they not have a say in the matter? The message sent is that their feelings are irrelevant, that they cannot be expected to be responsible, that they are not important in such decisions. If this is the prevailing attitude then no wonder there is such negativity among so many youth.

This is not to say that there aren't young men who successfully make it to maturity. In fact there are many extraordinary young people about at the moment. Nor is it to imply that the changes of the late twentieth century are all negative. Indeed there is much that is positive and exciting as we stand on the threshold of a new century and millennium. However it does seem that our progress has been bought at a cost, a part of which is the disaffiliation of a huge swathe of our youth. This disaffection, if unattended to, will cause grave problems in years to come.

Dave Hill (1997) puts it vividly in *Men*:

> *As for those at the bottom of the heap, the permanently casualised, they seem destined to remain there, spread across a spectrum of social exclusion which has insanity at one extreme and career criminality at the other, many a persistent and intractable menace to each other and the communities in which they live. The police have long been sick of them, the courts clogged with them, the hospitals full of them on Saturday nights. There hasn't been so much worry about working-class males for a hundred years, and there is no sign of it abating. Ten, twenty, thirty years from now all this will still be true. And the longer it goes on the more complete will be the detachment of such men from any sense of the greater good and the more absolute will be their separation from the rest of society. This will confirm the already prevailing perception of them as irrevocably mad and bad, as creatures from a blighted nether world, as a virtual sub-species whose very existence propagates dread.*

A solution

Although it is true that we live in a time of bewildering change it is also true that some things remain basically the same. The process of maturation, of growing up, of going from childhood through youth to adulthood, is one such unchanging thing. Of course many outer trappings of this period are different, but the fundamental inner journey is essentially the same. And so, in looking for 'solutions' to the present day 'crisis of youth', we may find it useful to examine how societies, since the time of Babylon and beyond, have dealt with 'coming of age'. It seems that most cultures recognised the potentially de-stabilising force of undirected youth, of young men in particular, and therefore devised clear, firm and creative ways to constructively channel these energies to bring about a purposeful and responsive adulthood. In many small scale cultures this process was focused in what has been called rites of passage. The crisis of contemporary youth is so extreme that we are forced by necessity to contemplate radical solutions. It is paradoxical that the most radical solution may be the remaking of a quite ancient and traditional practice, the adolescent 'rite of passage'.

Traditional rites of passage

Anthropologists have studied rites of passage practices in numerous societies and deduced a form which is widespread and which fulfils certain functions. (Though there were rituals to help girls become women the focus here is on 'boys becoming men'.) Generally, when a youth is deemed ready (some time between 13 and 17), he is removed from his cosy family circle and, with the co-operation of the grieving women, taken 'away'. He then becomes the dignified and highly valued focus for a series of ceremonies that, at times, involve the whole community. During this 'in between' time he is subjected to tests and ordeals that force him to confront his fears - especially his fear of separation from mother and the fear of death. Indeed, he will go through a 'death', the death of himself as a child. In the resulting state of openness he may be exposed to rapid-fire teachings on mythology which show him who he is, where he comes from, what he must do. The meaning of hitherto secret objects or symbols may be revealed. The beauty, power and responsibility of his sexuality will be affirmed. In some traditions he may be encouraged to seek a vision of identity and purpose by fasting alone in the wilderness. He may also be taught practical survival skills and the sacred topography of the surrounding landscape. When the time is right - anything from a couple of weeks to several months later - he will return to the community reborn. He is honoured for what he has been through and recognised as a man, self-possessed and responsible. It is a time of welcoming and celebration.

This rites of passage process achieves more than simply a transition to adulthood. It achieves transformation: transformation from an individual being to a social being, from someone living just in the present to someone who sees the past and the future, from someone who only consumes to someone who also creates. W.E.H.Stanner (1979), writing about the Australian Aborigines in *White Man Got No Dreaming*, summed up the functions of initiation as teaching boys to be men; to know pain and to ignore it; to feel fear and to master it; to want, but to bear the necessary costs; to grasp that outside society they are nothing and inside it, the masters.

I would further summarise the achievements of rites of passage as follows.

- The initiate learns how to survive independently and with confidence in the wider world.

- The initiate learns to deal with difficult emotions like fear, pain, anger, grief, greed, boredom, confusion, loneliness and doubt.

- He discovers feelings of appreciation, respect, courage, enthusiasm and love.

- The initiate experiences a 'spiritual awakening' where he meets with ancestral spirits (or God) and sees for the first time the beauty and splendour of the wider world and feels himself to be a significant part of that world.

- By being exposed to the strong presence of Nature and the powerful stories of his culture the initiate comes to feel a deeper sense of identity which contains within it his vocation or purpose.

- On his return to the community the initiate has come to recognise his responsibilities to himself, to others and to the land itself. Moreover, he knows that he has a respected place within that community and so is ready to begin his work.

There is one more extremely important, though less obvious, benefit of rites of passage. During the ceremonies the adults involved make an extra effort to purify themselves (by doing without or abstaining from improper behaviour) to be sure that the boys are reborn without danger of infection by evil. So, while the boys are learning adult values by which they will soon conduct their lives, adults try harder to practice those values. The importance of this was echoed at a recent UNESCO event in Paris when a 14 year old girl told an adult audience that teachers should "actually demonstrate values not simply talk about them" (Goodman, 1998). Conducting rites of passage encourages adults to do this and therefore benefits society at large. Indeed the growth of children into adulthood can be seen as part of the continued growth of society as a whole.

Why we need rites of passage for youth now

Modern education is pre-occupied with cramming intellectual knowledge and physical skill into the minds and bodies of young people. Such relentless pressure means that the fundamental aims of the traditional rites of passage, in particular, education of the heart (emotions) and cultivation of the soul (spirituality), are all but ignored. The complexity and detail of the National Curriculum means that the 'bigger picture' of Life in the Cosmos is hardly ever glimpsed let alone deliberately revealed. Consequently, high school usually achieves only transition to adulthood rather than transformation. All too often young people gain the rights of majority simply by reaching a certain age, rather than by virtue of having earned them. And those rights are seldom if ever accompanied by 'rites' to celebrate and honour the young person with the status of responsible and respected adulthood. That final, and crucial, stage of initiation - the return and re-incorporation of the initiate into the adult community - never happens, and we are therefore left with a world populated by 'eternal youths', immature boy-men who are driven by fear, anger, greed or desire, who have little idea of their place in the world or their purpose in life, who know only how to consume and not how to create and who may drift along aimlessly for years. Sometimes it is in mid-life that they suddenly wake up to ask themselves: 'Is this it?'

There is a great deal of concern, of course, with the condition of young men. Most solutions offered are of the 'more police on the street' or 'give them a short, sharp, shock in a boot camp' variety. It is thought that this will either prevent crime or 'make men out of' youthful delinquents. But here we are concerning ourselves only with the symptoms, mistaking them for the sickness. We cannot solve the problem or cure the sickness by repressing the symptoms.

In the absence of structured and elder-led rites of passage young people, especially boys, will try to initiate themselves anyway. Unfortunately the pseudo-initiations offered by peer groups in gangs, prisons, boarding schools and other youth sub-cultures do not have the wisdom of elders guiding them to bring about true masculine maturity. They may 'toughen' up the initiates but they have few of the other redeeming features of true rites of passage. Instead they inculcate a masculinity that is skewed, stunted and false, that is often abusive of self and others. And yet this fiery, daring, shocking, rebellious energy so characteristic of youth is natural enough. It is nothing if not an increasingly desperate cry for initiation.

Re-creating rites of passage

Interest in creating contemporary rites of passage has been growing slowly in Britain over the last ten years, though most 'practitioners' have been operating in isolation. In America, however, the practice of creating new rites of passage is further advanced. This is partly because America is more experimental and ground-breaking in these things generally, but also because they have the immediate presence of the First Nation-Native Americans who still do Vision Quests with their youth, and the Afro-American community who have looked to their African roots to find models of rites of passage for their youth. This has rubbed off on the wider population and there is now, for example, a National Rites of Passage Institute in Cleveland, Ohio and a School of Lost Borders which runs wilderness vision quests in California. In 1996 *Crossroads: The Quest for Contemporary Rites of Passage* (Mahdi, et al., 1996) was published.

In Britain we don't have the same closeness to a rites of passage practice which can be resurrected from our recent past. (We shouldn't forget, though, the apprenticeship system which had elements of rites of passage, especially in the mentoring role of the 'journeyman', an employee responsible for the welfare of a certain apprentice.) But perhaps we can see this as an advantage and start with a relatively clean slate. We can draw from traditional practices elsewhere and there are many other helpful disciplines, so we can also build new forms of our own, designed to fulfil the functions we think rites of passage should achieve.

The contemporary rites of passage movement in Britain has its roots in:

- Anthropology - drawing on an understanding of the process and importance of rites of passage in small scale non-industrial societies as well as direct teachings from Native American, African and Australian Aboriginal elders; also looking to rediscover some of the traditional practices of the early British people such as the Celts.

- Psychology - working with various models of group dynamics and personal development which are applicable to youth (including communication skills and emotional expression), as well as exploring current approaches to gender identity.

- Youth Work - utilising experience of working 'on the ground' with youth on issues such as sexuality, conflict and dealing with anger, racism, drug and alcohol use, survival skills, work and relating to adults.

- The Arts - using drama, storytelling, mythology, music, poetry, sculpture, dance and mask-making as ways to develop aesthetic appreciation, explore personal experience and build confidence in creative expression; also for use in making rituals.

- Environmental Movement - developing awareness of self and culture in relation to the wider natural world and recognising personal responsibilities in terms of taking care of the Earth for future generations.

- Survival Skills - learning traditional arts of survival like map reading and navigation, making fire and building shelters, finding wildfood and cooking, as well as more contemporary skills such as communication and self-presentation.

- Spiritual Approaches - using ways of stilling the mind, centering the body, expanding awareness of self to include the wider world; recognising life as a journey, looking for signs of the 'call to adventure'; working with symbol, metaphor and ritual; learning about timeless human values; experiencing nature as a teacher.

The people who founded organisations like Brathay and Outward Bound focussed on month long courses which fulfilled many of the traditional functions of rites of passage. Unfortunately, commercial pressures have meant these longer courses are now largely defunct. However, some groups representing the approaches mentioned above have now picked up the baton and are working to develop a contemporary rites of passage experience. Outdoor and adventure education, with its emphasis on nature, challenge and survival, is ideally positioned to work with such approaches to create transformative experiences for young people and so help them navigate the uncertain pathways to adulthood.

Conclusion

We live in exciting, but dangerous, times. As the Earth is assailed by an unprecedented array of de-stabilising forces, so society is being unpicked from below by a chronic lack of heart, particularly in the downcast and the young.

If we are to reweave the web we need to spend more time and effort with our youth. We need the growth of people to be higher in value than the growth of material wealth. At the moment there is something desperately important missing in the way we bring up our children. It has to do with how much we challenge them, how much we love them, how much we guide them. It has to do with spiritual values and ritual practice. It has to do with putting people first.

The special challenge is to work with those who are in the testing time of moving from childhood dependency to being self-reliant, inter-dependent, creative, active adults. We believe that a rites of passage perspective adds invaluable potency to this work, and ultimately not just for disadvantaged youth, but for all.

If only we could get this transition right, if only we could bring about a genuine transformation from youth to adulthood, then how much else would fall into place. We wouldn't have to keep sucking at our mother's breast any more; we wouldn't have to keep playing tin soldiers. We could live together on a healthy, wholesome, humming little planet that would still be beautiful one thousand years from now.

Notes

This chapter is condensed, by permission of the author, from notes written in March 1999 as a submission to the Home Office to promote a rites of passage perspective in work with young people. These notes have also been used as a discussion paper for a rites of passage gathering at Cae Mabon, the 'village encampment' founded by the author.

References

Mahdi, L.C.; Christopher, N.G.; Meade, M. (eds) (1996) *Crossroads: The Quest for Contemporary Rites of Passage*. Open Court.

Goodman, M. (1998) address at 'Youth and Values' conference, Nov. 1998.

Katz, A. (1979) *Leading Lads - A report on what 1400 lads think about life in Britain today*. Oxford: Oxford University.

Hill, D. (1997) *Men*. Weidenfield and Nicholson General.

Phillips, M. (1992) 'Criminalising the Younger Classes' *The Guardian*. January 31st.

Stanner, W.E.H. (1979) *White Man Got No Dreaming*. Canberra: Australian National University Press.

Chapter 18: Exploring an outdoor adventure education experience with reference to young people at risk

Tom Lilley

Introduction

Underpinning this chapter is a belief and commitment to using outdoor adventure education as a tool to work with young people at risk, not one that dominates or provides an easy solution but one which seeks to complement other strategies within the social/educational context. There is also a conviction that the use of outdoor adventure education can make a difference. The first part of the chapter explores the values, relationships and strategies of outdoor adventure education and places it in the context of the wider community or society. The second part looks at an outdoor adventure education qualitative research project with young people at risk based in a 'school' community.

Values for education and the wider community

In the context of the current debate on citizenship as part of the curriculum in schools and the present government's commitment to 'education, education, education' it is worthwhile to examine the contribution outdoor adventure education can offer as part of the education of the 'whole' person. The National Forum for Values in Education and the Community was set up (SCAA, 1996) to make recommendations on agreed core 'values, attitudes and behaviour that schools should promote'. Ron Dearing, in the introduction to the National Forum consultation document, stated,

> *We share a concern for the quality of our civilisation and the values that underpin it. We all have a positive role to play, in safeguarding and enhancing the quality of our childrens' lives.* (SCAA, 1996: 1)

The Forum identified a statement of values and principles for action based on four core areas; society, relationships, the self and the environment. The holistic nature of the statement offers a window of opportunity for outdoor adventure education particularly in the area of working with young people at risk. Indeed, many practitioners believe that these values are critical to any outdoor education experience and that outdoor adventure education can support the use of educational values and principles to facilitate teaching and learning (Royce, 1987; Humberstone, 1993; Keighley 1991, 1996). Cooper (1994; 11) states,

The development of self-esteem, co-operation and environmental
awareness encourages a holistic approach to learning. Outdoor education
is concerned with the development of the whole person through mind, body
and spirit. We need this holistic approach to achieve the changes required
for a more sustainable lifestyle.

Birmingham's chief education officer Tim Brighouse (1996: 15) also supports the
above view,

Education is concerned with the relationship with self and with self and
others, or intrapersonal and interpersonal development. Outdoor
education is central to this. It offers almost unique opportunities for the
development of inter and intra personal intelligences.

He challenges educationalists to seize the opportunity offered by the millennium to
become 'energy creators' and develop the potential of outdoor education in helping
to create 'a better future'. According to Brighouse (1995), energy creators are those
people who are naturally optimistic and have the drive to create 'pockets of optimism'
to facilitate change and focus on teaching and learning.

Multi-faceted education

In *Strategy 2000* Brighouse (1997) offers a vision of quality and achievement in
education and identifies several principles to guide action to improve Birmingham's
standards of educational provision and outcome,

*   Multi-faceted intelligence which means that there is no longer a
    concentration on just the literate, numerate, logical or scientific intelligences
    but a recognition of those with sporting, artistic, musical, dramatic, or
    interpersonal talents and intelligences.

*   Lifelong education, rather than just a one-off activity. All the participants
    involved in the educational process can continue to learn new things.

*   Ipsative 'to improve against previous best', not 'normative competition'
    competition against one's own previous best. This implies teachers/
    educators trying to differentiate the curriculum or provide challenges to
    meet or match needs of individuals.

*   Celebrating *success* rather than focusing on negative aspects; celebrating
    achievement at every possible occasion to highlight progress and
    improvements by groups or individuals.

These key principles can provide a foundation to emphasise the relationships of quality, equality of opportunity, and improvement in order to improve standards of education provision and outcome.

Brighouse (1994) suggested that the whole purpose of education was to unlock everybody's talent. He asks how teachers could give young people a moment to do something they never thought was possible, achieving 'priceless' personal growth and development. Brighouse highlights the components of outdoor education that can offer the potential to develop growth in the individual: new activities and skills; new areas of learning; holistic approach; cross curricula approaches; healthy lifestyles; residential experiences; personal and social development; environmental awareness and positive pupil/teacher young person/adult relationships, including the opportunity to have a meaningful conversation with an adult. He contends that, 'real issues had to be faced' in the outdoors. Thus, outdoor adventure education has a role in helping to develop values led programmes as part of a holistic approach.

Keighley (1996) called for personal qualities in education to be considered and re-established as an entitlement for the 'development of an education for life'. He argued that experienced-based learning out of doors had the potential to facilitate this valuable sphere of learning.

Building on Cumbria's (1984:9) 'major elements of outdoor education', Priest's (1986:15) 'relationships within outdoor education', Hopkins and Putnam's (1993:226) 'holistic model of outdoor adventure' and the author's personal research and experience, the author has developed the interdependent circles of outdoor adventure education which identify core relationships, values and strategies (Figure 1). The interlocking relationships between components of outdoor adventure i.e. outdoor adventure, environmental awareness and inter and intrapersonal development as well as core values and strategies are critical to developing successful programmes.

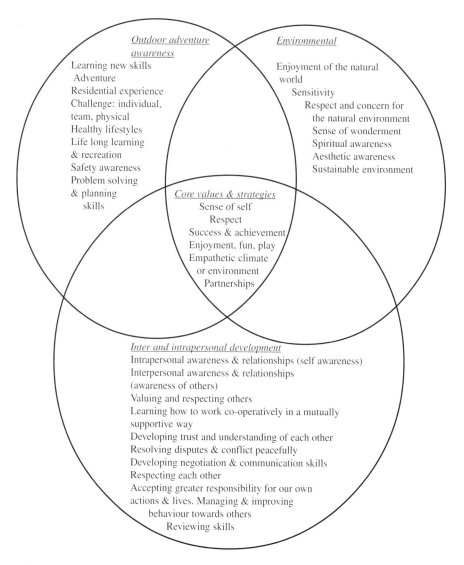

Figure 1. The interdependent circles of outdoor adventure education.
Developed from Cumbria LEA's model of 'The major elements of outdoor education'
(Cumbria 1984:9)

Research project with young people at risk based in a school community

The research addressed in this chapter focused on developing and evaluating programmes and strategies for young people at risk. This used the author's workplace; Oakdale Centre which is part of Birmingham's Education Service's Behaviour Support Service (BSS). The work is centre based, BSS cross service based and works proactively within schools.

The characteristics of young people at risk with a low self-esteem with whom the BSS work with may include many of the following indicators. These provide further confirmation of Huskins (1996) and Mosley's (1995) observations and signs.

- Low global self-esteem
- Poor academic ability and learning difficulties
- Exhibiting behavioural problems
- Involved in peer conflict, verbal and/or physical
- Exhibiting emotional problems
- Poor interpersonal relationships with peers and teachers
- Experiencing problems or difficulties concerned with their home or family background
- Excluded or refusing to attend school or at risk of exclusion or potentially refusing to attend school.

The factors above have a major impact on a young person's self-esteem. Their sense of self should not be seen as an isolated construct but as an multi-faceted organisation with interwoven structures as identified by Marsh and Shavelson (1985) and Lawrence (1996). Burns (1982), Mosley (1995) Margerison (1996) and Huskins (1996) all argue that self-esteem is a 'key' or 'core' factor in determining how a young person behaves, learns, achieves and interacts with others within a school or indeed, any other environment.

Hellison's (1990:38) work provides insight into how physical education may be used for helping youth at risk. It provides inspiration for outdoor adventure educators to draw on. It is a holistic education perspective which emphasises people and human values rather than bodies and winning, and a broad conceptualization of health education which prioritises social, emotional and spiritual health alongside physical health. Although the subject matter was sport or a physical education programme, the focus was on the goals and strategies of the programmes based 'in a values educational perspective'.

The intention of the research project (Lilley, 1998) was to identify, examine and comment upon the impact of outdoor adventure education on young people targeted at risk in mainstream education. It draws on three principal perspectives,

• An overview of academic literature.

• A body of research undertaken with young people involved in outdoor adventure education experiences. The research is based on an ethnographic case study.

• Qualitative evidence and commentary provided by teachers, the young people and the researcher.

The research approach adopted both interpretative and qualitative perspectives that focused on searching for meanings and interpretations of the processes and practices within this social/educational context. Interviewing and observation were significant components of the method. Reflexivity, reflection on the whole of the research process, is an important part of this ethnographic case study approach (Schon 1983, Hammersley and Atkinson 1983, Humberstone 1997a, 1997b). The case study approach further sought to provide insight into the intra and interpersonal relationships. Barrett and Greenaway (1995:53) in their comprehensive view of research literature in outdoor adventure concluded that, 'humanistic and qualitative approaches' to research may offer a 'more promising way forward'. Humberstone (1996) calls for more qualitative research which tries to '...understand and make sense of the outdoor experience' thus challenging the positivistic research tradition in outdoor education. Hopkins (1982, 1985) also considers the 'deeper question' of why or how changes in the individual occur in the outdoors.

This research sought to examine the data by utilising interpretative analysis. In particular the case studies of 18 young people participating in three separate outdoor adventure education courses formed the data sources. Using this approach the research endeavoured to identify meanings and interpretations of the processes and practices involved. The study sought to identify the relevant issues and relationships and also evaluated the impact of the outdoor adventure education course from the perspective of the young people, the participant teachers and the researcher.

The case study approach provides the organisational framework allowing insights into the issues and concepts raised within this study (Hitchcock and Hughes 1995). There is a broad outline of major categories issues or recurrent themes identified from the raw data of transcripts and observations which are used as a framework for the case studies. The case studies provide an in-depth study of the relationships involved within this social/educational setting. The interview forms a major part of the research methodology and is one of the research tools for gathering evidence in the social /educational study. The interview process was open enough to gain access to the interviewee's understanding and interpretation. A research diary was also used by the researcher recording his observations and personal reflections.

The young people involved were from two schools and were selected by the special educational needs co-ordinator (SENCO) with consultation from other teachers in the school and the researcher. The participants were characterised by low self-esteem, poor interpersonal relationships with peers, teachers and adults, emotional and behavioural difficulties, and problems concerning their home or family background. The pupils at the time of the course were still attending mainstream school although several were at risk of exclusion. Others were potentially school refusing pupils. The richness of the qualitative data is used to illustrate the relationships within the study.

The home background influence on the young people involved in the study was significant. The SENCO in discussing one of the participants said she was very concerned about David as she had evidence that he was 'mixed up' and depressed. In her opinion David was unable to deal with the "...awful sorts of problems, family problems". The SENCO commented that at times David had no idea where he was going to sleep that night. She added,

> ... in his head he gets so confused he can't think straight. He can't cope with anything... . He has so much coming in and is so confused inside he can't handle it, he can't handle anything. (Lilley 1998:313)

Nevertheless, poor and challenging behaviour were major issues for the teachers with the inevitable poor peer and peer/teacher relationships in some areas of the curriculum. A young person's low self-esteem can be further reinforced by negative perceptions/ relationships with peers, teachers or other adults (Marsh and Shavelson 1985, Lawrence 1996). These typical patterns of behaviour are indicators of children with low self-esteem (Mosley 1995, Margerison 1996). Many teachers argued that the course would be a reward for poor behaviour although the researcher emphasised in meetings and negotiations that,

> The course is not a reward for bad behaviour but a chance for the young people to learn something new and change their behaviour towards one another. (Lilley 1998:317)

The researcher emphasised that the course was aimed primarily to gain personal and social benefits for the young people involved. Green Hill's Head Teacher in an interview offered this view,

> Well, as you know I took a fair amount of 'stick' and criticism from people who saw these activities you were doing as a reward for poor behaviour.

Where as you and I had discussed the philosophy and thinking behind it,
that we could get them to take responsibility for their own actions and to
co-operate and communicate with each other. Then we were hoping there
would be a benefit and a spin off in class and behaviour in the community
in general. (Lilley 1998 : 317)

Self-esteem cannot be seen in isolation, it is a global concept. An individual develops as a consequence of relationships with the family, school, peer group, work and society. Lawrence (1996) maintains that young people continue to be affected by significant people in their lives.

These issues relating to low self-esteem in this study were categorised into the main areas,

- Low academic achievement;
- Disturbed family and home background;
- Behavioural problems;
- Poor social or interpersonal skills and relationships.

These factors are inter-related and help to define the inner picture a young person has of him/herself which will affect the way the person learns or behaves. The SENCO, during the interview with the researcher, expressed her concerns for one of the participants,

The real problem is that he has got his own problems and not many people
seem to see that...he is the one reason I have decided to do this[outdoor
course]... because he will get more out of this than anybody, but the way he
is behaving in school he might not be in school because he will be
suspended...When you show you like the boy, his face just lights up. I can
not understand why I like him so much, someone's *got to. He just responds*
to some love and care. (Lilley 1998: 335)

Another form tutor wanted one of the young people to go on the course because she felt that he needed, 'something to feel proud of' to build his confidence. The SENCO developed this perception,

I think he needs to be made to feel special, it's this self-esteem thing again, isn't it? He *really* needs to be made to feel special. (Lilley, 1998:338)

Issues and themes identified from the research concurs with the work of Schoel et al (1988), Kimball (1988), Hellison (1990), Cooper (1994), Van Welzenis (1994), and Duindam (1996), that successful responses to positive challenges in an outdoor adventure education course for young people at risk can:

- Break the 'failure cycle' to provide a 'powerful motivational tool'
- Be achieved at different levels for different individuals
- Provide opportunities for fun, enjoyment, excitement and satisfaction for the individual
- Achieve satisfaction in learning new skills (Lilley, 1998: 389)

The majority of the participants when interviewed stated they had enjoyed or gained satisfaction from the outdoor experience. Below are some typical responses:

> Kevin reflected, *"It's been exciting and fun and I'd really like to do it again".* *Several participants commented that they enjoyed learning new skills and activities. Darren felt that canoeing and skiing were new activities and 'different' from school. He commented, "I've never done them before and it's a change for me". When asked why he liked new and different activities he replied, "because it's a challenge."* (Lilley 1998: 340-352)

Simeon had displayed a responsible and supportive attitude throughout the programme. He stated that he was very proud of his achievements. The Long Moor SENCO overheard a conversation during which Simeon was being teased by some other boys about the course.

'You're going because you're naughty.' He replied confidently, 'I don't care why I'm going but it's great.' (Lilley 1998 : 346)

Another example of a young person succeeding was Monib who had found nearly all the activities difficult, however he was very determined to improve and learn new skills. The SENCO was asked if the others in the group were supportive of him, she observed,

Not always at first, but they got more and more supportive as he never gave up. (Lilley 1998 : 242)

It is evident from the research data that the young peoples' behavioural response to the outdoor adventure education programme suggested that the majority of the participants,

- Achieved an excellent behavioural response
- Achieved greater awareness of how to control their behaviour
- Experienced a transfer of positive behaviour into the school environment.

The improved behaviour and awareness of positive behaviours through a supportive outdoor adventure programme can have a significant impact on a young person's self-esteem (Kimball 1988). This also implies a young person is taking greater responsibility for his own actions with sufficient self-discipline to respect and consider others (Schoel et al 1988; Hellison 1990).

The Long Moor SENCO, who had participated in two programmes, identified one of the main achievements of the outdoor programmes,

> *I think that some of them hadn't even considered their behaviour or being able to control their behaviour. That they had not only the ability to do something about their behaviour but they had a responsibility towards each other.* (Lilley 1998: 353)

Nonetheless, it is evident from the research undertaken by the author that the young people at risk can achieve positive gains in interpersonal skills and relationships through an outdoor adventure education programme (Lilley, 1998). This supports the work and findings of Schoel et al (1988), Kimball (1988), Hooper (1992), Van Welzenis (1994), Duindam (1996) and Huskins (1996).

During a discussion on team building and problem solving exercises Simeon reflected,

I liked you had to use skill, and you had to rely on the back person and the front person and the person in between.

David was aware that he had learnt to,

... listen and get on with your friends, whilst getting on with different jobs and helping.

The research (Lilley 1998) also supported the assertion that an outdoor adventure programme can provide the opportunity for young people at risk to find alternative approaches to negative interaction through discussing, negotiating and listening (Schoel et al 1988, Kimball 1988, Hooper 1992, Huskins 1996).

A key element for the majority of the participants involved was, that they were capable of interacting positively with peers and adults given a facilitative supportive climate (Rogers 1983, Hopkins and Putnam 1993, Barrett and Greenaway 1995). It is evident from the case studies that many of the young people displayed co-operative and leadership abilities including being able to resolve disputes and help the group solve problems. It is important that these qualities should be recognised by educators as valuable skills and intelligences (Gardner 1983, 1994, SCAA 1996, Brighouse 1995, 1997).

John's case study provides evidence of the significance of interpersonal relationships for young people. When asked if he liked working in a group he replied, "It's all right sir, when people respect you". (Lilley, 1998: 180)

This was a mature observation from a young person and a guide that he was beginning to understand how to develop positive relationships.

The special educational needs (SEN) class had all participated in the outdoor adventure education research project. The in-school support teacher from the BSS had noticed that her relationships with the SEN class had improved in several ways,

- she could communicate more easily with them;
- the young people were more confident to ask for her help;
- the group worked more closely together;
- the group were more able to organise themselves to complete a task or exercise in the classroom.

This underlines the positive developments and transfer of interpersonal skills and relationships within the group.

The research data identifies that many of the young people valued the opportunity to work or 'play' with their friends. This opportunity to play can have emotional health therapeutic benefits (Cattenach 1992, Williams 1993, Lilley 1996). There was evidence to suggest a positive transfer on improved interpersonal skills and relationships for the majority of the young people into their school environment. This was achieved through partnerships with the schools, the BSS and the outdoor adventure education course (Schoel et al 1988, Kimball 1988, Van Welzenis 1994, Barrett and Greenaway 1995, Duindam 1996, Huskins 1996).

The qualitative evidence in this study suggests the positive enhancement of self-esteem for young people through an outdoor adventure course which provides further confirmation of the research of Clifford and Clifford (1967), Payne et al (1970), Fletcher 1971, Roberts et al (1974), Karplan and Talbot (1983), Hopkins (1982, 1985), Yaffey (1992), Bunyan (1997), and Gibbs and Bunyan (1997). This positive intrapersonal development within this study also supports the views of several exponents of outdoor adventure education (Mortlock 1984, Cumbria 1984, Priest 1986, Hopkins and Putnam 1993, Cooper 1994, Brighouse 1996b, Huskins 1996).

One boy had a reputation and recognition from his peers of being 'tough' and aggressive. However, the SENCO felt that the outdoor course had given him a '...different quality of looking at things' which had enhanced his 'personal self-esteem'. She maintained he had gained recognition for his achievements on the course, 'from within himself'. When asked what was that 'something from within?' She replied,

I think it's realising that you're a human being, that you're unique and that although... it's easy to look at your failures isn't it? But we all have to look at our successes. ...everyone of us as teachers...have to concentrate on the positive things and not the negative things because that won't get you anywhere... will it? (Lilley, 1998:378)

This is an example of an 'energy creator' who can provide a positive role models for young people as opposed to others who provide negative reinforcement for perceived failure. When asked how taking part in the course had made him feel one participant replied, "It made you feel as if you're showing off but you're not" (Lilley, 1998:146).

It is evident from the qualitative research issues and themes identified that there were key qualities, strategies and characteristics required in order to enhance inter and intrapersonal development,

- A fresh start in a supportive, challenging and empathetic environment or climate (Jersild 1955, Rogers 1983, Hopkins 1985, Schoel et al 1988, Hopkins and Putnam 1993, Mosley 1995, Barrett and Greenaway 1995, Margerison 1996, Bunyan 1997).
- Focusing on success and achievement to break the failure cycle (Schoel et al 1988, Cooper 1994, Van Welzenis 1994, Brighouse 1995, 1997, Duindam 1996).
- Recognition and celebration of success by significant others e.g. peers, teachers and parents (Gardner 1983, 1994, Marsh and Shavelson 1985, Brighouse 1995, 1997, Lawrence 1996)
- Improved relationships with peers and teachers/adults (Marsh and Shavelson 1985, Hopkins and Putnam 1993, Mosley 1995, Margerison 1996, Lawrence 1996)
- The ability and opportunity to self-reflect in order to self-develop (Schoel et al 1988, Greenaway 1992a, 1992b, Hellison 1990, Hopkins and Putnam 1993, Van Welzenis 1994, Huskins 1996.)
- The importance of partnerships to facilitate effective transfer (Kimball 1988, Sakofs 1992, Van Welzenis 1994, Barrett and Greenaway 1995, Duindam 1996, Huskins 1996, DfEE 1997)

The research and conclusions provided insights into a number of key issues germane to the use of outdoor education with young people at risk. There was clear evidence that the improvement in the development of intra and interpersonal skills and relationships could be achieved in a supportive, facilitative environment. The perceptions that make a young person's sense of self-worth were multi-faceted and their sense of success and achievement must be recognised and celebrated by significant peers, teachers and leaders. These successes were best achieved by offering young people challenges that met their needs. An explicit recognition was that the impact of home and family life was critical to the well being and learning potential of a young person and that the intervention of multi-faceted strategies and partnerships was crucial. Although there are no guarantees of inter and intrapersonal development within an outdoor adventure education course for young people at risk, given an empathetic environment young people can learn to interact positively and respect and understand each other, adults and themselves more fully.

References

Barrett, J. and Greenaway R. (1995) *Why Adventure? The role and value of outdoor* adventure in young people's personal and social development. A review of research. Coventry: Foundation for Outdoor Adventure.

Brighouse, T. (1994) *The Value of the Outdoors,* Keynote conference speech a Taste of Adventure Project, September 30th Birmingham National Indoor Arena.

Brighouse, T. (1995) *Achievement and Quality in Education,* Keynote speech in the 'Learning Cities' Conference March 1995.

Brighouse, T. (1996) *'Creating Energy for a Better Future',* Keynote conference speech In: National Association for Outdoor Education (1996) *Outdoor Education Within Schools; An Agenda for Action. Conference Report,* West Hill College, Birmingham 18/19th April.

Brighouse, T. (1997) *An Education Development Strategy for Birmingham Towards the Year 2000.* Birmingham: Birmingham City Council Education Department.

Bunyan, P. (1997) Developing Self-Esteem through Adventure Moving from Theory to Practice. *The Journal of Adventure Education and Outdoor Leadership,* 14(3), 7-9.

Burns, R.B. (1982) *Self-Concept Development and Education.* London: Holt, Rinehart & Winston.

Cattenach, A. (1992) 'Play Therapy with Abused Children' Jessica Kingsley in Williams, J (1993) *No Bear Friend (Dramatherapy).* Support for Learning, *NASEN* 8(3), 118-124.

Clifford, E. & Clifford, M. (1967) Self-concepts before and after survival training. *British Journal of Social and Clinical Psychology,* 6, 241-248.

Cooper, G. (1994) The Role of Outdoor Education in Education for the 21st Century. *The Journal of Adventure Education and Outdoor Leadership,* 11(2), 9-12.

Cumbria (1984) *Outdoor Education in the Curriculum:* Cumbria Education Authority- A Statement of Policy. Adventure Education, 11(5), 8-10.

Department for Education and Employment (1997). *Excellence in Schools.* London: DfEE.

Duindam, T. (1996) Experiential Learning for Problem Children. *The Journal of Adventure Education and Outdoor Leadership,* 13(2), 27-29.

Fletcher, B. (1971) *The Challenge of Outward Bound.* London: Heineman.

Gardner, H. (1983) *Frames of Mind: The Theory of Multiple Intelligences.* Heineman.

Gardner, H. (1994) 'The theory of multiple intelligences' In: Moon, B. & Shelton Mays, A. (Eds.) (1994) *Teaching and Learning in the Secondary School.* London: Routledge & The Open University. pp 38-46.

Gibbs, C. & Bunyan, P (1997) The Development of Self-Esteem Through A Duke of Edinburgh's Award Scheme. *The Journal of Adventure Education and Outdoor Leadership,* 14(2) 3-5.

Greenaway, R. (1992a) Doing Reviewing. *The Journal of Adventure Education and Outdoor Leadership,* 9(1), 15-17.

Greenaway, R. (1992b) Reviewing by Doing. *The Journal of Adventure Education and Outdoor Leadership,* 9(2), 21-25.

Hammersley, M. & Atkinson, P. (1983) *Ethnography: Principles in Practice.* London & New York: Routledge.

Hellison, D. (1990) Physical Education for Disadvantaged Youth. *Journal of Physical Education, Recreation and Dance,* 61(6) 37-39.

Hitchcock, G & Hughes, D. (1995) *Research and the Teacher: A Qualitative Introduction to School-Based Research.* (Second edition.) London, New York: Routledge.

Hooper, D. (1992) MOBEX Merseyside: The Way We Work. *The Journal of Adventure Education and Outdoor Leadership,* 9(3), 6-8.

Hopkins, D. (1982) Changes in Self-Concept as the Result of Adventure Training. *Journal of Canadian Association of Health, Physical Education and Recreation.* 48(6), 9-12.

Hopkins, D. (1985) *Self-Concept and Adventure: The Process of Change.* Adventure Education, 2(1) 7-12.

Hopkins, D. and Putnam, R. (1993) *Personal Growth through Adventure.* London: David Fulton.

Humberstone, B. (1993) 'Equality, Physical Education and Outdoor Education: Ideological Struggles and Transformative Structures?' In: Evans, J. (Ed) (1993) *Equality, Education and Physical Education.* London: Falmer. pp 217-232.

Humberstone, B. (1996) Other Voices; Many Meanings? Technique and Philosophy for Outdoor Adventure: The Case for Women. *The Journal of Adventure Education and Outdoor Leadership,* 13(2), 47-51.

Humberstone, B. (1997a) Perspectives on Research in Outdoor Education: Values and Ethics. *The Journal of Adventure Education and Outdoor Leadership,* 14(1), 7-9.

Humberstone, B. (1997b) 'Challenging Dominant Ideologies in the Research Process' In: Clarke, G. & Humberstone, B. (Eds.)(1997) *Researching Women and Sport.* London: Macmillan.

Huskins, John. (1996) *Quality Work with Young People; Developing social skills and diversion from risk.* Bristol: Huskins.

Kaplan, S. & Talbot, J. F. (1983) Psychological benefits of a wilderness experience. *Human Behaviour & Environment: Advances in Theory and Research,* 6, 163-203.

Keighley, P.W.S. (1991) Education Out of Doors. *British Journal of Physical Education,* 22(2), 32-36.

Keighley, P.W.S.(1996) 'Learning through first hand experiences out of doors' Keynote conference speech. In: National Association for Outdoor Education (1996) *Outdoor Education Within Schools; An Agenda for Action. Conference Report,* West Hill College, Birmingham 18/19th April.

Keighley, P.W.S.(1997) The Impact of Experience out of Doors on Personal Development and Environmental Attitudes. *The Journal of Adventure Education and Outdoor Leadership,* 14(2) 27-29.

Kimball, Richard O. (1988) The Wilderness as Therapy. *The Journal of Adventure Education and Outdoor Leadership,* 5(3), 31-33.

Lawrence, D. (1996) *Enhancing Self-Esteem in the Classroom,* (Second edition). London: Chapman Publishing.

Lilley, T.S. (1998) *Exploring relationships and strategies in developing an outdoor adventure education experience with young people at risk based in a school community.* M. Phil Birmingham University.

Margerison, A.(1996) *Self-esteem: Its effect on the development and learning of children with EBD.* Support for Learning, NASEN, 11(4), 176-180.

Marsh, H.W. & Shavelson, R. J. (1985) Self-concept: Its multifaceted, hierarchical structure. *Educational Psychologist,* 20, 107-1.

Mortlock, C. (1984) *The Adventure Alternative.* Cumbria: Cicerone Press.

Mosley, J. (1995) 'Developing self-esteem' In: Moss, G. (ed)(1995) *The Basics of Special Needs.* London & New York: Routledge/Special Children Survival Guide.

Payne, J., Drummond, A.W. & Lunghi, M. (1970) Changes in the Self-Concepts of School Leavers who Participated in an Arctic Expedition. *The British Journal of Educational Psychology,* 40, 211-216.

Poels, V. & Van der Voort, C. (1991) 'City Bound' In: Van Welzenis, I. (1994) *City Bound: The big city as learning environment for societal-vulnerable adolescents.* The Journal of Experiential Education, 17(3), 16-19.

Priest, Simon. (1986) Redefining outdoor education: A matter of many relationships. *Journal of Environmental Education* 17(3), 13-15.

Roberts, K, White, G. & Parker, H. (1974) *The Character Training Industry.* Devon: David & Charles.

Rogers, C.R. (1983) *Freedom to Learn: For the 80's.* Columbus, Ohio: Charles E. Merrill.

Royce, R. (1987) Outdoor Education- Aims and Approaches an Inherent Dilemma. *Adventure Education,* 4(1), 12-14.

Sakofs, M. (1992) Assessing the Impact of the Wilderness Alternative for Youth Programme: An Outward Bound Programme for Adjudicated Youth. *The Journal of Adventure Education and Outdoor Leadership,* 9(4), 16-21.

Schoel, J. Prouty, D. and Radcliffe, P. (1988) *Islands of Healing: A Guide to Adventure Based Counseling.* Project Adventure: Hamilton, MA.

Schon, D (1983) *The Reflective Practitioner.* Basic Books

School Curriculum and Assessment Authority (1996) *National Forum for Values in Education and the Community,* (consultation document.) London: SCAA.

Van Welzenis, I. (1994) City Bound: The big city as learning environment for societal-vulnerable adolescents. *The Journal of Experiential Education,* 17(3), 16-19.

Williams, J. (1993) No Bear Friend (Dramatherapy). *Support for Learning,* NANSEN, 8(3), 118-124.

Yaffey, D. (1992) Personal Growth and Outdoor Experience: Some Empirical Evidence. *The Journal of Adventure Education and Outdoor Leadership,* 9(1), 32-34.

Chapter 19: Constructing Values - An Expedition Case Study

Pete Allison

"After taking a close look at myself and talking to those friends close to me, I believe that the expedition has had a large effect on me, I say entirely good effect but others might disagree."

This chapter describes the influence of a six week long British Schools Exploring Society (BSES) expedition to south west Greenland. It explores the values that participants, who were between the ages of 16.5 and 20 years old, attribute to the expedition.

Many authors have written on the value of expeditions and many organisations take people on expeditions based on their value (Hunt, 1990). For some these are purely recreational values and adventure holidays of a lifetime. Alternatively some expeditions have scientific objectives, and some, educational aims.

The word expedition is attributed a vast array of meanings and interpretations. For some it involves an overnight stay in a tent or perhaps a week away, such as for the Duke of Edinburgh's Award Scheme. For others it refers to environmental visits to clean up specific areas and for others it involves massive physical challenges such as Shackleton or more recently Fiennes and Stroud. For this reason it is important to consider the context of the expedition setting on which the information in this chapter is based.

Setting the scene

This information in this chapter comes from the naturalistic research paradigm, it is focused on understanding within a specific context (the expedition experience) and was collected using a hermeneutic approach (Packer & Addison, 1989). This involves considering participants in the study as co researchers and their contributions to the circularity of understanding and interpretive processes. During and post expedition, participants were asked to write, in unstructured personal journals, about the experiences and the value they attributed to them (assuming a constructivist ontology). The participants in the expedition have continued to write for two years following the expedition and an extensive amount of information has now been collated. Timing of writing has varied among individuals as the research has tried to accommodate the needs of the participants, their lifestyle and times when they want, and have been able, to write. This information has been summarised and returned to the 18 authors. They have then replied with comments and adjustments to the emerging themes.

Thus the approach uses the participants as a check on the validity of interpretation. The process has gone through three cycles (at the time of writing this chapter) during which the meaning of the experiences has been interpreted, communicated and understood in more detail.

Stake (1995) described the value of case study research as developing three types of generalisability. First, petite generalisations which can be made from individual case studies to other cases which are very similar in nature. Second, naturalistic generalisations which are made by the reader after understanding, in depth, the nature of the phenomena being studied and the processes which appear to be occurring. Finally, he refers to grand generalisations which can only occasionally be made and involve application of findings from case studies to broader contexts in a more rationalist 'law like' manner.

In order to understand the information presented here it is useful to describe the setting within which this research took place and the type of people who were participants in order to paint as clear a picture as possible. This has been referred to as giving a 'thick description' by Schofield (1993).

The British Schools Exploring Society is based at the Royal Geographical Society (RGS) in London and runs expeditions to remote areas of the world. In their promotional literature they describe themselves:

> *BSES Expeditions, a UK based charity, was founded in 1932 by the late Surgeon Commander G. Murray Levick, a member of Scott's Antarctic Expedition of 1910, and as such is one of the longest running organisations of its type. For over 65 years it has provided opportunities for young people from schools and many other walks of life to take part in exploratory projects in remote regions, led by experts drawn from universities, teaching and medical professions, industry and The Services. The Society's expeditions aim to help in the development of young people through the challenge of living and working in remote and challenging areas of the world.* (BSES, 1998)

The charity was previously known as the Public Schools Exploring Society (PSES) and has a rich and varied history. Until 1980 the expeditions were for males only, the society now has relatively balanced participation in terms of gender, social background and race although it still tends towards white upper-middle class males.

In 1997 one of the expeditions was to South West Greenland. This wilderness area had been identified during a previous expedition in 1992 and also on a reconnaissance in 1996. One common characteristic of expeditions is a degree of uncertainty and the 1997 expedition was not without its fair share. Originally planned for a fjord further north the expedition had to be moved in to Tasermuit Fjord. Prior to the arrival of the whole party and during the expedition, plans changed - this. as may be expected, led to an exciting but sometimes frustrating experience for many. As Arthur in Hunt (1990: 62) notes "The trouble is that on *real* expeditions the unexpected is always happening" (emphasis as original).

During the expedition participants did not have any contact with any people outside the expedition. The region is mountainous and of astounding natural beauty. Swaney (1997: 354) attempts to describe Greenland:

> *It's a challenge to describe this country. One can only repeat the words 'beautiful', 'spectacular', 'magnificent' so many times before they begin to sound flat and meaningless.... As one Greenlandic poet put it,' I get dizzy of all the beauty and shiver with happiness.'*

BSES expeditions are typically broken into two phases - science and adventure. The 1997 expedition was split in to six fires (groups) of 12 people with two leaders for each group. The first seven days of the expedition were spent transporting the groups from the airstrip to Tasermuit Fjord. Each fire then undertook a science project of some type. For some this involved mapping archaeology sites, for others botany and for others clearing rubbish left by previous climbing expeditions.

All groups received snow and ice training during this phase and later visited the ice cap undertaking a number of journeys and ascents of peaks. The remaining week of the expedition involved transport back to the airstrip, cleaning equipment and report writing. The focus of this chapter is to describe two ways in which expeditions facilitate the development of young people's values.

Theme descriptions

This section describes two of the themes that have emerged from the expedition in detail and lists the other emerging themes at the end. Quotations from the personal journals are in italics.

1. Self-Self
This overall theme refers to the relationship with the self. This involves the degree to which one is comfortable with self and the inner contentment of the individual. The category breaks down in to four sub categories which describe, in more detail, the emergent themes.

i. Confidence
Many of the comments regarding the expedition relate to self-confidence. Some people have used the word confidence while others have alluded to it in more subtle ways. Regardless of the different ways in which people have referred to it, the expedition experience appears to influence the confidence of some of the individuals.

*I really have confidence now - I can do anything. I can raise £3000 and go
on an expedition. I recently did a parachute jump for charity - is this due to
Greenland? Who knows...but there aren't many people my age who are
prepared to do things I'll do. It sounds cocky but I believe in myself
absolutely and I love the challenge. If anyone says you'll never do it - I
know I can.*

ii. Tolerance
Part of knowing the self appears to be associated with development of tolerance, for
many this means understanding ones own strengths and weaknesses. Once aware of
strengths and weaknesses then it becomes possible to work within these parameters
and to change them. This appears to occur in two primary areas. First, with regard to
understanding the self as needing to develop tolerance. Second, the practice of tolerant
behaviour in various situations.

*....if you can appreciate other people's ways and those of nature and not
let them bother you or you understand it, them, - you can appreciate the
situation for what it is. (Appreciate - to value greatly, to be grateful for). In
Greenland we had an overdose of positive - sites to value greatly,
situations, people to be grateful for and in time learned to appreciate them.
I now appreciate and I suppose value greatly the 'bad' things. The rude
boys in the fast cars, the traffic jams, hassle, getting started on whatever.*

iii. Perspective and Motivation
One of the very strong themes that has emerged from the expedition has involved
individuals perspective and motivation. For some this involves some kind of
paradigmatic shift in the way they see and experience the world around them on a
daily basis:

*A year since the expedition, I tend to notice the bigger picture, or what I
perceive the bigger picture to be. If stuck in traffic I'll look up at the clouds
and slowly bring my eyes back to the mayhem. I've got a picture of what
everything's about, sounds a bit vague, but looking at what's natural
(clouds, birds etc.) and what's not. I appreciate my position in the
pyramidal hierarchy and that of the bird, the bugs bouncing off the
windscreen etc. and get on with it.*

Another individual describes the changes that they have experienced in their overall
motivation:

*I also hold the belief, sparked from the exped, that if you do want to
succeed in what ever you want to do, then at times you have to be selfish,
not to the extent of self obsession or cruelty, but at times you have to set
goals and go for them regardless.*

iv. Authenticity

It appears that some of the participants on expeditions explore what has been described as authenticity. Taylor (1991: 28-29) describes one of the assumptions of authenticity:

> *There is a certain way of being human that is my way. I am called upon to live my life in this way, and not in imitation of anyone elses. But this gives a new importance to being true to myself. If I am not, I miss the point of my life, I miss what being human is for me. ... I can't even find the model to live by outside myself. I can find it only within. ... Being true to myself means being true to my own originality, and that is something only I can articulate and discover. In articulating it, I am also defining myself. I am realising a potentiality that is properly my own. This is the background that gives moral force to the culture of authenticity...*

Some aspects of authenticity can be seen in a number of the comments that individuals have made which suggest an exploration of what it is to be 'true to oneself':

> *I have been happier since the expedition although not necessarily more contented. I often feel 'trapped' living in the same place and want to travel elsewhere. I often find myself thinking about how to become a 'better person' and about what I want out of life. Generally more confident although I question myself more and question why I do things wondering if we really understand ourselves and our motives.*

> *Thinking too much has been a bit of a problem, well not really, just that I do think now I try to define the way I see myself more rather than just bumbling along - but at the same time the thought occurs that I am such a pin in a haystack - what really matters?*

2. Post-Expedition Adjustment

One of the themes that has emerged strongly is a period of readjustment after the expedition experience. On returning people have reported a number of adjustments that they have had to deal with - some of these tend to be more physically related while others tend to be more psychological, these two areas cannot and should not be seen as separate.

This has been described by many (e.g. Spencer Chapman 1953: 14-15) but explained by few. Gair (1997: 184-204) has likened post-expedition adjustment to post traumatic stress disorder (PTSD) which is unfortunate as this term has almost exclusively negative connotations. Rather than the negative aspects it appears that it is actually a positive sign, although difficult. If there were no signs of some type of post post-expedition adjustment then one could question if there had been any changes or examination of values during the expedition experience.

Another explanation likens the return to a form of grieving. This has typically been understood as the grieving of the deceased. Kubler-Ross (1970) wrote on this topic and explored the grieving process in her best known work, *On Death and Dying*. Complimenting this work, Scippa (1997) and Scott (1997) proposed that humans are in a constant state of grieving but that this grieving does not have to relate to death *per se*. Scippa argues that from an early age humans grieve the womb, the mother, school friends that move away, places that they have been to and numerous experiences. If this is accepted then it would seem reasonable to understand post post-expedition adjustment as a grieving process, perhaps the grieving of the environment, of the people and the community, of time alone or most likely a combination of these and other aspects of the expedition experience.

i. Physical Adjustments
Some participants reported physical difficulties in the readjustment from the expedition experience which typically lasted for around one week. The majority of these reports involve reference to the natural environment, to sleeping with the window open and or to sleeping on hard ground.

> *How can you explain to someone the reason you can't sleep is because the bed is too soft or the room is not smelly enough or even worse there are not three of you cramped into the area of a single bed kicking and snoring all night.*

> *I even found myself missing the things I hated but adjusted to: the flies, washing facilities etc.*

ii. Psychological Adjustments
Expeditions require that individuals make a number of psychological adjustments on return, for some this is more difficult than others. Stroud (1994: 32-33) has described this eloquently and suggests that " By stepping so far from normal existence, you see your life as a whole in a different perspective." This suggests an adjustment of values and a reassessment which leads to a new level of awareness and personal knowledge which can be seen in some comments:

> *I can honestly say that for the first few days I totally resented being put back in England. Life seemed boring and full of (although it sounds terrible) young people who had done nothing with their lives and valued 'Eastenders' and alcohol as important in their lives.*

3. Further Themes
This chapter has described in some detail two themes that have emerged from an expedition. Other themes which have emerged include self - other relationships, self - environment and comments regarding education and career plans.

Conclusions

From the two theme descriptions it is clear that the experiences which many people have on expeditions are profound and, for some, life changing. Individuals respond in different ways and grow in a multiplicity of ways during and after the expedition experience. Being aware and striving to understand the power of expeditions and outdoor adventure education within the context of individual narratives is critical to ensuring positive educational experiences. This is especially important when so many experiences occur at critical developmental stages. It is useful to remember the words of Smith (1990) 'anything powerful enough to do good is powerful enough to do harm'.

These themes are useful in understanding the multi-faceted nature of expeditions and the various benefits which individuals attribute to the experience. It would be naïve to think that these themes occurred without any connection to the others or in some type of systematic chronological order, rather expeditions are holistic and the benefits which individuals report are of a holistic nature. Patterson et al (1998: 427) describe the subjective holistic nature of wilderness experiences as "mutually defined (co-constituted) by the transactional relationships among settings, individuals with unique identities, and situational influences." This complexity acknowledges the subjective nature of experience and the importance of utilising appropriate research techniques to understand outdoor experiences.

It is important to note that these themes strip some of the comments from the narrative of the individuals and so do not paint a clear picture of the broader context of the individuals narrative, as this quote exemplifies:

> *After a couple of weeks, when I decided everyone in my fire, didn't not like me, were fun to talk to and wanted to talk to me, I began to think how different it was, to school, where I was ignored and disliked by most. Knowing people in the capacity of friends, rather than faces, was a new idea. I was also reassured, although not literally, that people wanted to talk to me. After 5 years at school, with no one talking to you, I felt somewhat unwanted and insignificant. Looking back to before the expedition I can also see the lack of self confidence arising from this.*

It is interesting to note some of the themes which did not emerge. For example, the physical challenges did not appear to be important to the participants. Participants reported that they found the social aspects of the expedition to be the most challenging. For example, living in a tent with 3 people for six weeks and the close proximity of the group in a challenging environment received extensive commentary. There is an overwhelming meta theme that the important aspect of the expedition is concerned with social relationships. Two quotations illustrate this:

The many activities that relied vitally on successful teamwork have increased my awareness of the importance of every individual as a member of a team and of communication within a team. This has helped increase my efforts as a team member in all manner of situations and made me look forward more to team activities. My patience towards others seems to have increased dramatically, I'm not saying that the four were testing, quite the opposite, but six weeks, twenty-four hours a day with the same people can not go incident free. As the expedition went on these incidents became easy for me to deal with and try to resolve in a logical and common-sense manner that would be satisfactory for everyone. This approach seems to have passed on into everyday life.

For the first few months I had flashbacks of events which took place in Greenland, but these are now overpowered by memories of discussions in the middle of the night underneath the stars, comments people said to me, and my overwhelming feeling that everyone will always be around, no matter where in the world they are, and primarily, that we will always be friends.

It is hoped that the case study has helped the reader to consider the nature of experience of individuals in a broader context and that the themes offered have helped to determine areas for further attention. Returning to the work of Stake, discussed earlier, it is easy to see that grand generalisations from this study are unlikely. Petite and naturalistic generalisations are the main aim of this chapter.

In his seminal book *After Virtue* Alasdair MacIntyre (1981) discusses moral theory and the state of society in the western world. He suggests that moral values and beliefs must be grown in communities and individuals can not be expected to 'be moral' unless attention is given to this 'growing people' process. It appears from this study that expeditions for young people *can contribute* to this process by facilitating the development of their values and therefore the values of society.

References

BSESE Brochure (1998) London: British Schools Exploring Society.

Gair, N.P. (1997) *Outdoor Education: Theory & Practice*. London: Cassell Education.

Hunt, J. (1990) *In Search of Adventure*. Guildford, Surrey: Talbot Adair Press.

Kubler-Ross, E. (1970) *On Death and Dying*. London: Routledge.

MacIntyre, A. (1981) *After Virtue*. Kings Lynn: Duckworth.

Packer, M.J. & Addison, R.B. (1989) *Entering the Circle*. State University of New York Press.

Patterson, M. E., Watson, A. E. Williams., D.R. Roggenbuck, J.R. (1998) An Hermeneutic approach to studying the nature of wilderness experience, in *The Journal of Leisure Research*. 30 (4): 423-452.

Schofield, J.W. (1993) Increasing the Generalisability of Qualitative Research, in M. Hammersley *Educational Research: Current Issues*. London: Open University Press.

Scippa, M. A. (1997) Conference Presentation. Heartland Region AEE Conference. Camp Tecumseh. March.

Scott, S.M. (1997) Grieving as a Dynamic Process in Transformation. 27th Annual SCUTREA conference proceedings.

Smith, T. (1990) *Wilderness Beyond...Wilderness Within*. WI: Raccoon Institute.

Spencer Chapman, F. (1953) *Watkins' Last Journey*. London: Chatto & Windus.

Stake, R.E. (1995) *The Art of Case Study Research*. London: Sage Publications.

Swaney, D. (1997) *Iceland, Greenland and the Faroe Islands*. London: Lonely Planet Publications.

Taylor, C. (1991) *The Ethics of Authenticity*. Harvard University Press.

Chapter 20: Why Outdoor Adventure Educators should use stories in transmitting values to their students

J.A. "MAC" McInnes

Introduction

It has been said (McInnes 1995, 1996) that outdoor adventure educators are inveterate storytellers.[1] They tell stories regularly and often, whenever - it seems - the opportunity to do so arises. They tell them to their fellow instructors during course debriefings or after returning from expeditions. They tell them to their students as a prelude to activities or in order to emphasize a teaching point or safety concern. They tell them while sharing meals with their fellow instructors and as 'bedtime stories' to their students. They tell them to amuse, to entertain, to scare and to teach. The common experiences and mutual acquaintanceships, shared by all outdoor adventure educators, makes the rapid movement from "random gossip or incidental circumstance to narrative account" (Benstock 1982:707) almost inevitable. As with the Dubliners of James Joyce's novels (Benstock 1982) this is so even during the most casual of meetings between otherwise complete strangers as they succumb to the temptation to build stories . . . from [natural] conversation" (Snow and Goldfield 1981).[2]

This chapter is a response to the above mentioned intuitive conclusions. It is simply a proposal of the case for making greater didactical use of the storytelling proficiency demonstrated by outdoor adventure educators. If outdoor adventure educators are inveterate storytellers, they should make a conscious effort to use narratives more competently in their pedagogical practices. Because morals cannot be forced upon others, the use of stories may be even more pertinent in inculcating moral and ethical values.

The universality of stories and storytelling

The first reason for making stories a significant pedagogical practice in outdoor adventure education is the universal nature of stories and storytelling. Outdoor adventure educators may have a particular propensity for telling stories. However, it must also be recognized that the general universality of stories, and storytelling should be "accepted a priori" (Georges 1969:313). "The products of narrative schemes are ubiquitous" (Polkinghorne 1988:14), "international, [sic.] transhistorical, transcultural: simply there, like life itself" (Barthes 1977:79). Indeed, storytelling occurs in "every age, in every place, in every society; [for storytelling] begins with the very history[3] of mankind and there nowhere is, nor has been, a people without narratives" (Barthes 1977:79).

As "everyone yields to the temptation to become a storyteller" (Reaver 1981:66), and as there is a "storymaker in each of us" (Abrahams, 1985:39), the ubiquitous nature of storytelling should be accepted unequivocally. However, stories and storytelling are more than simply ubiquitous in nature, they are also both uniquely and characteristically human.

The opinion that storytelling is uniquely and characteristically human has been circulating for some time. Micheal Novak stated in 1975 that "the human being alone among all the creatures on the earth is a storytelling animal" (Novak 1975:175). The philosopher Alasdair MacIntyre concurs with Novak in stating that "narrative ... turns out to be the basic and essential genre for the characterisation of human actions" (MacIntyre 1981:194). The psychologist Renee Fuller (1979) goes even further for she feels that "the need to make our life coherent, to make a story out of it is probably so basic" (Fuller 1979:1) to human existence that it may be stories "rather than 'bits' of information [that are] the intellectual . . . engram of our species" (Fuller 1979:2).

More recently these ideas have been gaining in strength. Visits to current web sites confirm that many authorities now believe that "we [humankind] are the story-telling animal" (MENO 1999:2) because "telling stories is how we create ourselves and the world around us" (*ibid.*). Indeed it is now claimed that "[people] cannot not make sequential events into a story" (McDaid 1999:1).[4] Since people are today accepted as being natural narrators and since outdoor adventure educators seem to be particularly adroit in this skill, then it surely behooves the discipline of outdoor adventure *education* to maximize the didactical nature of stories by using them as a tool of purposeful pedagogy.

The revival of interest in stories and storytelling

The idea, that human beings should be characterized as "*Homo Narrans*" (Gerbner 1985a)[5] has naturally been accompanied by a "revival [of interest] in the ancient art of storytelling" (Tanner 1988:1). This revival has occurred "not only [in] literary texts and ordinary language but also [in] scholarly [and] technical discourse" (Prince 1990:1) and in "scholarly circles" (Hauerwas and Jones 1989:1) in general. It has also occurred in various aspects of the popular press (Quarrick 1989:49; Tanner 1988:1).

The recent deluge of scholarly works with a focus on narratives attests to this current "renaissance of [interest in] storytelling" (Oberle 1983). Many academic disciplines (Mechling 1991) have benefited from this "abundance of recent narratological production" (Prince 1990:2) as authorities seek to verify the recent claims that narratives and stories are "a cure if not a panacea [for] a variety of . . . illness[es]" (Hauerwas and Jones 1989:1). The philosophical disciplines of epistemology (Cazden and Hymes 1978; Polkinghorne 1988; Metzger 1981; White 1981a), metaphysics (DeConcini 1990; Polkinghorne 1988; Fisher 1985), and political philosophy (Beiner

1984) have not escaped this movement towards narratological investigation. However, more importantly from the point of view of teaching values, is the fact that moral philosophy (McDermitt 1981; MacIntyre 1981; Gilligan 1982; Fisher 1984; Vokey 1988; Hauerwas and Burrell 1989) and education (Stein and Policastro 1984; Coles 1989; Egan 1988; Maguire 1988) have also benefited enormously from recent such exploration.

The use of stories in the field of outdoor adventure education has reflected this general re-emerging use of stories elsewhere (Leonard 1990:17). One repercussion of this growing interest in stories and storytelling was the formation, at the 1987 Conference on the Philosophy of Outward Bound, of a "task force" (Clarkson 1990:1) whose mandate was to "prepare a collection of stories to illustrate fundamental themes of the OB experience" (*ibid.*). Another, more recent, repercussion was the devotion of an entire issue of Ontario's Journal of Outdoor Education to the works of "Homo-marron[ic] [sic.] thinker[s]" (Henderson 1995:2).

There has, then, been a recent renewal of interest in the ancient art of storytelling within the field of outdoor adventure education. Outdoor adventure education stories have been used to examine such things as participant reactions (Horwood 1992; Villar 1984; Vokey 1985, 1986), transformative psychology (Stremba 1989; Brown 1989), storytelling techniques (Clarkson 1988; Sweda 1987; Johnson 1984), story types (Clarkson 1988; Bacon 1983), the importance and virtues of storytelling as an educational tool (Leonard 1990; Swimme 1987; Clarkson 1988; Bacon 1983) and the ritual use of contemporary legends in camp mock-ordeals (Ellis 1981, 1982). Nevertheless, this is only a scratching of the surface of the effectiveness to which stories may be put. It is a general rule that stories are rarely used in outdoor adventure education in any systematic pedagogical manner through which to educate those we instruct.

The most popular stories told by outdoor adventure educators are personal or near-personal experience stories.[6] These are stories of events involving the teller or someone the teller knows.[7] In fact, despite outdoor adventure education's renewed interest in storytelling, there is little to indicate an inclusion of these personal experience stories as part of this interest. This is a reprehensible oversight as these stories are often told, unbeknownst to the tellers (McInnes 1996), in order to teach both technical and ethical right practices. It is my contention that stories are a very powerful educational tool and that outdoor adventure educators should make a concerted effort to become more aware of the stories they tell and how they use them in order to affect the morals and values of their students.

The pertinence of the knowledge conveyed in stories

The pertinence and gravity of the knowledge gained through sharing stories has been known for some time. Indeed the fact that stories convey information has been known since people started telling stories (Nowlin 1929). This fact is a further reason for becoming more systematic in our use of stories to teach values, morals and ethics.

Some authorities[8] believe that stories are capable of addressing humankind's oldest, most abstract, and most perplexing problems. Indeed, Wittgenstein (1961:4.121) held that "certain metaphysical, ethical and logical truths could only be 'shown'" through such expressive means of language as stories, and could "never [be] 'said' or 'stated'" (Kirkwood and Gold 1983:342) in non-expressive language.

Stories have, then, in recent years gained a significant place in philosophical scholarship (cf. McInnes, 1996 for a more comprehensive analysis). Ethically, stories may be one of the principal ways in which human values are transmitted to the younger generation (Tappan and Brown 1989; Gilligan 1982; Briggs 1985; Coles 1989). They may "also function to give shape to our moral character ... and thus affect what we determine to be appropriate action as members of the community" (Hauerwas and Jones 1989:2-3 citing Gustafson 1988:19). Stories may also exist solely as a "function of the impulse to moralize" (White 1981a:14) and may be "what makes . . . values meaningful" (McGee and Nelson 1999:1). Indeed, some authorities (MacIntyre 1981; Beiner 1984; Stout 1988; and Hauerwas and Jones 1989) believe that stories are the very "embodiment of social and moral relevance" (Bennett 1985:67) and encapsulate "living traditions regarding the good and the just" (Mechling 1991:43). They may, therefore, be the ultimate medium through which we judge and comprehend the differences between right and wrong, good and bad, and as such should be used to better effect in encouraging moral behaviour in the young.

The number of scholars linking narratives to all the different aspects of philosophy makes it obvious that "to tell a story is not a modest undertaking, but engages the grand questions of human nature and human destiny" (Beiner 1984: 559). The information stories provide may be significant in addressing humankind's oldest and most perplexing problems. If we wish to promote a change in those we teach we should tell them stories for as Plato once said "those who tell stories also rule the society" (cited in Gerbner 1985b:73).

The educational impact of stories

The knowledge conveyed through stories has, then, a high degree of pertinence. Stories are also educationally significant because of the particularly impactful way in which they convey this information. It has been said that stories are the "*primary scheme* by means of which human existence is rendered meaningful" (Polkinghorne 1988:11 emphasis added). Maguire (1988) uses phrases such as "no other process" (*ibid*:6) and "provides a unique context" (*ibid* 1988:7), in describing the effectiveness of stories in transmitting information. Metzger (1981) simply refers to "the genius of the tale" (*ibid*:8) in imparting "otherwise inaccessible" (*ibid*.) knowledge. Stories, then, are thought to "connect with a part of the individual which cannot be reached by any other convention" (Ornstein 1972:170), and to "communicate with a ... truth beyond customary limitation[s] of our familiar dimensions" (*ibid*.). They are said to be capable of communicating notions few other mediums can communicate (Lamb 1981:11), and "possess a healing power almost without peer" (Leonard 1990:13 citing Cook 1976).

Despite the boldness of these claims, they do seem to have some veracity. Edward Blishen (1979:32), the English teacher and novelist, and the 1970 Carnegie Medal winner, says that "the greatest possible teacher in the matter of ideas about life, and in the matter of our constant quest to establish values, ... is the story". The tremendous and mischievous energies that lie in all marvelous stories, he says, provide stories with an "intense vigour of meaning" (*ibid*:28) that is denied to other forms of knowledge conveyance. These claims are made so boldly and unequivocally that one is apt to doubt their probity. Careful examination of these claims is necessary, therefore, before their acceptance can be confirmed.

The educational aspect of the knowledge provided through stories is well documented. Stories are known to be educationally "edifying and pedagogically useful" (Kirshenblatt-Gimblett 1978:15) and have informed "traditional education [both] formal[ly] and informal[ly] from the earliest times" (ibid.), "almost since the very beginning of human history" (Dégh 1957:91). Indeed, stories have "always been a fundamental mode of teaching" (Georges 1993:3) and have "even [been] extolled as the *primary* means of education" (Stone 1986:18 emphasis added).[9]

Stories have always been recognized as "oral transmi[tters] of knowledge" (Pentikäinen 1978:235). However, "with the rise of liberal and universal education in the late 1800s storytelling came to be regarded as an important pedagogic tool" (Stone 1986:18) within a formal educational setting. Furthermore, recent publications on education and storytelling (Baacke 1986; Calfee 1982; Cazden and Hymes 1978; Egan 1988; Georges 1993; Maguire 1988; Schön 1991); and education and folklore (Burack 1978; Coelho 1978; Haut 1991; Hufford 1978; Jackson 1984; Nusz 1991), a discipline in which stories are and always were "a principal focus" (Georges 1993:5) and one which recognizes that education is one of the three (Oring 1976) or four (Bascom 1954/65) major functions of stories, attest to the contemporary, pedagogical value placed on stories and storytelling. Scholarly expressions such as "teaching stories" (Ornstein 1972:170), used to describe Middle Eastern tales, or "stories whose main function is not to entertain or amuse but to convey knowledge" (Kirkwood and Gold 1983:342) and "pedagogical discourse" (Briggs 1985), used in describing New

Mexican treasure tales, further testifies to the current high regard that scholars have for the pedagogical value of stories.

Stories, then, have a pedagogical impact that is both historically and currently well recognized. Furthermore, because the importance of stories "as pedagogic devices has [also] been documented in many parts on the world" (Bascom 1954/65:293), this recognition may be extended to include a geographical dimension.[10]

The educational purpose of stories and of the knowledge they provide may be viewed in various different ways from the very simple Socratic maxim (Sahakian and Sahakian 1966:32) of knowing oneself (Metzger 1981:7) to the bombastic and perhaps even pretentious "install[ing] the young and regenerat[ing] the universe" (Swimme 1987:86). Other ways to view the pedagogical aims of storytelling include: to "bring [an] individual's position in line with ones own" (Briggs 1985:309); to "establish continuity with the [tellers'] own past lives and with the future lives of those who will listen" (Mullen 1992:269); "to serve as a psychological regulator or social control" (Sanderson 1981:164); to "transmit norms and values" (Järvinen 1983:27); to achieve the "socialization of children" (Kvideland 1989); to "inculcate general attitudes and principles" (Bascom 1965/54:293 citing Raum 1940:214); and even to "provoke acts of self confrontation in listeners . . . [in order] to recognize and overcome those thoughts and feelings, attitudes, and actions which impede their spiritual growth" (Kirkwood 1983:58-59). Despite these differences, stories and storytelling convey a knowledge and wisdom that is undeniably educational. Furthermore, "storytelling is a unique educational process, . . . an especially valuable . . . [and] dynamic learning experience" (Maguire 1988:6) that conveys wisdom and knowledge in a very distinctive and impactful manner. Using the story format, "one can accomplish certain pedagogical goals that are more difficult to accomplish through other means" (Kirkwood and Gold 1983:342).

Stories, then, have a high degree of educational, "informational" (Maguire 1988:6), "and indeed, moral efficacy" (Metzger 1981:7). However, it is not the educational, informational and moral efficacy, considerable though that undoubtedly is, that is the most significant aspect of stories and storytelling in regard to the development of values. What is, in all probability, the most significant aspect of stories and storytelling is the enormous extent of this efficacy. Stories have a power to convey knowledge and information and moral efficacy far in excess of other forms of such conveyance.

Both those who tell stories and those who listen to them are affected by the efficacious power that stories possess. As we have already seen, some authorities are glowing in their praise of the effectiveness of stories in activating this power (Polkinghorne 1988; Maguire 1988; Metzger 1981). Livo and Reitz (1986) believe that "there is more profound real truth in 'story' than in the common motif of daily experience" (Livo and Reitz 1986:15); Robert Downs (1979), in citing Stephen Vincent Benét, is of the opinion that "legends and yarns and folk tales are as much a part of the real history of the country as proclamations and provisos and constitutional amendments" (Downs 1979:xi-xii); Sherry Smith (1990:1 citing Lieutenant W. H. Carter) feels that stories are better at shaping our attitudes and beliefs than the real truth, and Brian Swimme (1987) says that stories are "the fundamental unit of intelligibility for advanced hominid intelligence" (Swimme 1987:83). Even a myth - according to Mircea Eliade (1975) - is "understood in the archaic societies ... [as being] a 'true story'" (Eliade 1975:1). How can such seemingly extravagant claims regarding the profoundness and real truth of stories and storytelling be justified?

Undoubtedly, stories sometimes educate, counsel and shape our beliefs and attitudes through the examples provided by the stars of the stories (Leonard 1990; Clarkson 1988; Bruner 1986:4). However, many authorities believe that stories achieve much greater impact through "double or hidden meaning" (Polkinghorne 1988:66; Ricoeur 1975) effects that "evoke a zestful imaginative play" (Bruner 1986:4) upon words, ideas and symbols.

The source of a story's power to promote learning through double or hidden meanings was recognized and used to good effect by some of the world's most renowned teachers. Plato, Socrates, Buddha, Christ and Aesop (see Kirkwood and Gold 1983:341) often taught by "insert[ing]" (Ricoeur 1967:165) the hidden meanings contained in myths, allegories, and parables into their lessons. Certain contemporary scholars and teachers (Clarkson 1988; Leonard 1990; Bacon 1983; Lankton and Lankton 1989) believe that a story's power to provide educational double meaning is housed in that story's metaphorical content.[11]

Metaphors are "figures of speech in which a word or phrase denoting one kind of object or action is used in place of another to suggest a likeness or analogy between them" (Lankton and Lankton 1989:1). Metaphors create meaning when "similarity emerges out of an initial perception of difference" (Polkinghorne 1988:55). This meaningfulness, "results primarily from a clash between [the] literal meanings" (Ricoeur 1981b:170) and the figurative meaning of words. There may be considerable difference between a word or expression's meaning in a story, and that word or expression's literal meaning. New and insightful illuminations are generated by these similarities and differences as appropriate, and perhaps unusual, relationships and connections mitigate between them. (Bacon 1983).

A story's metaphorical content provides the mental challenge which gives the story one of two sources of educative and therapeutic power derived from metaphors. This mental challenge centers around the discovery of the connections hidden in the metaphorical content of the story. Such a metaphorical challenge can only be met when "*all* the functions of the mind" (Clarkson 1988:3, emphasis added) become involved in the "nontypical [problem solving] strategies" (Bacon 1983:6) promoted by the challenge. In this way stories provide a "metaphorical looking glass" (Leonard 1990:12) through which the mind reflectively searches for an understanding of the metaphor's hidden connections. This "complex cognitive . . . transderivational" search (Bacon 1983:6) provides the different "images of the world" (Leonard 1990:12) that make, through stories and storytelling, "new perceptions, emotions and behaviors" (ibid.) possible. Metaphors have a specific nature which provides the second source of the efficacious and educational power they invaginate into a story. Metaphors, by their very nature, make "conscious the unconscious" (Clarkson 1988:3) because they use the language of the unconscious. Stories hide their metaphorical meaning behind a veil of unconsciousness. Through the use of "symbols" (Voigt 1983:318), "primordial images" (Poulsen 1985:156), "archetypes" (Livo and Reitz 1986:15), "psych[ological] interpret[ations] of the experiential world" (Metzger 1981:8) and physical embodiment of internal expressions (Abrahams 1979:401), stories have - because of their metaphorical content - a unique power to promote the "release of repressions" (ibid.), the "struggle for individuation" (ibid.) and the confrontation of projections (Horner 1971; Dundes 1976; 1985).

There is a certain uniqueness, then, in the way that stories convey information, wisdom and knowledge. Not only is this knowledge of particular salience and pertinence in its own right in that it addresses some of humankind's most perplexing problems, it is also conveyed in a manner that is highly impactful. Some authorities believe that these factors make storytelling activities "the most important political and economic act of our time" (Swimme 1987:83), "the dominant power source for . . . the health of the people" (Victor 1987:2), and that which make us "progressively more capable of perceiving ever new truths . . . [and of] experiencing personal growth" (Heuscher 1974:x-xi). If we add to these factors the previously mentioned appropriateness of using stories for the investigation of such information, then we have a very powerful mandate for examining stories.

Summary

It is clear from the foregoing analysis that there are a number of very powerful reasons for using stories to promote morality. First, the profuse existence of stories and storytelling among outdoor adventure education instructors is sufficient initial reason for using them to teach others. Second, the renaissance of interest in stories indicates to some extent their worth as a tool of pedagogy.

The third and fourth reasons for encouraging the telling of stories in the transmission of moral values to others has to do with the type of information they provide. This information is - first, highly impactful - being ensconced in the unconscious - and second, highly pertinent, addressing - as it does - some of humankind's most perplexing moral problems. All in all, then, a convincing case has been made for encouraging outdoor adventure educators to use their natural propensity to tell stories in a more pedagogically systematic manner in the transmission of morals and values to those they educate.

Notes

1. This, intuitive, conclusion has been drawn with some confidence. Seventeen years of international involvement as an instructor at a number of outdoor adventure education

establishments, with indirect experience of at least ten different countries spanning four continents, gives rise to this confidence. During this time numerous informal observations were made of the social discourse of those with whom I worked, my fellow outdoor adventure education instructors. These observations, though unsystematic, provide powerful evidence supporting the claim that outdoor adventure educators are inveterate storytellers. When compared intuitively to other populations with whom I have had some dealings, (ten years in higher education, seven years in secondary education and nine years in coaching) the conclusions are similar. Outdoor adventure educators seem particularly inclined to tell stories.

2. Abrahams (1985) says that this movement from conversational to narrative discourse is a "representatively human" (ibid:39) process. "We are able," he says, "to relate, by storytelling, with people with whom we have never otherwise had a relationship because stories . . . give us some sense of engagement with others that we may not even know" (ibid:35). These ideas are also expressed by Helen Mary Brown (1985).

3. Strange as it may seem, this may be too late for some authorities. Scholes and Kellogg (1966) believe that language, and presumably, by implication, storytelling, has a longer history than "man himself, having been invented by some missing link . . . between man and the gibbon" (ibid:17). Additionally, on the one hand, "it may have been as many as a million years ago that man first . . . invented literature" (ibid) "not as an affair of pen and ink [but as] warning examples naturally told by a mother to her children" (Nowlin 1929:1); and not as written texts but as physical gestures (Boremann 1980), and on the other "the oldest confirmed fossils from modern humans are [only] 120,00 years [old]" (Lemonick 1994:45 citing Christopher Stringer) we can claim, with considerable confidence, that stories have been a part of our human heritage since *before* even the beginnings of human history.

4. Indeed, according to one authority, presumably speaking ironically, it would be impossible for man not to tell stories for, telling stories is the exact purpose for which "God . . . [who] loves stories" (Wiggins 1975:ix citing Elie Wiesel) created human beings.

5. The origins of the use of the expression *Homo Narrans* to capture "the ideas that homo sapiens, faber and ludens is by nature also a narrator" (Dégh 1994:245) is somewhat contentious. Mechling (1991), Nicolaisen (1984:260) and Gerbner (1985a and b) have all used the expression with something of a disregard for its origins. Linda Dégh (1985a:235) states that "Rank's interpretation, . . . of Jolles' Geistesbeschaftigung [sic.] concept led to the generalization of the *homo narrans* idea. However, the modern use of the expression was probably initiated by Barbara Myerhoff (1978) as "she characterizes our species as *Homo Narrans*, humankind the story-teller" (Turner 1978:xi) in the conclusions to her book *Number Our Days* where she categorically states that storytelling is a human constant (Myerhoff 1978:272).

6. Initially the term personal experience stories has been used to refer to those stories that are "based on [the] real experiences" (Stahl 1989:ix) of the teller. The term near-personal experience stories is applied to those experience narratives which the teller, perhaps because of close acquaintanceship with the story's protagonist, "may still regard as personal" (Gwyndaf 1985:224). These near-personal experience stories retain their "personal nature as much as if the teller had stated: 'This happened to me" (Dégh 1985b:102). Personal and near-personal experience stories may therefore be viewed as one and the same.

7. Gwyndaf (1985), Dégh (1985b), Stahl (1989), Robinson (1981) and McInnes (1996) have provided comprehensive definitions of the exact nature of the personal and near personal experience stories.

8. It must be noted that there is a vast amount of scholarship demonstrating a link between narrative discourse and humankind's oldest, most abstract and most perplexing problems. Barbara DeConcini (1990) has summed up this work in her book *Narrative Remembering*.

9. A number of authorities (Cazden and Hymes 1978:27; Barnes, Britton and Rosen 1971:25-6; Kirkwood and Gold 1983:341-2; Robinson and Hawpe 1986:123) have noted a recent repression, decline, wide disparagement and, indeed, abandonment of storytelling in the formal pedagogical environment. This "bias against narrative" (Robinson and Hawpe 1986:123) is thought to be the result of a scholastic emphasis on "definition, abstraction, conceptual analysis, and rigorous canons of evidence or proof" (ibid.). Whatever the reasons for such repression and disparagement, the results are unequivocal. A failure to use stories in the pedagogical process does enormous disservice to the "richness of human experience" (Egan 1988:7) they make directly accessible (ibid.) to the student.

10. It must be remembered, however, that "stories can be [as much] instruments of indoctrination" (Tappan and Brown 1989:200) as education. This "century's manipulating of folklore for governmental or commercial ends" (Jabbour 1989:296) offers a more than adequate illustration of the way "ideological propaganda" (Dundes 1975:8) is used in folklore, and by implication in stories, "to demonstrate the validity and correctness of a particular political point of view" (ibid. citing Dorson 1963) or to support "political ideology and virulent nationalism" (Dorson 1972b:16). Kamenetsky (1972, 1977), Mieder (1982) and Zipes (1986, 1988) have all produced works that further illustrates the indoctrinating aspects of folklore and stories.

11. Other scholars acknowledge that metaphors are just one of four ways in which a story generates meaning (Polkinghorne 1988:55; White 1973:31-37; Ricoeur 1975:55-59). The three other "master tropes" (Polkinghorne 1988:55) of "poetic language" (White 1973:x) are metonymy, synecdoche and irony. Despite differing from metaphors in the "kinds of reductions or integration they effect on the literal level of their meanings and by the kinds of illuminations they aim at on the figurative level" (White 1973:34), they are all generally recognized as being different "kinds of Metaphor" (ibid.). Whereas "Metaphor is essentially representational, Metonymy is reductionist, Synecdoche is integrative, and irony is negational" (White 1973:34). All three act, as do all metaphors, by facilitating understanding through the generation of connections. Metonymy promotes understanding by providing contiguous connections "characterized by part-to-part relations[ships]" (Polkinghorne 1988:55); synecdoche, promotes understanding by means of the integrative connections "characterized by part-to-whole relationships" (ibid.); and irony, generates meaning through negative connections by "say[ing] things about something in alternative ways" (ibid.).

References

Abrahams, R.D. (1979) Folklore in Culture: Notes Towards an Analytic Method. In *Readings in American Folklore*, edited by Jan Harold Brunvand, 391-403. New York: W. W. Norton and Co.

————. (1985) Our Native Notion of Story. *New York Folklore* 11(1-4):37-47.

Baacke, D. (1986) Narration and Narrative Analysis in Education and Educational Science. In *Narrative Analysis: An Interdisciplinary Dialogue*, edited by Gülick, E. & Quasthoff, U.M. 57-72. Poetics (Sp Iss) 15(1-2):1-242.

Bacon, S. (1983) *The Conscious Use of Metaphor in Outward Bound*. Denver, Co.: Colorado Outward Bound School.

Barnes, D.; Britton, J.; Rosen, H. (1971) *Language, the Learner and the School: A Research Report by Douglas Barnes with Contributions from James Britton and a Discussion Document Prepared by Harold Rosen on Behalf of the London Association of the Teachers of English*. London: Penguin.

Barthes, R. (1977) Introduction to the Structural Analysis of Narratives. In *Image, Music, and Text: Essays Selected and Translated by Stephen Heath*, 79-124. London: Fontana/Collins.

Bascom, W.R. (1954/65) Four Functions of Folklore. Reprinted in *The Study of Folklore*, edited by Dundes, A. 279-98. Englewood Cliffs, N.J.: Prentice-Hall.

Beiner, R. (1984). Philosophical and Narrative Truth: The Theorist as Storyteller. *Queen's Quarterly* 19(3):549-559.

Bennett, Gillian. (1985). What's Modern About the Modern Urban Legend? In Kvideland and Selberg (eds) (1985)

Benstock, S. (1982) The Dynamics of Narrative Performance: Steven Dedalus as Storyteller. *ELH* 49(3):707-738.

Blishen, E. (1979) The Impulse to Story. In *Through Folklore to Literature: Papers Presented at the Australian National Section of IBBY Conference on Children's Literature*, edited by Saxby, M. 27-41. Sidney: IBBY Australia Publishers.

Boremann, E.G. (1980) *Communication Theory*. New York: Holt, Rinehart and Winston.

Bottigheimer, R.B. (ed) (1986) *Fairy Tales and Society. Illusion, Allusion and Paradigm*. Philadelphia: University of Pennsylvania Press.

Briggs, C.L. (1985) Treasure Tales and Pedagogical Discourse in Mexicano New Mexico. *Journal of American Folklore* 98(389):287-314.

Brown, H.M. (1985) That Reminds Me of a Story: Speech Action in Organizational Socialization. *Western Journal of Speech Communication* 49(Wi.):27-42.

Brown, M.H. (1989) Transpersonal Psychology: Facilitating Transformations in Outdoor Experiential Education. *Journal of Experiential Education* 12(30):47-56.

Bruner, J. (1986) *Actual Minds Possible Worlds*. Cambridge, Mass. and London: Harvard University Press.

Burack, L. (ed) (1978) *Folklore and Education* Keystone Folklore (Sp Iss) 22(1-2): 13-105.

Calfee, R. (1982) Some Theoretical and Practical Ramifications of Story Grammar. *Journal of Pragmatics* 6(5-6):441-50.

Cazden, C. & Hymes. D. (1978) Narrative Thinking and Storytelling Rights: A Folklorist's Clue to a Critique of Education. In Burack. (ed) (1978) 21-35.

Clarkson, A. (1988) *Stories for Outward Bound: Themes and Interpretation*. No City: Soundway Press.

————. (1990) Personal Correspondence.

Coelho, D. (1978) The Folklorist and the Folk Artist-in-the-Schools Program: A Case for Involvement. *Keystone Folklore* 22(3):1-15.

Coles, R. (1989) *The Call of Stories: Teaching and the Moral Imagination*. Boston: Houghlin Mifflin.

DeConcini, B. (1990) *Narrative Remembering*. New York: University Press of America.

Dégh, L. (1957) Some Questions of the Social Function of Storytelling. *Acto Ethnographica* 6(1-2):91-147.

————. (1985a) The Theory of Personal Experience Narratives. In Kvideland and Selberg, (eds) (1985) 233-46.

————. (1985b) "When I Was Six We Moved West . . .;" Theory of Personal Experience Narrative. *New York Folklore* 11(1-4):99-108.

————. (1994) The Approach to Worldview in Folk Narrative Study. *Western Folklore* 53(3):243-52.

Dorson, R.M. (1963) Current Folklore Theories. *Current Anthropology* 4:93-112.

Dorson, R.M. (ed). (1972a) *Folklore and Folklife: An Introduction*. Chicago and London: University of Chicago Press.

————. (1972b) Introduction: Concepts of Folklore and Folklife Studies. In Dorson, (1972a) 1-50.

————, (Ed. 1978) *Folklore in the Modern World*. The Hague and Paris: Mouton.

————, (Ed. 1983) *Handbook of American Folklore*. Bloomington: Indiana University Press.

Dorson, R.M. & Stahl, S.D. (eds) (1977) *Stories of Personal Experiences*. Journal of the Folklore Institute (Sp Iss) 14(1-2):5-126.

Downs, R.B. (1979) Introduction: The Oral Tradition. In *The Story Experience*, by Wilson, J.B. vii-xiv. Metuchen, NJ. and London: Scarecrow Press.

Dundas, A. (1975) The American Concept of Folklore. In *Analytic Essays in Folklore*, by Dundes, A. 3-16. The Hague/Paris: Mouton.

————. (1976) Projection in Folklore: A Plea for Psychoanalytic Semiotics. *MLN* 91(5):1500-1533. John Hopkins University Press.

————. (1985) The Psychoanalytic Study of Folklore. *Annals of Scholarship: Studies of the Humanities and Social Sciences* 3(3):1-42.

Egan, K. (1988) *Teaching as Storytelling. An Alternative Approach to Teaching and Curriculum in the Elementary School*. London, Ont.: The Althouse Press.

Eliade, M. (1975) *Myth and Reality*. (Trans. by Trask, W.R.). New York and Cambridge: Harper Torchbooks.

Ellis, B. (1981) The Camp Mock-Ordeal: Theater as Life. *Journal of American Folklore* 94(374):486-505.

————. (1982) "Ralph and Rudy": The Audience's Role in Recreating a Camp Legend. *Western Folklore* 41(3):169-91.

Fisher, W.R. (1984) Narration as a Human Communication Paradigm: The Case of Public Moral Argument. *Communication Monographs* 51(1) 1-22.

————. (1985) The Narrative Paradigm: In the Beginning. In Gerbner (1985a). 74-89.

Fuller, R. (1979) *Making Stories May Be Fundamental to Human Thinking*. Brain/Mind Bulletin 5(2):1-2.

Georges, R.A. (1969) Towards an Understanding of Storytelling Events. *Journal of American Folklore* 82(326):313-28.

———, (ed) (1991a) Taking Stock: Current Problems and Future: [sic] Prospects in American Folklore. *Western Folklore* (Sp Iss) 50(1):1-126.

———. (1993) Using Storytelling in University Instruction. *Southern Folklore Quarterly* 50(1):3-17.

Gerbner, G. (ed) (1985a) Homo Narrans: Story-telling in Mass Culture and Everyday Life. *Journal of Communication* (Sp. Sect.) 35(4):73-174.

———. (1985b) Introduction. In Gerbner, (1985a) 73-4.

Gilligan, C. (1982) *In a Different Voice: Psychological Theory and Woman's Development*. Cambridge, Mass.: Harvard University Press.

Gwyndaf, R. (1985) Memorates, Chronicates and Anecdotes in Action: Some Remarks Towards a Definition of the Personal Narrative in Context. In Kvideland and Selberg. (1985) 217-24.

Hauerwas, S. & Burrell, D. (1989) From System to Story: An Alternative Pattern for Rationality in Ethics. In Hauerwas, and Jones, (1989) 158-90

Hauerwas, S. and Jones, L.G. (eds) (1989) *Why Narratives? Readings in Narrative Theology.* Grand Rapids, Mich.: William B. Eerbman's Publishing Co.

Haut, J.E. (1991) Folklore in the Classroom: 19th-Century Roots, 20th-Century Perspectives. In Georges, (1991a) 65-73.

Henderson, B. (1995) Editor's Log Book. *Pathways: The Ontario Journal of Outdoor Education* 7(5):2.

Heuscher, J.E. (1974) *A Psychiatric Study of Myths and Fairy Tales: Their Origins, Meaning and Usefulness.* Springfield, Ill: Charles C Thomas.

Horner, G.R. (1971) Folklore as a Psychological Projective System. *The Conch* 3(1): 3-13.

Horwood, B. (1992) The Goat Portage. Students' Stories and Learning from Canoe Trips. *CAHPER Journal* 58(4):18-22.

Hufford, M. (1978) Reply to Dennis Caelho. *Keystone Folklore* 22(3):15-16.

Jabbour, A. (1989) Values of American Folklorists. *Journal of American Folklore* 102(405):292-8.

Jackson, B. (1984) *Teaching Folklore.* Buffalo, NY.: Documentary Research (For the American Folklore Society).

Järvinen, I. (1983) Transmission of Norms and Values in Finnish-Karelian Sacred Legends. *ARV Scandinavian Yearbook of Folklore* 39:27-33.

Johnson, E.J. (1984) High Touch: The Personality of Storytelling. *Journal of Physical Education, Recreation and Dance* 55(8) 52-4.

Kamenetsky, C. (1972) Folklore as a Political Tool in Nazi Germany. *Journal of American Folklore* 85(337):221-35.

———. (1977) Folktales and Ideology of the Third Reich. *Journal of American Folklore* 90:(356)168-78.

Kirkwood, W.G. (1983) Storytelling and Self-Confrontation: Parables as Communication Strategies. *The Quarterly Journal of Speech* 69(1):58-74.

Kirkwood, W. &Gold, G. (1983) Using Teaching Stories to Explore Philosophical Themes in the Classroom. *Metaphilosophy* 14(3-4):341-52.

Kirshenblatt-Gimblett, B. (1978) Introduction. In Burack, (1978) 15-20.

Kvideland, R. (1989) Stories of Death and the Socialization of Children. In Kvideland, R. & Sehmsdorf, H.K. with Simpson, E. (eds) (1989) *Nordic Folklore: Recent Studies.* 232-7. Bloomington and Indianapolis: Indiana University Press.

Kvideland, R. & Selberg, T. (eds) (1985) *Papers I-IV. The Eighth Congress for the* International Society for Folk Narrative Research, Bergen June 12th-17th, 1984 Bergen: Forlaget Folkekultur.

Lamb, S.P. (1981) Shifting Paradigms and Modes of Consciousness: An Integrated View of the Storytelling Process. *Folklore and Mythology Studies* 5(Sp): 5-19.

Lankton, C.H. & Lankton, S.R. (1989) *Tales of Enchantment: Goal-Oriented Metaphors for Adults and Children in Therapy.* New York: Brunner/Mazel Inc.

Lemonick, M.D. (1994) How Man Began. *Time Magazine* 143(11, March 14th):38-45.

Leonard L.S. (1990). Storytelling as Experiential Education. *Journal of Experiential Education* 13(2):12-7.

Livo, N.J. & Reitz, S. A. (1986) *Storytelling: Process and Practice.* Littleton, Col.: Libraries Unlimited.

MacIntyre, A. (1981) *After Virtue.* London: Duckworth.

Maguire, J. (1988) Sounds and Sensibilities: Storytelling as an Educational Process. *Children's Literative Association Quarterly* 13(1):6-9.

Mandl, H.; Stein, N.L.; Trabasso, T. (eds) (1984) *Learning and Comprehension of Text.* Hilldale, NJ.: Lawrence Erlbaun Associates.

McDaid. (1999) Approaches. http://www.dstory.com/dsf1/story/ McDaid/approach.htm. Page 1 of 1.

McDermitt, B. (1981) The Belief System of a Scottish Traveler As Reflected in His Memorates, Legends and Tales. *ARV: Scandinavian Yearbook of Folklore* 37:43-51.

McGee, M.C. & Nelson, J.S. (1999) *Narrative Reason in Public Argument.* http://bradley.bradley edu./ ~ell/fisher.html. Page 1 of 2.

McInnes, J.A. (1995) The Fieldwork Methods Involved in Collecting Stories for Scholarly Investigation. In Walmsley, K.B. (ed) (1995) *Method and Methodology in Sport and Cultural History.* 127-136. Dubuque, IA: Brown and Benchmark.

————. (1996) *Conscious and Unconscious Use of Stories in Outward Bound: A* Folkloric Examination of the Personal Experience Stories of Outdoor Education *Instructors.* Unpublished Doctoral Dissertation: School of Health, Physical Education and Recreation, Ohio State University, Columbus, Ohio.

Mechling, J. (1991) Homo Narrans: Across the Disciplines. In Georges, (1991a) 29-40.

MENO (Multimedia Education and Narrative Oganisation). 1999. Website. http://www.svcc.cc.il.us/academ...sses/murray/ hum210/210note5.htm. Page 2/6.

Metzger, M.M. (1981) Preface. In Metzger and Mommsen, (1981) 1-10.

Mieder, W. (1982) Proverbs in Nazi Germany: The Promulgation of Anti-semitism and Stereotypes Through Folklore. *Journal of American Folklore* 95(378):435-64.

Mitchell, W. J. T. (ed) (1981). *On Narrative.* Chicago and London: University of Chicago Press.

Mullen, P.B. (1992) *Listening to Old Voices: Folklore, Life Stories and the Elderly.* Urbana and Chicago: University of Illinois Press.

Myerhoff, B. (1978) *Number Our Days.* New York: E. P. Dutton.

Nicolaisen, W.F.H. (1984) Names and Narratives. *Journal of American Folklore* 97(385):257-72.

Novak, M. (1975) "Story" and Experience. In Wiggins (1975)

Nowlin, C.H. (1929) *The Storyteller and His Pack.* Springfield, Mass.: Milton Bradley.

Nusz, N.J. (guest ed) (1991) Folklife and Education *Southern Folklore* (Sp Iss) 48(1): 3-84.

Oberle, M. (1983) The Renaissance of Storytelling. In Crouch, I.W.; Owen, G.R.; Anderson, K.E.; Kleinau, M. (eds) *Proceedings of the Seminar/ Conference on Oral Tradition.* 58-64.Las Cruces: New Mexico University Press.

Oring, E. (1976) The Three Functions of Folklore. *Journal of American Folklore* 89(351):67-80.

Ornstein, R. (1972) *The Psychology of Consciousness.* San Francisco: W. H. Freeman.

Pentikäinen, J. (1978) Oral Transmission of Knowledge. In Dorson, (1978) 235-52.

Polkinghorne, D.E. (1988) *Narrative Knowing and the Human Sciences.* Albany, NY.: State University of New York Press.

Poulsen, R.C. (1985) Legend: An Imagine in Time. In Kvideland and Selberg, (1985) 147-61.

Prince, G. (1990) On Narratology (Past, Present, Future). *FLS* 17:1-14.

Quarrick, G. (1989) *Our Sweetest Hours: Recreation and the Mental State of Absorption.* Jefferson, NC. and London: McFarland and Co.

Reaver, J. R. (1981) Socio-Psychic Levels of Narrative. *Fabula* 22(1-2):67-73.

Ricoeur, P. (1967) *The Symbolism of Evil* (Trans. Emerson Buchanan). New York/Evanston/London: Harper and Row.

————. (1975) *The Rule of Metaphor: Multi-disciplinary Studies of the Creation of Meaning in Language.* (Trans. Czerny, R.; McLaughlin, K.; Costello, J.) Toronto and Buffalo: University of Toronto Press.

————. (1981a) The Narrative Function. In Thompson (1981) 274-305.

————. (1981b.) Metaphor and the Central Problem of Hermeneutics. In Thompson (1981) 165-81.

Robinson, J.A. (1981) Personal Narrative Reconsidered. *Journal of American Folklore* 94(371):58-85.

Robinson, J.A. & Hawpe, L. (1986) Narrative Thinking as a Hueristic Process. In Sarbin T.R. (ed) (1986) *Narrative Psychology: The Storied Nature of Human Conduct.* (111-25) New York/Westport, Conn./London: Praeger.

Sahakian, W.S. & Sahakian, M.L. (1966) *The Ideas of the Great Philosophers.* New York, Hagerstown, San Francisco and London: Barnes and Noble Books.

Sanderson, S. (1981) From Social Regulator to Art Form: Case Study of a Modern Urban Legend. *ARV*: Scandinavian Yearbook of Folklore 37 161-6.

Scholes, R. & Kellogg, R. (1966) *The Nature of Narrative.* New York: Oxford University Press.

Schön, D.A. (ed) (1991) *The Reflect Turn: Case Studies In and On Educational Practice.* New York and London: Teacher's College, Columbus University, Teacher's College Press.

Smith, S.L. (1990) *The View from Offices' Row: Army Perceptions of Western Indians.* Tucson: University of Arizona Press.

Snow, C. & Goldfield, B.A. (1981) Building Stories: The Emergence of Information Structures From Conversation. In *Analyzing Discourse. Talk and Text*, edited by Tannen, D.F. 127-41. Washington, D.C.: Georgetown University Press.

Stahl, S.K.D. (1989) *Literary Folkloristics and the Personal Narrative.* Bloomington and Indianapolis: Indiana University Press.

Stein, N.L. & Policastro, M. (1984) The Concept of a Story: A Comparison Between Children's and Teacher's Viewpoint. In Mandl, et al. (1984) 113-55.

Stone, K.F. (1986) Oral Narrative in Contemporary North America. In Bottigheimer (1986) 13-31.

Stout, J. (1988). *Ethics After Babel: The Language of Morals and Their Discontent.* Boston: Beacon Books.

Stremba, B. (1989) Reflection: A Process to Learn About Self through Outdoor Adventure. *Journal of Experiential Education* 12(2):7-9.

Sweda, A.J. (1987) Storytelling. *Teacher's Outdoors* :7-8.

Swimme, B.T. (1987) The Resurgence of Cosmic Storytellers. *ReVision* 9(2):83-88.

Tanner, C.W. (1988) *The Criteria for Judging the Suitability of a Story for Telling.* Doctoral Dissertation: School of Library and Information Studies, Texas Woman's University.

Tappen, M.B. & Brown, L.M. (1989) Stories Told and Lessons Learned: Towards a Narrative Approach to Moral Development and Moral Education. *Harvard Educational Review* 59(2):182-205.

Thompson, J.B. (ed and trans) (1981) *Paul Ricoeur: Hermeneutics and the Human Sciences: Essays on Language, Action and Interpretation,* Cambridge: Cambridge University Press.

Turner, V. (1978) Forward. In Myerhoff (1978) ix-xiii.

Victor, K. (1987) Personal Correspondence.

Villar, R. N. (1984) So You Want to Climb Everest . . .? *British Medical Journal* 289(6460):1773-5.

Voigt, V. (1983) Folklore, Folklorism, Symbol, Symbolism. *Neohelicon* 10(2):305-20.

Vokey, D. (1985) *The Functions of Stories in Organizing and the Implications for Organizational Innovations,* Unpublished Paper. Queens University: Faculty of Education.

————. (1986) The Role of Story Telling in Innovative Organizations. *Journal of Colorado Outward Bound Wilderness School Education* (Feb.):21-26.

————. (1988) *Stories, Storytelling and Moral Judgment,* Unpublished Term Paper. Ontario Institute for Studies in Education: Dept. of History and Philosophy.

White, H. (1973) *Metahistory: The Historical Imagination in Nineteenth-Century Europe.* Baltimore and London: The Johns Hopkins University Press.

————. (1981a) The Value of Narrativity in the Representation of Reality. In Mitchell (1981) 1-23.

Wiggins, J.B. (ed) (1975) *Religion as Story.* New York: Harper and Row.

Wittgenstein, L. (1961) *Tractatus Logico-Philosophicus,* (Trans. by D. F. Pears and B. F. McGuinness). London:Routledge and Kegan Paul.

Zipes, J. (1986) Marxists and the Illumination of Folk and Fairy Tale. In Bottigheimer (1986) 237-243.

————. (1988) *Fairy Tales and the Art of Subversion: The Classic Genre for Children and the Process of Civilization.* New York: Methuen.

Chapter 21: Enhancing the Quality of the Outdoor Experience

David Hopkins

The theme of this text that focusses on "values" provides with me with an excellent excuse to quote from one of my favourite books, *Zen and the Art of Motorcycle Maintenance*. I am reminded of the question Robert Pirsig asks his *alter ego* Phaedrus: "And what is good Phaedrus, and what is not good - need we ask anyone to tell us these things?" This question and the rhetorical response directly addresses the central problem in any discussion of quality - how can we get beyond the subjective and relative in considering quality. Quality is unfortunately a concept that means all things to all people. In his essay *Quality in Education* David Hargreaves (1992) takes 'fitness for purpose' as the defining criteria of quality. This definition leads however, as Hargreaves admits, to difficult questions about, purposes or aims, the basis on which one judges whether goals are realised - the kind of evidence that is relevant to outcomes/inputs/processes, and the actions that might or should be taken to improve quality.

In considering the quality of the outdoor experience I shall follow Hargreaves' lead and address the following three issues:

- Essential Components of the Quality Outdoor Experience

- Researching the Quality Experience

- The Process of Quality Improvement

Essential components of the quality outdoor experience

It seems to me that there are some fundamental or defining characteristics of the 'quality' outdoor experience. If they are not present to some degree then the outdoor experience for the individual involved will inevitably lack quality. The following six characteristics are drawn from research, experience and common sense:

- Discovering the 'Self'

- Reciprocity of the Group

- Authenticity of the Facilitator or Instructor

- Confrontation Based Activities

- Outdoor Environment & Landscape

- Experience of Adventure

Space precludes an individual discussion of each of these factors, but they are all commonly known. They are the basic ingredients of a quality outdoor experience. Three qualifications need to be added however. The first is to re-affirm that the impact of this combination of factors is on the 'self concept' of the individual concerned.

Secondly, I should emphasise that these factors are necessary but not sufficient conditions for the quality outdoor experience for the individual concerned. They provide excellent guidelines for programme design but will not guarantee a positive experience for the individual - the gain in self-concept - unless the experience involves the individual concerned in *learning*. Quality learning not only involves the individual in an active construction of meaning but it also requires some interaction with prior experience. This means that in some way the learning experience for the individual has to be matched to their individual needs. This is what I have previously called the 'problem of the match' (cf. Hopkins & Putnam, 1993) - how an instructor or facilitator creates a unique experience for each individual in their group within the parameters of the six 'essential components'.

Thirdly, although it is self-concept that is the most usual beneficiary of the outdoor experience, there may be other positive outcomes. Many programmes claim a range of outcomes, but these are dependent on specific programme designs. I assume, for example, that quality management development programmes have a series of additional programme elements designed to promote specific management outcomes. All of these outcomes will tend to be relatively short term unless the individual need and the experience were closely matched or unless the programme design involves follow up and on-going feedback.

I should also add, particularly in a book on values, that when considering the quality of the outdoor experience it is important to identify what the values we are transferring consist of. Are they always positive, or is it possible to transfer negative values through the outdoor experience? Do we teach that success, in a climbing session for example, is all-important or do we also teach the values of caring for others more than worrying about the overall success of a project?

Professional judgement and research

The second point concerns the evaluation of success and the researching of programme effects. The commitment to quality involves participants, process, as well as outcomes. The surest way of ensuring quality is for those involved in delivering the programme to be using their 'professional judgements' to evaluate programme success. 'Professionals' do this through (adapted from Hargreaves & Hopkins, 1991):

- individual reflection

- discussion with others about the extent of progress or success

- establishing agreements on standards used to make judgements

- mutual observation

- the use of informed opinion

If these activities are commonplace within, say, an outdoor centre, then in my opinion it is well on its way to becoming a 'learning organisation' and to ensuring a quality culture. It is not a big step to elevate this 'reflection on practice' to more systematic research. In *Figure 1* I have indicated how an outdoor centre could more systematically research the impact of its courses on participants. This is done by evaluating the differential impact of individual programme elements upon desired outcomes. It is only through being self conscious about programme design that we can begin to understand what quality is and make efforts to improve it.

	Experience 1	
Participant	Experience 2	Outcome
	Experience 3	

Figure 1. Researching the Quality Experience - 1

In *Figure 2* I have suggested a way in which a larger research project could be undertaken with similar ends *i.e.* to identify those programme elements most consistent with desired outcomes. This is the approach being taken by the Foundation for Outdoor Adventure in collaboration with the Brathay Hall Trust in its second phase of research: the first phase being the commissioned review undertaken by Jon Barrett and Roger Greenaway - *Why Adventure?* (1995). It is only through enquiry that we refine practice.

Programme 1	Experience 1	Outcome 1
Programme 2	Experience 2	Outcome 2
Programme 3	Experience 3	Outcome 3

Figure 2. Researching the Quality Experience - 2

The process of quality improvement

There is much talk nowadays about quality assurance, a term I prefer to quality control. (Parenthetically it seems to me that outdoor adventure experiences are currently in danger of being circumscribed by too narrow forms of quality control rather than more positive schemes for quality assurance.) More consistent with my theme however is an emphasis on quality improvement. In our book *The Empowered School* (1991) David Hargreaves and I suggested a sequence of planning that fits well into a scheme for quality improvement, particularly when it is linked to a proactive approach to programme evaluation such as that mentioned above. The sequence goes something like this:

•   Clarify the Mission

•   Review Quality

•   Plan for Development / Quality Improvement

•   Implement & Evaluate the Plan

•   Report and Celebrate Success

•   Enter a New Cycle of Quality Improvement

•   And in so doing … Create a Quality Culture

It is of course the establishing of a quality culture that guarantees and sustains a quality outdoor experience for all participants. In the same essay I quoted from at the beginning, Hargreaves defined a 'Quality Culture' as having:

- an ethos which creates both pressure and support for its members

- a clear view of the organisation's main purposes and values

- a scepticism about its own rhetoric

- a pre-emptive approach to accountability

When an outdoor organisation is committed in its rhetoric and practice to quality, and develops structures to support reflection then it is no surprise that excellence results.

Coda

Such a brief summary of an already abbreviated talk[1] will inevitably only be a skeleton account. But I trust that the key point is clear - it is that in the pursuit of quality it is not good enough to do best practice. We must also reflect on and articulate good practice so that we can continue to do our best. This commitment to reflection and continuous improvement is at the heart of the quality outdoor experience.

Notes

1. This chapter is based on a keynote address given at the Third Outdoor Forum - "Quality 2000", Chorley, December 1996.

References

Barrett J & Greenaway R (1995) *Why Adventure?* Foundation for Outdoor Adventure
Hargreaves D (1992) "An Essay on Quality in Education" LEAP / BBC.
Hargreaves D & Hopkins D (1991) *The Empowered School*. London: Cassell.
Hopkins D & Putnam R (1993) *Personal Growth Through Adventure*. London: David Fulton Publishers.
Pirsig, R (1974) *Zen and the Art of Motorcycle Maintenance*. New York: Bantam Books.

Chapter 22: The Value of and the Values Within Outdoor Education for those With Disabilities and Special Needs

Phil Woodyer

Introduction

The values within a course of Outdoor Education and the value of these courses for the participants are well documented and are easy for us all to grapple with but how does Outdoor Education benefit those with disabilities and special needs. Does it have value for them, does it help to impart values for them? Do we assume that there is some intrinsic value which carries through into all areas of Outdoor Education? Do the leaders and the carers take responsibility for informing us that it is worthwhile? Do we take their word as the experts? Have they thought it through?

It is easy to ask the questions and, I think, it is easy to justify lots of this work with groups with disabilities and special needs but there are areas which perhaps need further thought and not all the answers will be found within these pages. This is not a scientific paper, my evidence is anecdotal and I do not even know if it is possible to measure such things or even if I would want to if it were possible.

Why am I doing this?

I am writing this partly to justify my own job. For those few occasions when I think, 'What value has this for someone with no demonstrable response, someone who cannot make their own decision about whether or not they want to be doing this thing?' What can be the value of taking this person – down an abseil, into a cave, onto the water?

There is a definite surge of energy and emotion coming from the Instructor/Carer transmitted towards the person with the disability when an activity/exercise is achieved. The hope is that this is somehow transmitted to that disabled person. Even if the Instructor sees no change in the participant, the Carer will often say, "She enjoyed that" or, "He really got a lot out of that."

Suppose this reaction is purely subjective and it made no difference to the person with the disability whether or not they did the activity; does it still have value? If it encouraged the Carer to continue caring in a positive way for the client and it encouraged the Instructor to carry on being positive about their job, does it have enough value so that we don't need to know whether or not it has value for the participant? Sometimes the effect of doing something with a person with a severe disability is not immediate and cannot be judged there and then in isolation. It may be part of a series of developments which together improve their lifestyle.

Sally had no use of her limbs, her head was floppy. To do an abseil she had to have complete support. It was easy in her case because, although she found it difficult to communicate, she had a big smile and when she had done the abseil once she smiled at the suggestion that she should do it again, and she smiled when she came the following year and did the abseil again. But was she reacting to the experience or just to the Instructor or was it to both? In the first instance there was a look of apprehension on her face and it was only when she was about half way down that the smile appeared. In her case she was well aware of what she was doing and her trust in her carers and in the instructor had enabled her to achieve something.

It's like the person being physically helped up a rock face by someone moving their feet, are they showing a determination to succeed? It is a matter of degrees, they may be showing great determination if they are pulling as hard as they can with their hands and arms. If they cannot do this they are still choosing to do the activity. If they can communicate a desire to do the activity again, they have made a choice based on experience and have learnt to like something which they had never done before.

Going up or down a vertical wall is a different experience and it may be that the person having this experience is helping themselves as much as they can because they want to get to the top or get to the bottom. Even if they are not helping themselves at all they are experiencing the outdoors, the rock face, the ropes, the harness, the encouragement; things that the person without a disability or special need would experience. To what extent they are experiencing or to what extent it may positively enrich their lives we may never know but we may never know this about any of the people we encourage into the outdoors.

The shared experience

In my experience everyone delights in the thought of two groups sharing a residential outdoor experience. A mainstream school group and a group from a special school; all the positive spin-offs; living together, sharing the building and facilities, sharing the activities. The mainstream pupils learn about disability or relating to someone with special needs. The special needs group learn to relate with mainstream students in a small, friendly setting which they are more able to deal with. At my own centre, Low Mill, we have various groups who have chosen to share their experience for three or four years. They place a high value on this.

However, the mainstream group may be learning consideration, care, patience, the need to help others and so on, but what about the special needs group? Could the experience be mis-educative, could it in fact reduce the need of those with special needs to take responsibility for themselves if there is a supply of willing helpers. From my experience this is where the skill of the leaders, teachers, carers comes in to maximise the experience for all concerned. Undoubtedly what has been expressed above does sometimes occur but I think overall the benefits outweigh the drawbacks.

There has to be thought and care in the matching of groups to share. Some groups who need their own space in order to develop their confidence in 'Life Skills' may be better on their own without the added burden of having to form relationships with strangers, the sharing may reduce the value for them. Some groups sharing may create a heady cocktail that would be difficult to contain and may produce unwanted outcomes which have little value. I am thinking of some of our more volatile groups with emotional/ behavioural difficulties who have enough problems relating to each other within their own group without giving them another volatile group to contend with. Sometimes, these groups may benefit from another mainstream set of individuals to distract them from the complexities of their own group dynamics but sometimes this mixture may be to the detriment of the mainstream group. Their experience may be reduced in value by a disturbed group whose agenda is not understood by the mainstream group.

Positive outcomes

After wrestling with some of the possible negative aspects of outdoor education with those with disabilities and special needs what about positive outcomes? Do they exist, what are they and do they have value, do they impart values? What are the opportunities for personal development, confidence building? Are there building blocks which will lead to further developments, to more independent living? Are there opportunities to stimulate changes of behaviour or changes of attitudes?

a) Personal Development
In a lot of circumstances in their everyday lives, people with special needs or physical disabilities are not encouraged to do things; in some cases they may be actively discouraged. The reasons for this are many and varied, mainly because it is physically more difficult to accommodate a physical disability or it takes more time to explain to someone with an educational special need. It takes longer, needs more patience, may need special equipment and cannot be achieved in the normal run of things.

This means that some of these people are missing out on many opportunities for personal and social development. In a setting of a course of outdoor education there is more time to spend with people and their needs. Instructors in this branch of the industry tend to have more patience, be more laid back in their approach to life. To be fair they do not have the constraints of a rigid timetable or a demanding curriculum, they are often not even too bothered about specific times for meals. This unhurried but concentrated approach can bring out the best in those with special needs and physical disabilities.

b) Confidence Building and Independent Living

As has been already stated that people with special needs or physical disabilities are often discouraged rather than encouraged to do things for themselves.

In a setting of an outdoor residential course people can be encouraged to do more for themselves; wash up, set tables, choose the correct clothing for the activity. Even going to the local village pub and ordering a drink is something which is not so daunting in a small, friendly rural setting with plenty of positive support.

One boy in his late teens when asked what he had learnt which was of most benefit from his course said that he had learnt to shave himself. Formerly he had always been shaved by his father but away on a residential the leaders and carers had too much to do for others and encouraged him to shave himself. This he did and could now go home a little more independent than when he arrived. This may even change his attitude to his father and his father's attitude to him and lead to more independent living.

When discussing this chapter with colleagues, one of the things we found, which this last story illustrates, was that once the participants had finished the course and left that was often the last we ever saw or heard of them. Some of the changes which took place and were stimulated by the course were never followed up to see what the long term effects were. There may be some more academic work here for someone to follow up the long-term benefits of courses of outdoor education on those with disabilities and special needs.

c) Building Blocks

Some of the changes brought about by an outdoor education course are dramatic but others are evolutionary and present building blocks for further development.

I have always thought that gorge walking/gill scrambling is a great medium for confidence building and personal development. It requires co-ordination and balance, making decisions about which rocks are slippery and which aren't, which water will come over the tops of your wellingtons and which won't, the realisation that if the water does come over the top of your wellingtons you're not going to die. The moving together through a natural environment without technical assistance, only the encouragement and helping hands of others in the group.

This activity is not for those with more severe physical disabilities but for those with minor mobility problems and some with special needs, I have witnessed a growing in confidence from those first tentative steps to a more confident movement and a loss of inhibitions about walking on stones and walking in water.

What confidence does it give someone who may have been excluded from PE and games lessons at school to be able to abseil down a sheer rock face or to journey through a cave, a seemingly hostile environment? These experiences present building blocks in physical confidence for people to try things not previously attempted.

d) Stimulus

It is a privilege to work in outdoor education and to witness some of the changes our courses can produce in people. Because it is intense and the challenges are so different from the routine of ordinary everyday life these changes can sometimes be instant and dramatic.

Two examples of this are of two elective mutes. These are people who are physically capable of speech and have spoken but for some reason have now chosen not to speak.

The first instance is of a girl who was an elective mute. About two thirds of the way through the course it was noticed that she was missing from a briefing. Questions were asked, 'where is she?' To the astonishment of all concerned she was found on the telephone talking to her mother excitedly about the course. Her mother was also shocked because she did not formerly speak to anyone including her. The heightened stimulus and excitement of an outdoor course had made her want to communicate again.

The second instance is also of a girl who was an elective mute. She was at a climbing session at a local quarry. She had been kitted up with harness and helmet and was at the bottom of a climb belayed on a bottom belay. She was standing with her head down seemingly ignoring all encouragement from the laid back, sympathetic instructor to coax her to climb up the rock face. After about two minutes of this coaxing she turned to the instructor and muttered her first immortal words, "Why don't you **** Off?" The power of speech returned. This time it was a negative reaction but the fear of what she was being asked to do provoked her to speak.

Again we do not know if this speech continued after the girl returned home but we do know that what she was doing made her speak again.

e) Change of Attitudes

I have tried briefly to describe some of the ways in which outdoor courses would seem to have value for those with physical disabilities and special needs but do they also impart values?

I think for a lot of these participants they gain or regain the pleasure of a physical experience. None of us like to continue trying things which we conceive we are no good at or at which we always fail. Because these courses always go for a positive outcome and are about what you can do, not what you can't do there is a lot of positive encouragement about what is achieved, no matter how little this may seem to others.

Some achieve great things. Look at those who through some accident have become paraplegic and now do physical things they did not attempt when they were able-bodied. When your possibilities are curtailed it can make you more positive and determined about what you can achieve.

Does being in the outdoors and the countryside bring a love and respect for this environment? Again it is relative but a positive pleasurable experience in this environment should encourage a positive attitude towards it. Perhaps it is for others to devise ways to measure this attitude with clients who have varying degrees of difficulty with communicating.

The value of sharing, of helping others, of being part of a group both on the activities and within the residential setting: these are all part of a way of imparting values. Could this be done elsewhere? Probably, but it would be more difficult in a more everyday, routine setting where it would be easier to discourage rather than encourage and the strictures of time would make it easier to do things for people rather than to encourage them to do things for themselves or for others.

In conclusion

I believe that by writing this article and thinking about what we do I have convinced myself that outdoor courses for those with physical disabilities and special needs have value and can impart values. I would rather cite another few hundred examples to illustrate my claims than try to devise a system of measuring any long term benefits or changes. It may be that there is an opportunity for others to do this and the results could help to maximise the experience for the benefit of others.

VI
And finally

Chapters 23 - 24

And Finally: Chapters 23 - 24

Chapter 23:   Experiencing the Buzz of Dandelions Playing

Johnna Haskell

Quietly buzzing
Caressing, petal after petal
The bumble bee
Moves its abdomen
Exchanging dandelion pollen.

Does it matter
Where the dandelion grows?

I go out daily to interact with the thriving, buzzing business of the natural world in my own back yard. It keeps me in touch with what really matters. The robins hop, cock an ear to listen, then plunge beak first into the grassy earth bringing up morsels to devour. Four leaf clovers hide in patches of pastel green. Meanwhile, a male cardinal bellows out beautiful notes as his chest rhythmically fluctuates in and out. The wind blows white petals from the pear tree, one by one, floating to paint the ground. Dandelions seem to play, their plucky yellow flower heads absorbing the clear light of spring sunshine. The dandelion's brilliance radiates out in petal after petal. It amazes me how dandelions pop up with their strong erect stems above the manicured grass. I am fascinated by their persistence. Dandelions grow everywhere there is disturbed soil, on islands, in grassy meadows - wherever the wind blows their white seedlings. I wonder what it would be like to blow out into the world, to be taken along on a journey tucked into the fur of some animal and then deposited into an unfamiliar environment?

The outdoors is often that unfamiliar environment in traditional education. Outdoor education, on the other hand, encourages students to journey into extraordinary learning environments. Outdoor experiences can provide opportunities for students to follow their passions and flourish like the dandelion in new and different ways.

Passion moves you out of your comfort zone into a place of risk, adventure, of daring. You meet the circumstances and challenges of your life boldly. It's not that you don't feel doubt or fear - it's that your passion is stronger than your fear. It allows you to see beyond that which is in the way of your dreams, your desire, your destiny, and to go forward with enthusiasm. (De Angelis, 1998: 72)

Passionate teaching and learning compels us into an animated way of being, becoming, and living much like the persevering dandelion.

As a teacher, I experienced an environment we call 'school.' The dusty shelves, ordered desks, and little windows of my room keeping us shut off from the outside world. In good weather we would wander outside to complete a science lesson, but what, really, was I teaching? We think that outdoor education is some separate subject; the outdoor living planet as separate from our existence. Even the air we breathe we talk of as separate from who we are and whom we interact with. Experience teaches us that when bringing together school curricula and the outdoors, students learn so much more about human interaction and the real world around us. We can experience and taste, touch, and be mindful of the sensuous, bodily feelings of exchanging air with each other and the living world. The ecology of the outside classroom reconnects us to a space, where we come in tune with the 'more-than-human world' (Abram, 1996).

From students' perspectives, what is the value of adventuring and learning with/in[1] the outdoors? This question was one of many at the heart of my doctoral research. I began by looking at an outdoor adventure education programme based within a public secondary school. I interviewed ten current students, staff, and past students near the end of my five months as a participant/instructor/researcher to gain insight into the significance of outdoor, experiential learning on outdoor trips within the programme. Common themes include: pushing limits, being persistent to achieve goals, encountering new friendships, learning respect, and connecting to the natural world. The themes arose not only in these particular conversations but were offered by the many participants along the way as I camped, hiked, paddled, climbed and talked with them around bustling camp stoves.

The benefits of outdoor adventure education became clear while listening to those who shared their thoughts and experiences. Along with exploring how students discover passionate ways of being with the 'outdoor' world, I intertwine the adventures of dandelions playing in my own backyard.

Where is the 'Classroom'?

The programme, located in a Vancouver secondary school, is an outdoor adventure and environmental education classroom for 108 grade ten students. Students participate in two half-year semesters. In the first semester, from September to January, half of the students are in the regular academic classroom, while the other half are in the outdoor portion of the programme. In the second semester, February to June, the two halves of the programme switch. The outdoor adventure education classroom is distinctively decorated with couches instead of desks. On the walls are paintings, pictures, and environmental posters from previous programme students. Students spend the first month of the programme learning basic outdoor skills such as camping, cooking, self-rescues, and belaying. Students are randomly assigned tenting/cooking partners and are responsiblefor packing all their own signed-out gear and food for outdoor trips. At the end of the first outdoor semester, I spoke with ten participants about the value of outdoor education from their experience in the programme.

What happens when we directly connect and integrate what we call subjects in to the doing or experiencing? Students begin to relate their goals into academics and realize the integration and importance of a healthy mind and body. Outdoor activities bring together the learning and the physical. Ben, a student, explains, 'Most people are happy in the outdoors, so you are creating a happy learning experience.' This does not mean that learning is necessarily easy or comfortable. Dan adds an example, 'You have to learn to experience . . . like tying knots in the freezing cold.' If you have not practiced and learned the knot tying of tarps, then when you are out in the pouring rain, you experience firsthand the value and importance of knot tying.

A way of being, becoming, living

Dandelions seem to persevere everywhere I travel, even though their life cycle is a short two years. In that time they focus on attracting pollinating bees, regrowing new flower heads after being cut by the lawn mower, and forming mature seeds for dispersal. During three or four trips in the outdoors students become like dandelions. Beth, who could not go on the last two trips due to a broken leg, describes what she learned in the outdoor programme:

> *I guess I have learned ... that I can do anything really. Anything I set my mind to ... In [the programme] you learn how ... to push ... be persistent in your goals ... When you do something individual in the outdoors you learn more about yourself and what you want to do. You learn how to persevere.*

Outdoors, students begin to see that by pushing their limits and being persistent they can achieve their goals. Such an approach to learning, living, and being opens up possibilities for students to becoming anything they dream imaginable.

Inter-action——collecting pollen together

I continue to adventure out into the natural world to enliven the simplicity of life, to refamiliarize myself with what matters. I attend to the essentials of food, shelter, water, and being harmonious with the natural world. I come back renewed after a trip, letting go of all the things that do not really matter. I focus on each moment as it emerges. I embody an awareness through my interactions with paddling, eating and tasting, really tasting the food, the crunch of leafy vegetables, or the spark and snap of a good bite into an apple. Focusing on the immediate seems to be easier for students to practice when outdoors. As Sara describes:

> *When you go on trips, you really realize what your priorities are ... All that matters is what you have in your pack and what's around you ... You're*

*there in the moment and all that matters is what you are doing at that
moment ... You realize that people are so much more interesting than you
would have thought. There are people that maybe you wouldn't have been
friends with before. But, because you are working so closely with them,
you realize that everybody has something to offer and that we are all
people.*

In addition to learning what is really important and how to keep focused, students,
while working together so closely on outdoor trips, also learn how to communicate,
read people, and develop lasting friendships.

Group interaction in the outdoor programme fosters communication and trust. In
the outdoors, barriers come down; students learn to be open to people they otherwise
would not have befriended. As Abram (1996) writes, our human actions and
interactions are influenced not only by each other but by 'experiencing forms' with/
in the environment. When we connect our senses and our sensual beings with the
'more-than-human world,' we shape our perceptions.

Opening 'doors', stepping outside to play with dandelions

While I sit in the middle of a patch of dandelions today, I begin to rethink the words
out-door edu-ca-tion. The word 'outdoor,' for example, implies that there has to be
a door to go out when in fact we can never truly separate ourselves from the buzzing,
dandelion world. The in-doors is merely an illusion where we educate and learn
'about' more-than-human inter-action. When students experience inter-actions with
peers, teachers, and the outdoor environment, they bring to light the values of
motivation and respect. It is not as if motivation or respect can be obtained like a
diploma but they emerge through the actions of doing. Alex talks about learning
within the outdoor environment and the programme as a methodology, a way of
being that 'lets you motivate yourself to achieve.'

*It wasn't a competitiveness but it was more of a self motivation that I got
from the programme toward life in general. I found it to be really valuable
... In the programme, you also learn self respect, respect for others, and
respect for the environment ... If you respect your environment, you are
respecting the environment you live in, therefore you respect yourself and
you are respecting that of your peers and whoever lives in the environment.
[If you are in a classroom] then you are so removed.*

Learning in the outdoors motivates students to stretch their limits and their connections
to each other and their environment.

This particular outdoor programme opens up potential for students to be leaders and
seek their best. They learn to motivate themselves through setting achievable goals

and to be persistent. This steadfastness is connected to their interactions with peers and their interactions with the natural world. Being outdoors opens the minds of young individuals as they connect and experience learning through bodily exchange, just as dandelions pollinate, where a way of being and becoming with the living world matters.

The Vancouver programme provides an opportunity to experience and learn not only subject matter but an interconnection to achieving goals, following your own choices, and becoming who you want to be. I have read many vision statements of schools wanting their students to realize and reach their potentials. Students who focus on reconnecting their bodies with the wilderness move toward a new understanding of goals and choices.

What is school for?

If education is the pursuit of knowledge, theories, and the coupling of the known and the unknown, how do we get people excited about learning, lifelong learning, to ask questions, to taste learning? We sometimes become caught up in the economics of education and what might benefit students or society. These answers are not contained separate from our own experiencing of the world, but we may need to take the time to experience our world in new ways. A previous teacher in the programme, Barry suggests the following:

> One of the main focuses of the school system is to produce well adjusted, enthusiastic individuals who are well connected socially. If they don't have that, they are really handicapped. We can pump all kinds of academics into them, but if we don't focus on their development as people, they can come out with straight A's, but they may not do well in life. I already see the outdoor education component as focusing on those core human skills besides the whole environmental awareness, which I think is critical too ... [the values] you know, the sense of belonging. The big thing for me was the sense of trust and working with each other ... They [kids] need that. The ideal programme would be to do all the academics like science in the outdoors. The community support, parents, raising of funds ... Kids are involved in their own funding to keep the programme going. Idealistically as an educator, I would rather produce a well adjusted, happy individual. What else is there?

Students struggle with this notion of happiness, not only in their participation within the programme, but also in their daily choices of living. Students talk about happiness as a choice to portray a positive attitude. If they focus on positive thoughts and encourage one another on outdoor trips, students begin to experience a happy learning experience as well as a positive way of being.

Why teenagers? why not teachers?

At times, the outdoors can be wet, cold and appear unwelcoming, just like life, with all its many forces beyond our control. All we can control is our attitudes: do we curse the rain or do we embrace the rain with all our senses, smelling the earthy warmth and marveling over the pockets of perfect water droplets balancing on blades of grass? The dandelions seemingly use many ways to produce many seeds for new plants. Students, on the other hand, are bored in classrooms because, as Beth adds, 'you don't have a goal or know what you want to do.' Holly explains what it is about outdoor education that makes learning so stimulating:

> *The programme is a hard struggle and fun. The value, especially for teenagers, is that your life as a teenager is often really confusing. It's filled with like a billion different decisions, especially teenage girls. They probably have the most things to deal with out of any other group in the entire world. Like people try to trivialize it, being a teenager ... It's a huge joke or it's funny or it's like the awkward years. And thank god that's over and everything. They don't really realize what they don't remember, the feeling that there should be something more ... It makes life so much less confusing if you all of a sudden have these goals ... this potential ... I know so much more than when I started this ... not just more about nature, but more about everything, more about life in general. Teenagers are the people that need to know the most about life ... because they are just figuring out their place in the world. You can't teach that in a career and personal planning class. Not only are those things so boring... They don't take you anywhere where it's real. The outdoors is the most real place you can be.*

The programme is participatory, not illusionary, virtual, or watched on the latest technology. It requires bodily interactions with people and the sentient landscape. How might such an experience open possibilities for teacher education, where teachers could experience the passion of full interaction with the living world? If teachers themselves experience the passion of dandelion patches, they might provide more opportunities for students to experience the buzz of the natural world.

> *"It is the first glimmerings of a precious realization so essential for student-teachers to undergo——that understanding erupts out of life itself and not simply as a response to our concerted acts of teaching, and therefore, that teaching must first and foremost attune itself to what is already at work in our lives and the lives of the children we teach."*(Jardine, 1998: 60)

Students in the outdoor portion of the programme push their limits so they can see, who could I become? what are my choices? where will I go? They are forced into situations where they learn interpersonal skills; they experience a sense of independence, adventure, confidence, friendships, a positive attitude, and a willingness to try. Students develop a sense of belonging where they connect socially and individually which, as Alex points out, 'occurs in the outdoors when things aren't so comfortable.'

How do dandelions grow?

I sneak out into the back yard seeking the power of words to express a way of living, being, or becoming with/in a world of interaction and relationship. I am looking for impassioned interplay where the encounter between teachers, students and the outdoor environment is like the buzz of dandelions playing. How do we make the choices to bring forth and enact[2] compassion for the unfolding, breathing, sensuous world? I think we must be mindful not to continue to perpetually objectify phenomena and, in so doing, separate our sensuous involvement, as Abram (1996: 69) suggests,

> ... *when consciously acknowledged ... surroundings are experienced as sensate, attentive, and watchful, then I must take care that my actions are mindful and respectful, even when I am far from other humans, lest I offend the watchful land itself.*

I invite you to throw off your shoes, live on the edge, and experience the wonders of the natural environment. Dare to live like the dandelions, pop up with persistence in new environments, and you may experience growing with full potential. I can teach and learn no other way.

The sky glows a crimson pink through trees moving with the wind while the dandelions are busy closing up for the night to protect and ensure germinating pollen grains. Silently, a ripe flower head releases its mature fruit, which fly to new environments. Outdoor education offers students opportunities to experience the unfamiliar within a happy learning environment and to adventure into a passionate way of being with the whole world.

Notes

1. I use the word *with/in* instead of in as I am really referring to how the environment is not seperate and that we co-emerge with the interactions of the world and not seperate where we are placed in a world. Our world is brought forth through the interactions 'with' our sensual being.
2. By *enact*, I am refering to the enactive approach where cognition and human experience coupe and co-evolve through a way of being mindful of our social history and interactions with/in the world (Varela et al., 1991)

References

Abram, D. (1996) *The spell of the sensuous.* New York: Vintage Books.
De Angelis, B. (1998) *Passion.* New York: Delcorte Press.
Jardine, D, W. (1998) *To dwell with a boundless heart: Essays in curriculum theory, hermeneutics and the ecological imagination.* New York: Peter Lang.
Varela, F, J., Thompson, E. & Rosch, E. (1991) *The embodied mind: Cognitive science and human experience.* Massachusetts: MIT Press.

Chapter 24: Has Outdoor Education any Future?

Harold Dradso

In terms of an old educational analogy the child is considered as clay, jug or flower. Character building may be seen as closest to typifying the first possibility - the educator has decided what he wants and he is going to shape the raw material to his design. The teaching of techniques and the communication of factual information, whether about Nature or about recreational skills, comes closest to the second - the educator has the empty vessel before him and he is going to fill it to the brim. These are crude metaphors and no doubt unfair but they bring out the third possibility. All clay can be moulded and every vessel can be filled in identical fashion. Living things, however, are never identical and they contain their own programmes; they must simply be protected from what is harmful to them.

It has been proposed from studies of animal behaviour that the level of a species' evolutionary development may be judged from how hard the mentality of an individual differs from others of the same species. Correspondingly, Read[1] takes the purpose of education to be to foster the growth of what is individual in each human being, at the same time harmonising the individuality thus enduced with the organic unity of the social group to which the individual belongs. This definition admittedly has the properties of a see-saw, to be weighted as one pleases: but it has the merit of allowing individual claims the same potential importance as social claims.

Has outdoor education any future? In one sense, of course it has. In the idiomatic sense I am less certain that outdoor education has a future. But a number of years ago it felt like the most promising experiment in British education. There was a degree of freedom about it which made it more progressive than the Progressive Schools. But an unimaginative pressure for standardisation (in the interests of consistency - why?) has exercised a repressive influence upon the experiment.

In the outdoor pursuits approach, in order to take the fullest advantage of all possiblities we must arrange first that the teachers are not processed. We must restructure the various outdoor pursuits qualifications to encourage variety and experiment rather than to secure uniformity of approach. We must abandon any qualification system which is becoming insubordinate to the experiences it attempts to measure. We must take steps to ensure that Centre Wardens and Instructors are drawn from as many different fields of teaching as possible and that we do not suffer from a preponderance of scientists and physical educationalists. It is high time that, to keep the balance, Colleges of Art began to run outdoor education courses.

If the teachers are not processed it will be easier to ensure that the students are not processed. We must diversify the progammes and arrange, with adequate safeguards, that young people are able to spend a little time alone without any project whatsoever: no difficult map and compass scheme, no huge sack filled with survival gear, no insulation by the company of others from the personal confrontation with Nature. We should try to arrange that they see a particular area at different seasons, even if only briefly, rather than see it only once for a longer spell. We must always try to prevent our programmes from turning what should be natural, direct and immediate into a contrived experience.

We should try to retain at least that degree of autonomy that already exists in Outdoor Centres. Above all, we should turn for our interpretation of the values of outdoor activities to men and women who have enjoyed and are enjoying wild country outside any teaching context - to those who have written about it in the past and to the climbers, sailors and naturalists of today.

Sometimes, there is a temptation to propose outdoor education itself as an autonomous province, incorporating recreational and travel skills, biological and geographical studies, matters of aesthetics, ecology, conservation and whatever. But some of the more specialised of these disciplines belong partly to the classroom or laboratory. And since many classroom teachers now agree that theoretical work is essentially completed by practical experience, it seems likely, as well as right and good, that these teachers will extend their own spheres of action to include the use of wild country: rather than hand over to yet another emergent priesthood.

The writer's prepossessions will have become obvious by now. If I have a sympathy for any new model or ideal it is for something like the Incidental Education of Paul Goodman[2]. Unluckily, the subject of this pamphlet was one of the very few areas of contemporary education and culture on which Goodman did not express himself. Nevertheless, any young instructor in an outdoor centre will feel on familiar ground in Goodman's world. He will recognise himself in the teacher who abandons the classroom and who, with ten youngsters, explores his neighbourhood intensively day after day - like 'the Athenian pedagogue, touring the city with his charges'. And he may see himself again in the artist, artisan or scholar who is spared all self-questioning about the proper use of his authority. 'He says do or don't do with a clear conscience' - because he has a real stake in the enterprise; and the group having once accepted the commitment, the value of his experience, underscored by criteria of safety, is clear to everybody. Above all, Goodman's insistence that virtually all trades and professions are better learned by apprenticeship than by college courses has urgent relevance for outdoor education - which is showing a tendency to imitate all the absurdities of ordinary teacher training. It may be that in the long run Ivan Illich[3] and the de-schoolers will have most to say to outdoor educationists; unless, not impossibly, the ideas begin to flow the other way.

In the end I have to say why I put such a high value upon the aspects of outdoor education I have tried to describe. It seems to me that the formal approaches originally outlined would be considered worthy of encouragement - with minimal modification and subject to the availability of capital - by every Minister of Education on earth. This leads me to suspect that there is nothing very unusual or revolutionary about their content. But I can imagine that more profound and experimental approaches might be attempted, starting with the widest possible freedom of choice and allowing time for reflection about nature and man. These, I think, would not gain so wide an assent. ('I deny altogether that idleness is an evil' Jefferies[4] said, 'or that it produces evil, and I am well aware why the interested are so bitter against idleness - namely, because it gives time for thought and if men had time to think their reign would come to an end.') To my surprise I find myself reflecting that this country may be one of the few in the modern world in which humanistic, multi-cultural, politically useless educational experiments can be argued for, could be afforded, and might even be overlooked.

In the end, whether we choose to treat Nature as a Greased Pole or as a Visual Aid or as a Personnel Selection Test may be a matter of predilection. But the ultimate virtue in each approach depends primarily, to my mind, on how far it leaves us able to enjoy two discrete aspects of our relationship with Nature: those ancient, subversive, anarchistic values, beauty and freedom.

Notes/References

This chapter has been condensed, by permission of the author, from the original text, *Education and the Mountain Centres*, first published in 1972 and now reprinted as a new edition (1998) by Adventure Education, Penrith. It is reproduced here with their permission. The original text was unreferenced and is referenced here, as far as possible, by the editor.

1. Probably from the text *Education Through Art*.
2. There are three collections of essays by Paul Goodman which refer to political, literary and psychological subjects, they are: *Drawing the Line; Creator Spirit, Come!* and *Nature Heals*. There is a paperback set edited by Taylor Stoehr and published by E. P. Dutton, New York (1979).
3. Illich, I. (1971/76) *Deschooling Society*. Harmondsworth: Pelican.
4. Probably from the text *The Story of My Heart*.

Appendices

Appendices

| **Appendix i.** | **Ethical Guidelines for Outdoor Leaders (From Chapter 5)** |

Professionals conduct experiences with an appropriate level of competence. Outdoor leaders promote and conduct activities within their level of competence. They provide services within the boundaries of their education, training, supervision, experience, and practice. They take reasonable steps to ensure the competence of their work. They avoid situations where personal problems or conflicts will impair their performance or judgment. They stay abreast of current information in the field. They participate in ongoing professional efforts to maintain their knowledge, practice, and skills.

Professionals conduct experiences with integrity. Outdoor leaders conduct activities with honesty, fairness, and respect, both in interactions with clients and peers. They avoid false, misleading, or deceptive statements when describing or reporting qualifications, services, products, or fees. They are aware of how personal belief systems, values, needs and limitations affect clients.

Professionals conduct experiences with responsibility. Outdoor leaders uphold the ethical principles of their work. They are clear with clients as to everyone's roles and obligations. They accept responsibility for their behavior and decisions. They adapt methods to the needs of different populations. They possess an adequate basis for professional judgments. They do not begin services when the constraints of limited contact will not benefit client needs. They continue services only so long as it is reasonably clear that clients will benefit. They conduct experiences in a manner that results in minimal impact (or temporary damage) to the environment.

Professionals conduct experiences with respect for the rights and dignity of clients. Outdoor leaders respect the fundamental rights, dignity, and worth of all people. They respect clients' rights to privacy, confidentiality, and self determination within the limits of the law. Outdoor leaders also strive to be sensitive to cultural and individual differences - including those due to age, gender, race, ethnicity, national origin, religion, sexual orientation, disability, and socioeconomic status. Outdoor leaders do not engage in sexual or other harassment or exploitation of clients. They respect clients' rights to make decisions and help them understand the consequences of their choices. They provide clients with appropriate information about the nature of services and their rights, risks, and responsibilities. They provide an opportunity to discuss the results, interpretations, and conclusions of the adventure experience with clients. They respect clients' rights to refuse consent to services and activities. They obtain informed consent from clients and, when appropriate, their parents or guardians before beginning services. They accurately represent their competence, training, education, and experience relevant to the program being delivered.

Professionals conduct experiences with concern for the well being of clients. Outdoor leaders are sensitive to client needs and well being. Outdoor leaders provide for the appropriate physical needs of clients, including necessary water, nutrition, clothing, shelter, rest, or other essentials. They monitor the appropriate use of emotional and physical risk in adventure experiences. They assist in obtaining other services if the program cannot, for appropriate reasons, provide the professional help clients may need. They plan experiences with the intent that decisions made during and after are in accordance with the clients' best interest. They respect clients' rights to decide the extent to which confidential material can be made public, except under extreme conditions (as required by law to prevent a clear and immediate danger to a person or persons).

Professionals conduct experiences with recognition for their level of social responsibility. Outdoor leaders are aware of their responsibilities to community and society. They appropriately encourage the development of standards and policies that serve their clients' interests as well as those of the public. They respect the property of others.

Professionals conduct experiences with objectivity by avoiding dual relationships with clients that impair professional judgement. Outdoor leaders do not exploit or mislead clients (or other leaders) during and after professional relationships. This includes, but is not limited to: business relationships, close personal friendships, family relationships, sexual relations, and inappropriate physical contact.

Appendix ii. Statement Of Brathay's Current Values - as prepared in 1994 by staff in consultation with colleagues and Trustees (From Chapter 13)

MISSION -   TO EXCEL IN DEVELOPMENT TRAINING AND SO FACILITATE OUR COMMITMENT TO YOUNG PEOPLE

PEOPLE -   People are the reason for our existence and our most important resource.
Developing people is our business: we seek to practice what we preach.
We aim to provide equality of opportunity.
We value the physical and emotional safety of our customers and staff.

TEAMWORK - We value everyone's contribution to our success.
We value commitment, trust, integrity, openness and respect.
We expect to give and receive support and loyalty.
We strive to communicate effectively, and particularly value listening.

QUALITY -   We value excellence in all we do.
We express pride in our mission and our history.
We endeavour to provide excellent service to our customers.
We encourage and celebrate success.
We strive for continuous improvement.

ENVIRONMENT -
We value the environment within which we work.
We wish to ensure that our actions conserve the beauty of the Estate and of the Lake District.
We aspire to making our impact on the global environment sustainable.

Appendix iii. The Code of Ethics published by the Association for Outdoor Learning

Code of Professional Conduct

A fundamental principle of membership is an undertaking that the conduct of each member can be justified ethically and morally at all times and will bring credit to themselves, AfOL and the outdoor profession.

The purpose of this Code is to set out the standards of behaviour agreed to and upheld by members of the Association as they cultivate and promote the special values and importance of outdoor learning experiences. The revision, updating and use of the Code shall be the responsibility of the Association Trustees. Changes are subject to ratification at an AGM.

1. Professional Integrity

1.1 Members should maintain the highest of standards and values. Members should demonstrate fairness, consistency, honesty, tolerance, compassion, truthfulness and discretion during their work out of doors.

1.2 The Association may be judged by the conduct of its Trustees, Officers and Members. Consequently all members of the Association should conduct themselves in a befitting manner.

1.3 The logo of the Association may not be used for personal or commercial purposes.

2. Professional Responsibilities and Relationships

2.1 Members have a duty of care to each participant and should accept their responsibility to protect the dignity, privacy and safety of all those for whom they are responsible. Members should define and respect the boundaries between personal and working life and never misuse a leadership position whatever the age of the client.

2.2 When dealing with other members, agencies, clients, students, sponsors or the general public, members should present themselves as responsible persons and in a manner which inspires confidence and trust.

2.3 Members should manage the activities for which they are responsible with due regard to student, client and staff emotional and physical welfare, complying with all legal requirements and Health and Safety guidelines.

2.4 Members should accept that discrimination on the grounds of race, gender and sexual orientation have no place in outdoor learning and should be challenged if they are displayed.

2.5 Members should safeguard confidential information relating to participants and use discretion when there is a particular need to share essential information with professional colleagues.

2.6 Where a member delegates any activity or welfare responsibilities they should understand that the ultimate responsibility remains with themselves.

2.7 Members should respect fellow members. Public or private reference to the conduct, integrity or quality of service of another member should be expressed with due care, accepting that there is a clear moral obligation to challenge unprofessional conduct.

3. Professional Standards

3.1 Members should work only within the limits of their competence and experience, acknowledging and adhering to commonly accepted, current, best practice and standards.

3.2 Members should maintain and develop their personal, professional competence and when possible share their expertise with other members and contribute constructively to debate on professional matters.

3.3 Members should respect the needs, traditions, practices, special competencies and responsibilities of other institutions, associations, agencies and professions which share a common interest in Outdoor Learning

4. Environmental and Cultural Responsibilities

4.1 Members should conserve the natural environment, endorsing the principles of sustainable use and minimum impact.

4.2 Members should be sensitive to the impact of their operation on the local community and cultural setting within which they work and minimise any adverse effect.

4.3 Members should encourage knowledge, understanding and respect for the cultural setting within which they work.

About the Authors

About The Authors

The editor, **Peter Barnes** has had a varied career which has included military service, youth work, designing radar systems and many years of outdoor work with Outward Bound and others in a variety of countries. He now works as the lecturer responsible for implementing the new outdoor education programme at the Newton Rigg Campus of the University of Central Lancashire. He continues to do occasional freelance work as an outdoor instructor. Following an M.A. in 'Tourism and Social Responsibility', he took his Ph.D. in 'The Motivation Of Staff Working In The Outdoor Industry', he is also a Fellow of the Royal Geographical Society. Peter has published a number of books about outdoor education, particularly on outdoor leadership and theory. Staffing issues within the outdoor industry continue to be his primary interest and he works with both the Association for Outdoor Learning and the English Outdoor Council when these issues are involved. He lives in the Cumbrian Eden Valley with his partner, Sue, a manic household of children and cats and struggles to remain an active caver and mountaineer.

Pete Allison is senior lecturer in adventure education at University College Chichester and is finishing his Ph.D. from University of Strathclyde. Outdoor interests are in running, mountaineering and expeditions while research interests are in philosophy of outdoor education and leadership training. Pete works with British Schools Exploring Society, is a Fellow of the Royal Geographical Society and is co-editor of the Journal of Adventure Education and Outdoor Leadership.

Geoff Cooper is head of Metropolitan Wigan's two outdoor education centres in the Lake District. He has introduced many young people to the outdoors through a range of experiences and regularly runs training courses for youth leaders and countryside staff. He has organised workshops on environmental education for teachers and leaders in Britain and across Europe. Geoff has recently published *Outdoors with Young People - A Leader's Guide to Outdoor Activities, the Environment and Sustainability*.

Steve Deeming is Warden at Swarthmoor Hall in Ulverston, Cumbria. The Hall is owned by the Religious Society of Friends and was the powerhouse of the early Quaker Movement, it is currently nearing the end of a period of major restoration. Steve is a climber and canoeist with a long term interest in human involvement in the outdoors.

Harold Drasdo started climbing shortly after the Second World War, formerly an English teacher he worked for many years as head of an outdoor pursuits centre in North Wales. As well as serving on various committees of the British Mountaineering Council he has been a judge for the Boardman-Tasker award. Harold has written articles, reviews and guidebooks while his 'autobiography', *The Ordinary Route,* was published in 1997.

Maurice Dybeck is a retired comprehensive school head and a Trustee of Brathay Hall. His works include a history of Brathay Hall, a study of village/community colleges and a series of geography textbooks. Formerly a chairman of the Young Explorers' Trust he is a photographer and educational film producer.

Michael Gass Ph.D. is a leading researcher and writer on the topics of facilitation and metaphoric transfer in experiential programming. He consults for leading global organisational learning providers and his consulting expertise lies primarily in facilitator training and isomorphic training.

John Halliday Ph.D. is a Reader at the University of Strathclyde, Glasgow. He is qualified as a philosopher and publishes widely in the area of educational theory. His recent publications include *Values in Further Education* published by Trentham Books and *Back to Good Teaching; diversity within tradition* published by Cassells.

Ian Harris is the course leader of the Maritime Leisure Management degree at Southampton Institute having previously worked as a physical education teacher in Hampshire and Essex. As well as outdoor pursuits in general he has a particular love of watersports with experience of working as a freelance instructor at many centres around the South of England in the last ten years. Ian is also a helmsman on the Hayling Island Lifeboat.

Johnna G. Haskell is a doctoral candidate in the Department of Curriculum Studies at the University of British Columbia. Johnna's research focuses on the phenomena of experiencing of students in outdoor adventure education within schools.

Peter Higgins Ph.D. is Senior Lecturer in Outdoor and Environmental Education at Moray House Institute of Education, University of Edinburgh, UK.

David Hopkins Ph.D. is Professor and Dean of Education at the University of Nottingham. He has previously worked as an Outward Bound Instructor and Schoolteacher. He writes extensively on educational issues, among his books are: *School Improvement in an Era of Change* (Cassell, 1994); *Models of Learning - Tools for Teaching* (Open University Press, 1997). David was also one of the ten British Mountain Guides to first receive the International Mountain Guides (UIAGM) carnet in 1978, and is currently Chair of the Mountain Guides Professional Standards Committee. In recent years, he has led a number of expeditions to Nepal in support of charities for those with disabilities.

Barbara Humberstone Ph.D. is Reader in outdoor education and critical sociology of sport at Buckinghamshire Chilterns University College (BCUC). Her Ph.D. thesis was an ethnographic study of teaching and learning in an outdoor education residential centre. She has written widely on equity, equal opportunities and outdoor education and continues to develop new courses such as a new outdoor degree at BCUC. Barbara is currently the AfOL co-ordinator for higher education and research and a board member of the European Institute for OutdoorAdventure Education and Experiential Learning. She is involved in collaborative work concerning European women's experiences of outdoor education.

Tom Lilley is a teacher of outdoor adventure education, currently working with excluded pupils as part of Birmingham Education's Behavioural Support Service. He has recently completed a part time M.Phil degree exploring the use of outdoor education with young people at risk and has two young children - which is undoubtedly his greatest adventure yet!

Chris Loynes has worked in outdoor education for 26 years. He first started as a teacher before leading the Brathay Hall Trust's Youth Development Programme. He then established Adventure Education providing training and publishing services. He edited *Horizons* until December 1999, the field's professional magazine, and offers consultancy services. His first loves are coastal sailing and wilderness exploration.

Eric Maddern made a ten year journey round the world which climaxed in working in the Aboriginal communities of Central Australia. He is a storyteller, author, musician and teacher who has written chapters and articles on Aboriginal issues. Over the last ten years he has set up Cae Mabon, a village encampment beneath the high mountains of Snowdonia, North Wales, where visiting young people can directly experience the woodland and water and live in simple, elemental dwellings.

Mac McInnes Ph.D. graduated from Carnegie and Charlotte Mason College before taking his Ph.D. in Outdoor Pursuits at Ohio State University. He has worked for Outward Bound in the USA, Great Britain and Germany. Mac has spent the last nine years teaching post-secondary education in Canada and the US and is currently an Assistant Professor at Unity College, Maine.

Geoff Nichols worked for Outward Bound in the UK in the 1980's. For the last ten years he has been a lecturer at Sheffield University. His current research interests include the role of adventure education in programmes to reduce youth crime.

Simon Priest Ph.D. is a leading researcher and writer on the topic of corporate experiential training and development. He consults for a handful of progressive corporations interested in staying ahead of their international competition by focusing on the development and maintenance of human resource relationships. His consulting expertise lies primarily in leadership, executive programmes and creating internal corporate universities.

Julie Rea is a doctoral student at Indiana University School of Counseling and Educational Psychology. She holds an MS in counseling and has worked with experiential and cognitive therapy models. Her research interests are experiential learning and instruction, semiotics and moral reasoning, and leisure behavior.

Michael Slavkin is currently completing his Doctorate in Educational Psychology. His teaching areas of interest are in child development, adolescent development, and social and cultural bases of behaviour. His areas of research interest are the development of gender identity in pre-adolescence, violence and maladaptive uses of fire across childhood and adolescence as well as the intersection of gender and race in understanding personality.

Phil Woodyer has been head of Low Mill Centre for seven years. This centre is a member of the 'Adventure for All' association which promotes outdoor adventure for people with special needs. Previous to his work at Low Mill, Phil was deputy head at Prior House LEA centre and has worked in the outdoor industry for some twenty years. He is secretary for the Northern Council for Outdoor Education, Training and Recreation. Phil continues to be active in caving, including working as an assessor for the local cave leader scheme.

Judy Ling Wong F.R.S.A. is the Director of Black Environment Network, an organisation with an international reputation as the pioneer in the field of ethnic environmental participation. She has worked extensively in various sectors - in the arts, in psychotherapy and in community development. She was made a Fellow of the Royal Society of Arts in recognition of her contribution to contemporary environmental thinking.